MAKING MUR

K. J. Kesselring is Professor of History at Dalhousie University, Halifax, Nova Scotia. She is the author of *Mercy and Authority in the Tudor State* and *The Northern Rebellion of 1569*, as well as a number of articles and essays on homicide and criminal forfeiture. She has also edited or co-edited collections including *The Trial of Charles I*, *Married Women and the Law: Coverture in England and the Common Law World* (with Tim Stretton), and *Crossing Borders: Boundaries and Margins in Medieval and Early Modern Britain* (with Sara M. Butler).

Praise for *Making Murder Public*

'This is likely to be the definitive work on homicide in the early modern period [...] It is indispensable reading for legal scholars and historians of crime and the law as well as an invaluable introduction for non-specialists.'

Andrea McKenzie, *American Historical Review*

'a very smart and stylish book. Kesselring moves between and brings together legal, cultural, social, and political history like few can do.'

Paul Griffiths, *Cultural and Social History*

'a masterful synthesis...Scholars and students will undoubtedly find much that is both original and helpful here...Its masterful placing in conversation of a number of fields, including the histories of crime, violence, and law together with social and political history, alongside its accessible and lucid style, will make it highly valuable for students, as well as providing much scholarly food for thought.'

Joan Redmond, *English Historical Review*

Making Murder Public

Homicide in Early Modern England,
1480–1680

K.J. KESSELRING

OXFORD
UNIVERSITY PRESS

OXFORD

UNIVERSITY PRESS

Great Clarendon Street, Oxford, OX2 6DP,
United Kingdom

Oxford University Press is a department of the University of Oxford.
It furthers the University's objective of excellence in research, scholarship,
and education by publishing worldwide. Oxford is a registered trade mark of
Oxford University Press in the UK and in certain other countries

First published 2019
First published in paperback 2022

Published in the United States of America by Oxford University Press
198 Madison Avenue, New York, NY 10016, United States of America

British Library Cataloguing in Publication Data
Data available

Library of Congress Cataloging in Publication Data
Data available

ISBN 978–0–19–883562–2 (Hbk.)
ISBN 978–0–19–286374–4 (Pbk.)

Acknowledgements

A story told against the backdrop of declining rates of homicide is, ultimately, a hopeful one. Even so, the research for this book was at times grim, so I am all the more thankful for the generosity of time and spirit shown by all the many people who helped along the way. I am glad to have the chance to name and thank at least some of them here.

For their kindness in reading drafts of the manuscript, in whole or in part, I am deeply grateful to Sara Butler, Thomas Green, Cynthia Neville, Edward Powell, Tim Stretton, and Katherine Watson. The Press's anonymous reviewers also provided useful guidance. Cynthia Herrup, one of those reviewers, shared her comments with me directly and generously followed up with leads from her own research. If I have not been able to incorporate all of their suggestions, I hope I have done enough to show that I appreciate their assistance. Certainly, the book is much stronger for their interventions than it would otherwise have been.

Cynthia Herrup, Margaret Hunt, and Shannon McSheffrey invited me to present draft material from the project at the USC/Huntington Library early modern seminar, the University of Uppsala, and Concordia University, respectively. To them, and to their institutions for providing support, my thanks. The conversations with Margaret and her Swedish colleagues were particularly helpful in prodding me to think more about comparative contexts. Marianna Muravyeva's invitation to participate in her symposium on parricide proved similarly useful. The seminar Ethan Shagan hosted at Berkeley on violence and the state shaped my early thinking on this subject. The audiences at these presentations and at several conferences and seminars offered many thought-provoking questions and suggestions. A few of the people who provided especially pertinent pointers, aside from those already named above, include Susan Amussen, Marisha Caswell, David Cressy, Steve Hindle, Jennine Hurl-Eamon, Margaret McGlynn, Brendan Kane, Elizabeth Papp Kamali, Jonah Miller, Linda Pollock, Justin Roberts, James Sharpe, Debora Shuger, Malcolm Smuts, Courtney Thomas, and Rachel Weil.

In addition to sharing from their own expertise, Helen Good, Simon Healy, and Diana Newton fed, housed, or befriended me on my research trips to Britain. Bob Tittler was always a reliable font of knowledge as well, and I thank both Bob and his wife Anne for hosting me on my trips to or through Montreal.

Colleagues at Dalhousie University have helped in any number of ways. In addition to Cynthia Neville's welcome advice, I could always count on Ruth Bleasdale's encouragement and perspective, for example. Greg Hanlon was generous with references and suggestions. During my five years in administrative posts, I became ever more grateful to those colleagues who sustained the intellectual life of the departmental seminar series and the Halifax medieval and early modern studies reading group. I was also fortunate to have excellent research assistance from Dalhousie students Anne Cummings, Hilary Doda, and Andrea Shannon. Anne's work on the homicide database of inquests and indictments was especially invaluable.

My university also provided the two sabbaticals that enabled this project; on the first, I began the research, and on the second, I finished the writing. Other institutional support came from the Social Sciences and Humanities Research Council of Canada, which funded much of the travel to archives and the student assistance. For the final stage of the project, I was lucky enough to have visiting fellowships at Durham University, one sponsored jointly by the Institute of Advanced Studies and the European Union, and the other provided by the Institute of Medieval and Early Modern Studies and University College. Staff at a long list of libraries and archives provided much assistance. I am particularly indebted to those who tend the collections (and visitors) at the National Archives in Kew, the British Library, the Durham University libraries, the Institute of Historical Research, and Dalhousie's libraries, especially its special collections and interlibrary loans departments.

While working on this book, I published several articles and essays on related subjects: 'License to Kill: Assassination and the Politics of Murder in Elizabethan and Early Stuart England'; 'Bodies of Evidence: Sex and Murder (or Gender and Homicide) in Early Modern England'; No Greater Provocation? Adultery and the Mitigation of Murder in English Law'; '"Murder's Crimson Badge": Homicide in the Age of Shakespeare'; and 'Marks of Division: Cross-Border Remand after 1603 and the Case of Lord Sanquhar'. (The full publishing details for these pieces appear in the bibliography.) Some of the material from 'Murder's Crimson Badge' reappears here in chapters one and five; short selections from 'Bodies of Evidence' appear in chapter one as well. As such, I thank Oxford University Press and Wiley for permission to reuse parts of those papers. Brief passages from another essay also appear in chapter five: 'Crime, Punishment, and Violence in *The Tudors*', in *History, Fiction, and The Tudors*, edited by William Robison (Basingstoke, 2016), pp. 235–47, reproduced with permission of Palgrave Macmillan. I have not drawn upon passages of any substance from the other articles. I mention them here in part to note that readers particularly interested in the facets of homicide's history explored in them might want to consult the articles as well as the book, but mainly to thank again the people who helped in their preparation. While I decided not to reproduce much material that was already in print, the discussions and exchanges that preceded those publications have been helpful here.

My grandmother, Dorothy Kesselring, died while I was finishing this project. This is hardly the sort of book one dedicates to the memory of a loved one, but I do want to acknowledge her support and inspiration over all the years. She took me on my first visits to record offices, after all, when she brought my 12-year-old self along on her family history road trip. Having been a sensible sort, she must at times have thought that I was spending my time on strange subjects when I later returned to the archives, but she was always my biggest fan and best listener. She is missed. I am so grateful to her and to everyone else who helped along the way.

Contents

Abbreviations and Conventions   ix

1. Introduction: From the King's Peace to Public Justice   1

2. 'In *Corona Populi*': Early Modern Coroners and their Inquests   37

3. 'An Image of Deadly Feud': Recompense, Revenge,
   and the Appeal of Homicide   68

4. 'That Saucy Paradox': The Politics of Duelling in Early
   Modern England   94

5. 'For Publick Satisfaction': Punishment, Print, Plays, and
   Public Vengeance   120

   Conclusion   147

Appendix: The Records and the Database   157
Bibliography   161
Index   181

Abbreviations and Conventions

APC   *Acts of the Privy Council 1542–1628*, edited by John Roche Dasent, 43 vols. (London, 1890–1949).

BL   British Library, London

CAR   *Calendar of Assize Records: Home Circuit Indictments*, edited by J.S. Cockburn, 11 vols. (London, 1975–85) and *Calendar of Assize Indictments: Kent Indictments, 1625–1688*, edited by J.S. Cockburn, 4 vols. (London, 1989–95 for vols. 1–3; Woodbridge, 1997 for vol. 4).

CAS   Cumbria Archive Service

DUL   Durham University Library

EEBO   *Early English Books Online*

ER   *English Reports*, 178 vols. (London, 1900–32).

JP   justice of the peace

MCR   *Middlesex County Records*, edited by John Cordy Jeaffreson, 4 vols. (London, 1886–92).

MP   member of parliament

ODNB   *Oxford Dictionary of National Biography*, online edn, edited by David Cannadine (Oxford, 2004).

P&P   *Past and Present*

RPS   *Records of the Parliaments of Scotland to 1707*, edited by K.M. Brown et al. (St. Andrews, 2007–17).

SRP   *Stuart Royal Proclamations*, edited by Paul L. Hughes and James F. Larkin, 2 vols. (Oxford, 1973–83).

TRP   *Tudor Royal Proclamations*, edited by Paul L. Hughes and James F. Larkin, 3 vols. (New Haven, CT, 1964–69).

All manuscript citations are to the National Archives, Kew, unless otherwise noted.

I have modernized the spelling and punctuation in all quotations, except where the original seems particularly apposite. Dates appear in New Style, though the year is taken to begin on 1 January.

English statutes are cited by regnal date and chapter from *The Statutes of the Realm*, edited by A. Luders et al., 11 vols. (London, 1810–25). Citations for Scottish statutes use the original calendar year and reference number as provided by *The Records of the Parliaments of Scotland to 1707*, edited by K.M. Brown et al. (St. Andrews, 2007–17).

Biblical quotations come from the King James Version of 1611 unless otherwise noted.

1

Introduction
From the King's Peace to Public Justice

Murder is perhaps not the worst thing we do to each other, at least not in sheer numbers: globally, today, roughly a half a million people die in acts of criminal homicide every year, compared to the imprecise but far greater numbers of people who die in state-sponsored conflicts or from deprivation and need.[1] But murder potentially touches everyone, even those who do not live lives made especially precarious by war or poverty. It is something that we can all imagine happening to ourselves; perhaps, too, we might imagine ourselves doing it to others. We see killing as the worst of acts in the abstract, yet in some instances as excusable, justifiable, merciful, or maybe even commendable. We recognize it as being both individual and social in its roots: we look to an individual's greed, rage, sadism, warped sense of justice, or other such motive, while also knowing that some cultures and some societies produce distinctive kinds of killings or sustain more or less homicidal violence than others. We see it as being always with us, and yet also historical: while the impulses that lead to homicide might well be bred in the bone and shaped by evolutionary pressures, some societies in the past, as today, gave them freer rein than others. Whether as individuals, as members of societies, or as organized into states, we are capable of gross violence, but we use repertoires of action and interpretation that change through time.

The pages that follow seek to say something about homicide in a particular place and time: England in the early modern era, from the end of the 1400s to the late 1600s. Wales comes into the study occasionally, too, after the early sixteenth-century integration of its laws and administration with those of the English. In this very Christian society, attentive to biblical accounts of Creation, people traced the history of homicide back almost to the beginning. To paraphrase Milton, Eve's weakness in the Garden allowed Death in all his shapes to enter, but his very first appearance was called forth by the first man born, when Cain killed his brother Abel. The early modern English grounded in their scriptures a belief that of all the dismal ways Death might lead them to his grim cave, only this one required a response in kind: while God had allowed Cain to live, He later warned Noah that 'Who so sheddeth man's blood, by man shall his blood be shed: for in the

---

[1] United Nations Office on Drugs and Crime, *Global Study on Homicide 2013*: https://www.unodc.org/unodc/en/data-and-analysis/statistics/publications.html

image of God made He man'.[2] They believed, too, that the same passions, humours, and susceptibility to sin that made some people murderers existed in all people. As one 1573 news report on a killing observed darkly, 'Behold, we be all made of the same mould, printed with the same stamp, and endued with the same nature that the offenders are. We be the imps of the old Adam, and the venom of sin which he received from the old serpent is shed into us all.'[3] Yet even while early modern men and women traced murder's roots to Creation and saw it as a sin to which any might succumb, they believed that the propensity to such violence varied according to climate, complexion, diet, and environment.[4] Some observed, too, real novelties around them in an otherwise age-old problem. They commented that 'in this age' laws defined and punished homicides differently than they had done in days gone by and worried about the new ways of killing that had appeared amongst them.[5]

A few of the novelties upon which they commented make the homicides of their era worth studying in our own, together with one upon which they did not remark. Most particularly we might point to the redefinition of laws that shaped the ways people understood and responded to criminal killings well into the present day. Jurists, jurors, and others came more clearly to distinguish murder from manslaughter, with the more and less serious species of the broader class of criminal homicides coming to differ according to new formulations of provocation. The distinctions they formalized in the sixteenth and seventeenth centuries had earlier roots and endured for a very long time thereafter, perhaps making them seem natural; but the nature of those distinctions was unusual in Europe at the time and had important effects. One other fundamental change they did not notice has been revealed by scholars working over the past few decades: a significant and lasting reduction in the rates of interpersonal homicide. That is, the levels of fatal violence that individuals perpetrated on each other, rather than state violence or suicides, decreased over time. The nature of the records that survive do not allow us precise numbers, but show that over the sixteenth and seventeenth centuries, homicide rates fell dramatically, with the English the first to see what eventually and fitfully became a pan-European shift from more to less interpersonal homicidal violence.

Thus, beyond the enduring interest in a persistent fact of human behaviour, and beyond what killings in any time and place can tell us of the societies in which they happened, the new definitions and diminishing incidence of homicide give us particular reasons to study its history in early modern England. This book does not attempt to offer a comprehensive analysis of the subject in all its facets; instead, it focuses on a set of topics that highlight a development that connects and helps explain the two big changes noted above. It brings together the legal and the social

---

[2] Genesis 9:6; John Milton, *Paradise Lost*, edited by Barbara Lewalski (Malden, MA, 2007), vol. 2, pp. 466–7.

[3] Arthur Golding, *A Briefe Discourse of the Late Murther of Master George Saunders* (London, 1573), sig. C4r.

[4] For a classic example of such theories, see William Harrison's ch. 20, 'Of the General Constitution of the Bodies of the Britons', in *The Description of England*, edited by Georges Edelen (Ithaca, NY, 1968).

[5] See, e.g., John Wilkinson, *A Treatise Collected out of the Statutes... Concerning the Office and Authorities of Coroners and Sherifes* (London, 1618 and 1657), p. 10; DUL, MSP 49, p. 247.

histories of homicide, too often treated separately. It also follows the lead of medievalists who have shown the inextricable links between political history and the histories of justice, law, and order. Focusing on the politics of murder, the pages that follow seek to show how homicide became more fully 'public' in these years, and how its place on the spectrum between private and public moved in ways that mattered. Homicide became more effectively criminalized as the 'king's peace' increasingly became 'the public peace'. By the early modern era, the English had long treated slayings as offences not just against the victims and their kin, but also against the king. At the onset of modernity, even as the balance between kin and king tilted more firmly towards the latter, they also came to see murder as an offence against a state or public more broadly conceived.

THE POLITICS OF MURDER

England's history from the late 1400s through to the late 1600s moves from the conclusion of one period of civil conflict—the so-called 'Wars of the Roses'— through to the aftermath of the seventeenth-century revolutions. Quite aside from domestic conflicts, repeated bouts of military action abroad marked the era, with especially intense enlistment of men for the wars from the middle of Queen Elizabeth's reign in the late sixteenth century through to the beginning of her successor's at the dawn of the seventeenth. The English and Welsh produced dramatic increases in population from the early 1500s, with an estimated population of roughly two and a half million people in the early 1500s peaking at just over five million *c.*1650, when growth rates tapered off. This expanding population dealt with years of marked inflation and desperate hardship for many of its members, especially in the decades on either side of 1600. The period saw classical learning and civic humanism shape intellectual culture and normative political vocabularies. It witnessed a long religious reformation that began early in the sixteenth century as the country's official worship and the bulk of its population shifted from Catholic to Protestant, with all the theological, political, and cultural changes that this transformation entailed. Unstable dynastic politics saw the usurper king, Henry VII, bring a degree of order, but then lose his eldest son and be followed instead by the second. The much-married Henry VIII was in turn succeeded by a minor, two women, and then Scottish kings, the first of whom brought with him ideas and experiences nurtured in a rather different legal and social context. The period saw the spread of printing and the advent of the commercial stage. Legally, the era produced a huge growth in litigation, the consolidation of common law courts and modes of legal argument under noted jurists such as Sir Edward Coke, and the development—then demise—of bodies such as the Court of Star Chamber. The list could go on, of course, to highlight the commercial shifts that enabled corporations to embark on trade, conquest, and colonization efforts with global consequences; I only recall here those developments that might most usefully be kept in mind when reading the following pages, which focus on the politics of murder and changes to the rates and laws of homicide.

Why 'the politics' of murder? The study of crime is usually resolutely social or sociological in its focus and approach; why might adding a political lens be useful or appropriate? In what ways can we consider homicide 'political'? We might point to the early modern political theorists who so often saw the power to take life as either the foundation of sovereignty and political power or at least as one of its fundamental attributes. For the Protestant bishop and political theorist John Ponet, writing in 1556, God's declaration to Noah that manslayers must be slain by man created political power: 'By this ordinance and law He instituteth politike power and gave authority to men to make more laws. For He that giveth man authority over the body and life of man, because He would have man to live quietly with man that all might serve him quietly in holiness and righteousness all the days of their life, it cannot be denied, but He gave him authority over goods, lands, possessions, and all such things.'[6] Later, Robert Filmer and John Locke rested their very different theories of political power on similar foundations. For Filmer, the subjection of children to their fathers served as the basis of all regal authority by God's own ordination, the proof of which lay in the 'dominion of life and death' fathers once had over their children. He continued that 'these acts of judging in capital crimes, of making war, and concluding peace, are the chiefest marks of sovereignty that are found in any monarch'.[7] Locke, famously, carefully distinguished between political and patriarchal power, but still defined the former as 'a right of making laws with penalties of death, and consequently all less penalties'.[8] Others might in fact have the ability to take life, but the *authority* to do so was the sovereign's alone.

Stepping away from political theorists to look at politics in action, we see the king's council, then the Privy Council, frequently intervene in the investigation and prosecution of homicides throughout England and Wales. In fact, a statute of 1541 made it easier for councillors to proceed against suspected traitors and murderers they had brought in for examination: no longer did the king's agents need to return suspects to the county in which they had committed their crimes for trial by a local jury, but they could instead try them with a special commission at more speed and less expense.[9] Councillors tortured suspects in some murders, treating the crime as a danger to the polity similar to treason or heresy.[10] More routinely, the monarch's closest councillors called upon local officials for information about slayings, hauled suspects in for questioning, and issued admonitions; the council registers are full of such high-level interventions into homicides.

We might point to the key political figures of the age themselves tied up in slayings, or the utility of rumours of murder as devices to damage one's political

---

[6] John Ponet, *A Shorte Treatise of Politike Power* (Strasbourg, 1556), sigs. A4r–v.
[7] Robert Filmer, *Patriarcha, or, The Natural Power of Kings* (London, 1680), p. 13.
[8] John Locke, 'Second Treatise of Civil Government (1690)', in *Two Treatises of Government*, edited by Peter Laslett (Cambridge, 1988), p. 268.
[9] 33 Henry VIII c. 23.
[10] John H. Langbein, *Torture and the Law of Proof* (Chicago, 1977), pp. 73–4, 80. The Privy Council's offshoots, the Council in the Marches and the Council in the North, could also license torture for suspected murderers. See, e.g., SP 46/3, no. 10.

opponents: from the tales of Richard III's orders to kill his young nephews in the Tower, so advantageous to Henry VII after the new king's men killed the old on the field of battle, to the English 'trial' of Mary Queen of Scots for procuring her husband's death (and the scandal of his slaying of her private secretary), through to the rumours that King Charles I's favourite, the duke of Buckingham, had murdered King James. We might continue to the formal charge against Charles at his trial that he was not only a traitor to his people but a murderer as well, guilty of upholding a 'personal interest' against that of 'the public', with his judges thereafter to be tried as murderers in turn. (We should perhaps take a moment to remind ourselves that the political revolution of 1688/9 was, unusually, achieved without the deaths of any of its principals.) We might look to the fears and facts of assassination attempts that became so central to politics from the late sixteenth century on: in a new development, driven by confessional differences and signalled by the late sixteenth-century appearance of 'assassination' in English, people from a variety of backgrounds came to consider themselves licensed to act in the public interest, as they saw it, by killing (or trying to kill) their leaders.[11] Or we might look to the ways that the investigation and trial of homicides drew so many individuals— mostly men, but also some women—into the state's operations. Whether we adopt a narrow definition of politics as the conduct or philosophy of affairs of state, or a broader definition focused on relationships of power and authority, homicide was abundantly political.[12]

The particular thread followed here is how homicide became more fully 'public', a matter not for private vengeance or composition but increasingly understood as an offence against the king, and then gradually and tentatively as an affront to something conceived as 'the public' more broadly. Signs of this change appear in a number of different places, as the following chapters explore through a wide variety of sources of evidence. Records of practice such as coroners' inquisitions and court records as well as normative sources such as legal treatises, statutes, and proclamations are all drawn upon. Law reports—the summaries of cases that recorded judicial opinion on points of law, which legal professionals began to use in this period as precedents to guide subsequent rulings—are also used, as evidence of both pre-script and practice. Private correspondence as well as printed materials, such as the pamphlets that luridly detailed 'true stories' of crime and repentance, are mined as well; as Frances Dolan has urged, they are read as both sources and texts.[13] When

[11] See Kesselring, 'License to Kill: Assassination and the Politics of Murder in Elizabethan and Early Stuart England', *Canadian Journal of History* 48 (2013): pp. 421–40.

[12] For influential discussions of the broadening of political history, see, e.g., Keith Wrightson, 'The Politics of the Parish in Early Modern England', in *The Experience of Authority in Early Modern England*, edited by Paul Griffiths, Adam Fox, and Steve Hindle (Basingstoke, 1996), pp. 10–46 and Patrick Collinson, '*De Republica Anglorum*: Or, History with the Politics Put Back', in *Elizabethan Essays* (London, 1994), pp. 1–30.

[13] Frances Dolan, *True Relations: Reading, Literature, and Evidence in Seventeenth-Century England* (Philadelphia, 2013). As Dolan notes, a model of how to read the 'textual remnants' of the law for patterns of meaning and interpretation can be found in Cynthia Herrup, *A House in Gross Disorder: Sex, Law, and the 2nd Earl of Castlehaven* (Oxford, 1999). Another classic: Natalie Zemon Davis's *Fiction in the Archives: Pardon Tales and their Tellers in Sixteenth-Century France* (Stanford, CA, 1987).

records lend themselves to some reasonably reliable or useful quantification, their contents are quantified; the next section in this introductory chapter, 'The Incidence of Homicide', lays out much of the numerical scene-setting to be done in this book. Just as often, though, the focus here is on records as texts. Attentiveness to language, to terms and keywords, and to changes in vocabulary can reveal shared assumptions and social imaginaries. Without getting caught up in debates about whether language precedes or reflects a concept or experience, we can use changes in the words people spoke and wrote to track the contours of change more broadly.[14]

One very striking change in the vocabulary used to discuss homicide in this era was a growing density and intensity of references to 'the public'—a change evident in political discourse more generally. Distinctions between *res publica* and *res privata* go back, of course, to writers of classical antiquity. People thereafter revived this vocabulary at different times to different effects. In the revolution in canon law and the *ius commune* that unfolded over the twelfth and thirteenth centuries, Pope Innocent III notably invoked public utility for the prosecution of some sins as wrongs not just against God but also against the community. In doing so he offered a maxim that came to be frequently cited to justify various innovations, not least the shift towards inquisitorial modes of criminal prosecution: '*rei publicae interest, ne crimina remaneant impunita*'.[15] In England in the later middle ages people often tied talk of *res publica* to discussions of the 'common weal' or 'commonwealth' and by the late sixteenth century to talk of 'the state'. John Watts has argued that fresh engagements with Cicero and other late Roman republican writers in the mid-fifteenth century, together with the civil war's weakening of aristocratic independence, changed the language of politics by revitalizing consciousness of *res publica* and asserting its links to the commonwealth understood as a political community.[16] Christian humanists as well as evangelical reformers appealed to the 'common weal' over the early and mid-sixteenth century. Thomas Cromwell invoked this ideal in his efforts to promote the royal supremacy over the Church, as did the 'commonwealth men' who came to prominence in the circles of Protector Somerset with their projects for agrarian reform and a Christianized *res publica*. Paul Slack traced a shift from talk of the common weal and commonwealth, which often conflated both the purposes of political activity and the political structures in

---

[14] For particularly effective examples of the attentiveness to language amongst social historians, see, e.g., Keith Wrightson, 'Estates, Degrees, and Sorts: Changing Perceptions of Society in Tudor and Stuart England', in *Language, History, and Class*, edited by P.J. Corfield (Oxford, 1991), pp. 30–52, and Phil Withington, *Society in Early Modern England: The Vernacular Origins of Some Powerful Ideas* (Cambridge, 2010). For the distinctions some scholars draw between 'keywords' and 'terms', and language as constitutive or reflective, see, e.g., Raymond Williams, *Keywords: A Vocabulary of Culture and Society* (Oxford, 1976) and Quentin Skinner, 'Language and Political Change', in *Political Innovation and Conceptual Change*, edited by Terence Ball et al. (Cambridge, 1989), pp. 6–23.

[15] Richard M. Fraher, 'The Theoretical Justification for the New Criminal Law of the High Middle Ages: "*Rei Publicae Interest, Ne Crimina Remanent Impunita*" ', *University of Illinois Law Review* 3 (1984): pp. 577–96.

[16] John Watts, ' "Common Weal" and "Commonwealth": England's Monarchical Republic in the Making, *c.*1450–1630', in *The Languages of Political Society*, edited by Andrea Gamberini et al. (Rome, 2011), pp. 147–63.

which it occurred, to more frequent references to 'the public good' by the late sixteenth and early seventeenth centuries.[17] Such rhetoric was not confined to university scholars and royal councillors; Phil Withington has written of the 'vernacular humanism' that inflected city politics, increasingly viewed in terms of service to 'the public' and 'the public good' by people who were coming to act and talk 'like citizens'.[18]

With the adoption of a rhetoric of 'the public' and what served its interests came struggles over who or what that public consisted of. Historians have written of the 'monarchical republicanism' that emerged in Queen Elizabeth's reign, as men worried about the lack of a successor (or, more precisely, the lack of an English, Protestant successor) embraced concepts of a headless body politic, an 'acephalous monarchy', or a polity that had an existence somewhat independent from that of the monarch.[19] Within this context, Richard Cust has tracked the arrival of 'the public man' from the 1580s to 1620s, a member of a self-consciously active citizenry for whom the contrast between 'public' and 'private' summarized the principles that ought to guide service to commonwealth and country. Drawing upon zealous Calvinism, classical republicanism, and—one might add—a native rhetoric of the common weal, the distinction between public and private, and the valorization of the former, provided a normative political vocabulary 'through which contemporaries sought to legitimate their actions and make sense of the political world around them'. Furthermore, as Cust notes, 'in the political vocabulary of the day, these were highly charged terms with a moral force and potency which allowed them to stand for fundamentally opposed approaches to government and magistracy'.[20] As Ann Hughes and Geoff Baldwin have shown, this praise of 'the public' became entrenched over the civil war years of the mid-seventeenth century: sometimes gendered male but other times used more inclusively, the term was employed in imprecise, sometimes overlapping or contradictory ways, but

[17] Paul Slack, *From Reformation to Improvement: Public Welfare in Early Modern England* (Oxford, 1999), esp. p. 75.

[18] Phil Withington, 'Public Discourse, Corporate Citizenship and State Formation in Early Modern England', *American Historical Review* 112.4 (2007): pp. 1016–38, quote at 1036.

[19] The notion of a 'monarchical republic' prompted by the Elizabethan 'exclusion crisis' derives from Patrick Collinson's work, especially 'The Monarchical Republic of Queen Elizabeth I', *Elizabethan Essays* (London, 1994), and has been explored at length in the essays in *The Monarchical Republic of Early Modern England*, edited by John McDiarmid (Aldershot, 2007). Notes of caution have more recently been expressed by Norman L. Jones and Peter Lake, who dispute the existence of a 'monarchical republic' while acknowledging the influence of ideas or an ideology that might go by the label of 'monarchical republicanism'. See Jones, *Governing by Virtue: Lord Burghley and the Management of Elizabethan England* (Oxford, 2015) and Lake, *Bad Queen Bess: Libellous Politics, Secret Histories, and the Politics of Publicity in the Reign of Queen Elizabeth I* (Oxford, 2016).

[20] Richard Cust, 'The "Public Man" in Late Tudor and Early Stuart England', in *The Politics of the Public Sphere in Early Modern England*, edited by Peter Lake and Steven Pincus (Manchester, 2007), pp. 116–43, quotes at pp. 121 and 123. In the same volume, see also Ann Hughes, 'Men, the "Public" and the "Private" in the English Revolution', pp. 191–212. For the addition of native common weal traditions, see David Rollison, 'The Spectre of the Commonalty: Class Struggle and the Commonweal in England before the Atlantic World', *William and Mary Quarterly* 63 (2006): pp. 221–52; Andy Wood, *The 1549 Rebellions and the Making of Early Modern England* (Cambridge, 2007); and Ethan Shagan, 'The Two Republics: Conflicting Views of Participatory Local Government in Early Tudor England', in *The Monarchical Republic*, pp. 19–36.

generally betokened interests deemed collective and thus of broader value than the singular or private. In time, a notion of 'the public' as an active body or community of people was added to the adjectival use of 'public' to denote something of common concern.[21]

Writers linked 'the public' with justice, peace, and order, with varying inflections. As a base here, we might turn to the judge Sir John Davies and his charge to the grand jury at York in 1620. He praised the 'fair and full assembly' before him, with special care for the jurors, representatives of their fellow freeholders who performed an important public service. That service was 'to maintain and continue the public peace, by the execution of the public justice, a work so noble and so worthy as I doubt whether any temporal business that can be done in the life of man be comparable unto it'. The public peace he defined as a well-ordered concord that reflected the divine order. He likened it to 'that which is called harmony in music, when the strings of an instrument are all in tune without jarring and without discord'. Davies continued:

> The public peace is the cause that your fruitful fields are so well manured, your barren wastes converted, your herds and flocks increased, your cities and towns enlarged, trade and traffic by sea and land freely entertained, and all the commodities of the earth improved. In these halcyon days of peace all arts and sciences, liberal and mechanical, have been brought to perfection and have produced and daily do produce innumerable things, as well for pleasure and ornament as for the necessary use of the life of man, the commonwealth, and in the commonwealth the church of God doth flourish, the gospel hath a more free passage, and religion itself takes deep root. In a word, every man doth sit under his own vine, and under his own fig tree, and enjoy the fruits of his own labours, which are the chiefest felicities that the heart of man desireth in this life.

How was this public peace maintained? Through the execution of 'public justice', the scope and end of which was 'to appease all tumults, to end all controversies, and to repose and settle all men and matters in quiet and safety'. Justice maintained order in all its senses; without it, 'the land would be full of thieves, the sea full of pirates, the commons would rise against the nobility, and the nobility against the Crown'. Drawing towards the more practical business of the day, Davies told the jurors gathered before him that, 'therefore, the law of England doth put into your hands who are the grand inquest, and the public inquisitors for this county, the very key of justice'.[22] In his enumeration of offences, Davies continued to treat homicide as an offence primarily 'hurtful to particular persons', in contrast to acts of treason which endangered all, but depicted its punishment as necessarily public. Private vengeance must give way to public justice.

---

[21] Ann Hughes, 'Men, the "Public" and the "Private" ', and Geoff Baldwin, 'The "Public" as a Rhetorical Community in Early Modern England', in *Communities in Early Modern England*, edited by Alexandra Shepard and Phil Withington (Manchester, 2000), pp. 199–215.
[22] BL, Harleian MS 7581, ff. 61–77.

The increasingly insistent talk of 'the public' and the contrasting of public and private accompanied references to 'the state', another term new to these years.[23] People still conceptualized the 'state' as something of a public/private hybrid that included the personal 'estate' of the monarch but also, for some, denoted a polity or body that might in some ways be separate or separable from the person on the throne. Such claims to collective and common interests had the potential to mask unequal power arrangements in society at large and to shape high political conflict. Claims to serve a public good were ideological at base, contested and contestable, and resolutely tied to interests. The chapters gathered here, though, focus on how homicide fits into this conceptual world, how killings came to be understood as something of concern to this 'public'. Much of the historiography of homicide's past focuses on the state—as an entity and not as a concept that was itself being developed and refined in the early modern era. Looking at this state not just through modern sociological definitions and lenses, but also through the political vocabulary in use at the time, and the closely related rhetoric of public and private, can provide fresh insights into the history of homicide.

First, though, we begin with discussions of the two broad changes that prompt attention to homicide in early modern England, with a section on the incidence of criminal killings, followed by one on the laws relating to murder and manslaughter, before moving to a brief overview of the chapters that follow.

THE INCIDENCE OF HOMICIDE

What do we already know of the incidence of homicide in early modern England? Most significantly, as noted above, the period witnessed a marked and lasting reduction in the rate of interpersonal slaying. In the 1970s, new interest in social history opened the floodgates of research into the experiences and activities of people long overlooked in accounts of the past. A particularly powerful torrent of this 'history from below' was directed at crime and criminals and their treatment by the courts: scholars counted indictments and incorporated material from older institutional legal histories to produce rich studies of social relations.[24] T.R. Gurr assembled numbers produced by some of these historians of crime to create a graph that suggested a staggering decline in lethal interpersonal violence from the

[23] On the emergence of the concept and language of 'the state' by the late sixteenth century, see especially Quentin Skinner, *The Foundations of Modern Political Thought* (Cambridge, 1978), 2 vols., esp. vol. 2, pp. 349–58.

[24] See, e.g., J.M. Beattie, 'The Pattern of Crime in England, 1660–1800', *P&P* 62 (1974): pp. 47–95; J.S. Cockburn, 'The Nature and Incidence of Crime in England, 1559–1625: A Preliminary Survey,' in *Crime in England, 1550–1800*, edited by J.S. Cockburn (Princeton, NJ, 1977), pp. 49–71; James Buchanan Given, *Society and Homicide in Thirteenth-Century England* (Stanford, CA, 1977); P.E.H. Hair, 'Deaths from Violence in Britain: A Tentative Secular Survey', *Population Studies* 25 (1971): pp. 5–24; Carl Hammer, 'Patterns of Homicide in a Medieval University Town: Fourteenth-Century Oxford', *P&P* 78 (1978): pp. 3–23; Barbara Hanawalt, *Crime and Conflict in English Communities, 1300–1348* (Cambridge, MA, 1979); Joel Samaha, *Law and Order in Historical Perspective: The Case of Elizabethan Essex* (New York, 1974); Douglas Hay et al., *Albion's Fatal Tree: Crime and Society in Eighteenth-Century England* (New York, 1975).

middle ages to the modern era, with the steepest slide between *c*.1500 and 1700. Adopting the standard expression of homicide rates as *x* number of victims per year per 100,000 people (with the latter number often implicit), Gurr estimated annual homicide rates of about 20:100,000 in the late thirteenth century, down to about seven in the late sixteenth, and then to two in the eighteenth. This decline occurred before modern medicine or modern policing might have affected the numbers.[25]

Lawrence Stone's speculations about the significance of Gurr's graphs, and in particular the evidence for an interruption of the downward trend in the late sixteenth and early seventeenth centuries, provoked a vibrant debate on the levels and meanings of violence in early modern society.[26] Aware that violent acts exist within historically specific systems of meanings and values, as Susan Amussen compellingly demonstrated for the era, some historians of crime turned to the ways in which cultural context informed reactions to crime and to violent behaviour.[27] What counts as violence depends on the context, and our definitions. Do we focus only on force deemed illegitimate by the conventions of its own time— much of what we might consider 'violent' would not have been seen as such in the sixteenth-century—or do we include any intentional act of physical harm, for example? Historians engaged in this discussion expressed serious and legitimate reservations about seeing signs of the declining homicide rate as evidence of declining levels of 'violence' more generally, and often moved on to other areas of focus. Some turned to detailed studies of individual murders, or murderers, seeing the crimes and the resulting trials as 'social dramas' that reveal otherwise submerged aspects of social and political life when closely examined.[28] A particularly rich vein of scholarship incorporated the early work on crime into studies of political culture and state formation. Interested in the interpretative frameworks and codes of conduct within which political action (broadly defined) took place, these historians highlighted the broad participatory base of the early modern state. Behaviours became effectively criminalized not solely by parliamentary statute, but also by

[25] T.R. Gurr, 'Historical Trends in Violent Crime: A Critical Review of the Evidence', *Crime and Justice* 3 (1981): pp. 295–353.

[26] Lawrence Stone, 'Interpersonal Violence in English Society, 1300–1980', *P&P* 101 (1983): pp. 22–33; J.A. Sharpe, 'The History of Violence in England: Some Observations', *P&P* 108 (1985): pp. 206–15; Stone, 'A Rejoinder', ibid., 216–24; J.S. Cockburn, 'Patterns of Violence in English Society: Homicide in Kent, 1560–1985', *P&P* 130 (1991): pp. 70–106; Susan Amussen, 'Discipline and Power: The Social Meanings of Violence in Early Modern England', *Journal of British Studies* 34 (1995): pp. 1–34; and more recently, Sharpe, 'Revisiting the "Violence We Have Lost": Homicide in Seventeenth-Century Cheshire', *English Historical Review* 131 (2016): pp. 293–323.

[27] Amussen, 'Discipline and Power', and see, e.g.: Garthine Walker, *Crime, Gender and Social Order in Early Modern England* (Cambridge, 2003); Stuart Carroll, ed., *Cultures of Violence: Interpersonal Violence in Historical Perspective* (Houndmills, 2007); Paul Griffiths, *Lost Londons: Change, Crime and Control in the Capital City, 1550–1660* (Cambridge, 2008). For discussions of 'violence' and how historians have defined it, see, too, Pieter Spierenburg, 'Violence: Reflections about a Word', in *Violence in Europe: Historical and Contemporary Perspectives*, edited by Sophie Body-Gendrot and Pieter Spierenburg (New York, 2009), pp. 13–26.

[28] e.g. Angus McLaren, *A Prescription for Murder: The Victorian Serial Killings of Dr. Thomas Neill Cream* (Chicago, 1993); John Brewer, *A Sentimental Murder: Love and Madness in the Eighteenth Century* (New York, 2004); Paul Monod, *The Murder of Mr Grebell: Madness and Civility in an English Town* (New Haven, CT, 2003); Martin Wiener, *An Empire on Trial: Race, Murder and Justice under British Rule, 1870–1935* (Cambridge, 2009).

locals' willingness to indict and convict. Jurors, constables, bailiffs, and others used the law as a resource to their own ends and in so doing brought the state into the locality.[29] Malcolm Gaskill, for example, included a substantial section on murder in his *Crime and Mentalities* but disavowed any interest in counting crime: he focused instead on the cultural consequences of homicide, in particular on the methods of investigating the offence.[30] In Gaskill's work, as with others from this stream of study, the emphasis moved from crime to the ways in which its prosecution allowed people to participate in state formation and thus to extend the scope and functions of governance.

Meanwhile, the evidence for a declining homicide rate remains. Early dissections of efforts to chart homicide statistics over time expressed reservations about the reliability or comparability of rates derived from both patchily surviving court records and uncertain estimates of population, with especially strong qualms about rates derived from scarce medieval records. Early doubts seem to have resolved in favour of seeing such rates as imprecise, yes, but as valid indicators of broad patterns of change. J.S. Cockburn focused on the county of Kent, for which records survive in reasonably complete runs from 1559 forward, and suggested a homicide rate of fewer than 4:100,000 for the 1560s and 1570s, with an increase to 6:100,000 dating from the 1580s, and a lasting decline setting in by the 1680s. Noting the existence of regional and short-term variations, and plumbing carefully the 'shifting sands of statistical uncertainty', Cockburn nevertheless argued that the data provided 'strong support for the thesis that the four centuries after 1560 saw a decisive decline in the incidence of homicide in England. The secular trend is unmistakeably downward.'[31] John Beattie's prodigious work on Surrey's court records began only in 1660, but showed declines in rates of homicide from an average of 6:100,000 in the two decades after the Restoration to fewer than 4:100,000 in the early 1700s.[32] More recently, James Sharpe's close study of Cheshire records suggests a rate of about eight to twelve killings per 100,000 people in the 1620s, dropping to 2:100,000 in the 1690s. While he treats such rates individually as tentative, he notes that as a series, they show that homicidal violence in Cheshire unambiguously diminished.[33] Can we assert with confidence a precise rate of homicide prosecutions, let alone of homicides committed, in any given year before modern record keeping? No. But we can be confident of the broad pattern of significant decline.

Historians of a sociological bent studying places beyond the shores of England and Wales have also shown a continued commitment to counting and to fleshing out Gurr's homicide graph. Manuel Eisner compiled and analysed over ninety

---

[29] e.g. Michael J. Braddick, *State Formation in Early Modern England, c.1550–1700* (Cambridge, 2000); Steve Hindle, *The State and Social Change in Early Modern England, c.1550–1640* (Basingstoke, 2000). An important transitional work: Cynthia Herrup, *The Common Peace: Participation and the Criminal Law in Seventeenth-Century England* (Cambridge, 1987).

[30] Malcolm Gaskill, *Crime and Mentalities in Early Modern England* (Cambridge, 2000).

[31] Cockburn, 'Patterns of Violence', pp. 76, 78, 101.

[32] John Beattie, *Crime and the Courts in England, 1660–1800* (Oxford, 1986), esp. p. 107.

[33] Sharpe, 'Revisiting the "Violence We Have Lost" ', p. 301. See, too, his *A Fiery & Furious People: A History of Violence in England* (London, 2016).

quantitative studies of pre-modern homicide in Europe: his findings confirm a decline in lethal violence over the early modern period, first in England and the Netherlands beginning in the sixteenth century and then in other areas of north-western Europe.[34] He suggested two main routes to better understand this pattern: the accumulation of more data to allow better comparisons by location and date, and the disaggregation of the data to detect changing patterns within the incidence of homicide. Much work to date suggests that disproportionate declines in elite violence and in lethal conflicts between unrelated men lie behind the overall pattern of change.

A number of historians have confirmed such declines in their own studies and offered possible explanations for this historic shift, with many focusing on state formation, especially as viewed through Norbert Elias's concept of the 'civilizing process'. A sociologist whose key work first appeared in German in 1939, Elias had argued from the premise that the structure of society and structure of behaviour are linked, given that 'social structures' are nothing more than 'figurations formed by large numbers of interdependent individuals'. Over the long span of Western history, he argued, people came to restrain the entire 'affect structure' of instincts and drives—manifested in such things as table manners, bodily functions, and violence—as webs of interdependence tightened with the development of an increasingly differentiated economy and an increasingly centralized state. Historians of violence who draw upon Elias have focused particularly on his discussion of the centralizing state: violence does not disappear, but its expression is moderated as the threat any one person poses for another is lessened and more calculable when the state concentrates to itself the possession of arms and use of force. Partly through conscious self-control and partly through habit, individuals less often act upon their violent urges and in time the whole structure of human relations changes.[35]

Pieter Spierenburg and Randolph Roth have both drawn upon Elias. Spierenburg, in particular, has emerged as the champion for seeing the 'civilizing process' as the key to explaining the pattern of elite violence and the decline of feuds and vendettas at all social levels, also incorporating anthropological work on honour and its varied forms. Drawing primarily upon his own research in Amsterdam's archives, Spierenburg suggests as a working hypothesis that we can 'expect the murder rate to be highest, and traditional male honour to be most intense, when the monopolization of violence by state institutions and economic differentiation are at their lowest point'. Homicide was criminalized only slowly and patchily over the late middle ages and early modern period, as the state's sanctions came to replace private settlements.[36] Roth also privileges the state in his explanation for patterns in lethal violence in America, but in a rather different way. He notes that

[34] Manuel Eisner, 'Long-Term Historical Trends in Violent Crime', *Crime and Justice: A Review of Research* 30 (2003): pp. 83–142.

[35] Norbert Elias, *The Civilizing Process*, trans. Edmund Jephcott (Oxford, 1994).

[36] Pieter Spierenburg, 'Violence and the Civilizing Process: Does it Work?', *Crime, Histoire & Sociétés* 5.2 (2001): pp. 87–105, and *A History of Murder: Personal Violence in Europe from the Middle Ages to the Present* (Cambridge, 2008).

types of killings move along different trajectories, but hypothesizes that patterns in overall homicide rates correlate with changes in people's feelings about government. Roth privileges political events in triggering changes in feelings of national belonging and perceptions of government legitimacy, and thus in altering levels of violence in society. Like Spierenburg and some others working in the field, Roth acknowledges that evolutionary psychology and its cognate disciplines can offer useful insights, though in his epic study of homicide in America, his focus remains on the *historical* aspects of culture, politics, and state formation that are necessary to explain changing patterns within the incidence of homicide and in levels of lethal violence more generally. As Roth asks, 'Why, if humans have roughly the same capacity for violence, does murder claim 1 in 100,000 adults in some societies, and 1 in 20 in others?... History holds the key.'[37]

Studies done to date, then, tell us that rates of interpersonal homicide in late seventeenth-century England were lower than those of the late sixteenth century, which were in turn quite likely lower than medieval rates. Unfortunately, the nature of records that survive from the years between *c*.1480 and 1680 leaves the precise contours of the decline and what seems to have been a brief reversal poorly delineated.[38] Coroners submitted some of their records of inquests into suspicious deaths to the central Court of King's Bench from 1487 onwards; from 1559 on, some of the files of the travelling English assize justices survive.[39] The patchy survival of such records, compounded by uncertainties about population numbers, means that we cannot use them to calculate even moderately useful homicide rates. We need to wait until we get to solid runs of all court records from a given county or district in the late sixteenth century. We can, however, use the earlier records as a sample, to reveal patterns within the broader incidence of homicide and to provide context for qualitative discussions of murder.

Thus, while insufficient records remain to allow precise calculations of homicide rates throughout the early modern period, enough survive to serve as a sample of

---

[37] Randolph Roth, 'Homicide in Early Modern England, 1549–1800: The Need for a Quantitative Synthesis', *Crime, Histoire & Sociétés* 5.3 (2001): pp. 33–67, and *American Homicide* (Cambridge, MA, 2009). On this point, see also Sharpe, *Fiery & Furious People*, pp. 19–22. For a review of the influence of evolutionary psychology and other behavioural sciences in the field, see Gregory Hanlon, 'The Decline of Violence in the West: From Cultural to Post-Cultural History', *English Historical Review* 128 (2013): pp. 367–400, and the essays in the special issue of the *British Journal of Criminology*, 51 (2011). Martin Daly and Margo Wilson's *Homicide* (Hawthorne, CA, 1988) is a classic and thought-provoking work in the field.

[38] Matthew Lockwood has recently queried the notion, expressed by Stone, Sharpe, Cockburn, and others, that the downward trend in homicide rates was interrupted or reversed from *c*.1580–1620, arguing instead that the decline set in from the 1530s and stayed fairly consistent thereafter: *The Conquest of Death: Violence and the Birth of the Modern England State* (New Haven, CT, 2017), ch. 7. For a discussion of this point, see Appendix.

[39] See especially Cockburn, *Assizes* and *CAR*. While the statutes of 1534–43 largely integrated English and Welsh law and administration, the Court of Great Sessions, not King's Bench, dealt with most criminal business there. Good runs of Welsh records survive from the 1540s. On the integration, see, e.g., Peter Roberts, 'The English Crown, the Principality of Wales, and the Council in the Marches, 1534-1641', in *The British Problem, c.1534–1707*, edited by Brendan Bradshaw and John Morrill (Basingstoke, 1996), pp. 118–47. On the records, see Glyn Parry, *A Guide to the Records of Great Sessions in Wales* (Aberystwyth, 1995). Murray Chapman has produced useful calendars of the Montgomeryshire gaol files.

the larger, deadlier whole to give insight into the cases people brought before the courts as suspected homicides, and whom they identified as the killers in their midst. My dataset, compiled from coroners' inquisitions and court indictments produced in England between *c*.1480 and 1680, includes information on 3,601 people identified as victims of homicide and 4,374 people implicated in their killings.[40] This is not a complete set of records for a given area of the sort that might allow the generation of homicide rates expressed as *x*:100,000, but it should serve as a reasonably representative guide to what was common or uncommon. One must take care in using these records, of course. Not least to be borne in mind is that they document accusations, not 'actual' killings. Trial juries later decided that some of these supposed victims died from natural or accidental causes, and they deemed a good number of the people charged with killings not guilty. Some other homicides presumably went undetected. Reasons for caution in how one reads these records certainly exist, but as an indication of the claims that came before the courts and in what proportions and patterns, they can provide useful context.

Of all the supposed killers and victims in this sample, 80 per cent were men: 3,522 men were implicated in the deaths of 2,859 other men. This means, of course, that 20 per cent of people suspected of being killers and of the putative victims were women. This preponderance of men among the killers and victims accords with the results of studies of other times and places. The proportions did vary over time, though, with a peak in the percentage of killings attributed to women in the late 1500s and early 1600s, when indictments for killings of infants and by means of witchcraft began to proliferate. Already here we get a sense of the care that we need to take when interpreting such numbers: presumably almost all of the supposed victims of killings by means of witchcraft died of causes other than murder, and all by means other than magic. Some scholars opt to remove killings of infants from their surveys of homicides as they think that the motives and implications of such deaths distinguish them from the kind of violence they wish to study. It is worth noting, though, that early modern observers treated killings both of infants and by means of witchcraft as murders—indeed, as amongst the most egregious of cold-blooded, calculated killings against which defence was impossible—and so might have been less sanguine about women's lower levels of violence than broad averages might suggest.[41]

Women were disproportionately charged with domestic killings, but if we can assume that the indictments and inquisitions note familial and master–servant relationships when they existed, only about 16 per cent of these supposed homicides might be counted as 'domestic'. This is in stark contrast to today's rates: the proportion of domestic homicides typically goes up as the overall rates of homicide in a society decline, and is now somewhere between 30 and 50 per cent of all

---

[40] See Appendix for a description of the database.

[41] Explored at greater length in Kesselring, 'Bodies of Evidence: Sex and Murder (or Gender and Homicide) in Early Modern England', *Gender & History* 27 (2015): pp. 245–62. Given that this point is sometimes misunderstood, it is perhaps worth noting here that the killing of infants *did* count as homicide even before the 1623/4 passage of the so-called 'infanticide act', more properly the 'Act to prevent the murdering of bastard children' (1 Jac. I c. 27).

homicides in England, depending on whom one counts.[42] Almost all of the killers identified in these records were adults, whereas nearly 16 per cent of victims were infants (9.3 per cent) or children between the ages of one and fourteen (6.4 per cent). The majority of these young victims were the children of the killers, and most were killed by their mothers. Only five individuals were said to have killed a parent. A similar disparity existed in the master–servant relationship: fifty of the 3,601 victims were described explicitly as the servants or apprentices of their killers, with twenty-eight killed by women and twenty-two by men. Only eight servants or apprentices were said to have killed their masters or mistresses, often in self-defence during a beating. In keeping with the power dynamic in the familial relationships between parents and children, masters and servants, more husbands killed their wives than vice versa—the one subset of domestic killings in which men dominated: sixty-six men in this set of records were charged with killing their spouses, with thirty-two women accused of doing the same. Subordinates who intentionally killed someone to whom they owed obedience—whether wives their husbands, or servants their masters or mistresses—faced charges of petty treason rather than murder, with law protecting hierarchies of power. In practice, though, the realities of those relationships of inequality left the subordinate more likely to suffer deadly violence.

Status designations in such records are often unreliable, unfortunately, but may serve as a rough guide.[43] For women, the only such designation reflected marital status—spinster, wife, or widow—and provides no hint of economic or hierarchical standing, quite aside from seeming a bit randomly applied in some records. (More than a few ostensible 'spinsters' are also described as 'wife of...'.) Of the indictments and inquisitions that identify male killers, comparable numbers labelled their subjects as labourers (24 per cent), as yeomen (22 per cent), and as tradesmen (21 per cent). Gentlemen, despite the name, ostensibly accounted for 13 per cent of the killers over the period as a whole, and their share of the total actually increased over time. Relatively few of the records gave the status of the male victims—only 914—but of that smaller group, labourers purportedly accounted for 11 per cent, yeomen for 18 per cent, tradesmen for 22 per cent, and gentlemen for 16 per cent. The numbers of gentlemen named amongst the killers and victims are disproportionate to their numbers in the population more generally, suggesting that elite men still had some way to go in turning from violence to law to settle their disputes.

As for weapons, people often used whatever was at hand, though with a few tools new to the period. Bladed weapons were most commonly used: 19 per cent of the fatalities were attributed to knives and daggers, with another 14 per cent the work of swords and rapiers. Staffs and cudgels accounted for another 15 per cent of victims; unarmed beatings, kicking, strangling, and suffocating for another

---

[42] See also J.A. Sharpe, 'Domestic Homicide in Early Modern England', *Historical Journal* 24 (1981): pp. 29–48, and Susan Amussen, ' "Being Stirred to Much Unquietness": Violence and Domestic Violence in Early Modern England', *Journal of Women's History* 6 (1994): pp. 70–89.

[43] J.S. Cockburn, 'Early Modern Assize Records as Historical Evidence', *Journal of the Society of Archivists* 5 (1975): pp. 215–31.

13 per cent; and agricultural or work tools for nearly 9 per cent. Pitchforks, scythes, and hedging bills took many lives. Poison accounted for less than 2 per cent of the accusations. Some means of killing were new to this period: witchcraft was identified as the cause of a little more than 10 per cent of all these deaths, but such charges only appeared in any numbers (as one would expect) after the passage of the witchcraft statute in 1563. Rapiers were new, too: the first to appear in this sample were in 1549 and 1550, with the novelty perhaps signalled by a switch from Latin to English in noting that the killer used a '*gladio vocat[ur]* a rapier'.[44] So, too, were firearms new to criminal homicide: while coroners' files identified firearms as the cause of a steady stream of accidental deaths, the first in this set of records to identify one being used with murderous intent was in 1591.[45] The shooting death of London mercer Robert Packington in 1536 provoked much comment at the time in part because of the very novelty of the weapon used, and it was decades yet before guns came to be used with any frequency in criminal homicides.[46]

Spierenburg has hypothesized that killings over time inclined from the impulsive to the planned, and from the expressive to the instrumental.[47] The laconic nature of the English records does not lend itself to such a quantification, unfortunately. Clearly, some people planned to kill. Observers at the time would have identified all the killings by means of witchcraft and poison as premeditated. The report of the coroner's inquest into Thomas Sampson's 1549 death tells us explicitly that his killer lay in wait outside Sampson's home; this attack evidently was planned.[48] But the records too rarely give the amount of detail one would need to make any determination. What of the monk Thomas Grave, who was whipped to death by three of his brothers in 1525; was this an intentional, premeditated murder?[49] Or what of Philip Luca, a Genoese mariner who killed John de Monte (described as 'nigro gunner') in a fight on New Year's Day, 1531?[50] What of the death of Robert Alye in 1541 at the hands of a group of men who broke in to burgle his home?[51] From the available records, we could easily read any of these killings, like many others, as either impulsive or carefully plotted. Roughly 15 per cent of the victims in this sample died in incidents that involved multiple killers; perhaps we can assume that the perpetrators of a significant number of these deaths planned to kill. A few were simply sadistic. But the impression gained from reading these records—and it can be no stronger than an impression—is that throughout the period, most of the killings were unplanned, whether intentional or not,

---

[44] KB 9/576, m. 99, and Hunnisett, *Sussex Inquests, 1485–1558*, no. 145.

[45] *MCR*, I. 208.

[46] See, e.g., Raphael Holinshed, *Chronicles of England, Scotland, and Ireland* (London, 1586), vol. 3, p. 944.

[47] Spierenburg, *History of Murder*, pp. 6–7. For a discussion of some of the difficulties with distinguishing 'instrumental' and 'expressive'—either as a dichotomy or as ends of a spectrum—see Shani D'Cruze, Sandra Walklate, and Samantha Pegg, *Murder: Social and Historical Approaches to Understanding Murder and Murderers* (Cullompton, 2006), pp. 126–8.

[48] KB 8/18, m. 154.   [49] KB 9/500, m. 80.

[50] KB 9/515, m. 36.   [51] KB 9/550, m. 100.

done in the course of drunken brawls, workplace disputes, and sudden angry responses to a slight of some sort.

Clearly, the frequency of some types of killing compared to others changed over time. Women's perceived involvement in homicide waxed and waned. Guns came in time to be feared more than witchcraft or rapiers, and killings outside the home diminished in number to leave domestic slayings responsible for a greater proportion of victims. A variety of factors, themselves subject to change, shaped the incidence of homicide, including gendered and household structures of power, codes of honour, the availability of weapons and drink, the general legitimacy of some uses of force to chastise subordinates, and more besides.

The biggest shift in the incidence of interpersonal homicide, though, remains the decline over time charted by previous studies of medieval and modern court records. As noted above, explanations for this shift tend to focus in one way or another on the growth of 'the state'. True, some scholars point to eighteenth-century developments or movements associated with the Enlightenment, such as Steven Pinker's novel-reading participants in a 'humanitarian revolution'.[52] Such changes in sentiment and sensibility may well have entrenched and deepened the decline in homicidal violence, but cannot explain the beginnings of that decline. Nor can we identify a single, monocausal, explanation. Instead, as Sharpe has noted, we must fall back on a 'nexus of interacting developments', which we might call the rise of urbanity (as Paul Langford proposes) or, as Spierenburg suggests (drawing from Norbert Elias), the 'civilizing process'.[53] Some aspects of Elias's arguments for greater emotional restraint and self-control over time have been effectively set aside: most obviously, as other historians have demonstrated, violence in the middle ages was not simply impulsive, but was itself shaped by particular cultural conventions and expectations. And anger can drive one to law as much as to violence; aggression endures in different forms.[54] But the elements of state formation intrinsic to Elias's notion of a 'civilizing process' clearly played some part in this shift. Some proponents of explanations rooted in evolutionary psychology see this 'rise of Leviathan' as congenial to their understandings of human behaviour: as the state assumes responsibility for vengeance, individuals can free themselves from this dangerous biological imperative.[55] The use of force does not necessarily diminish, but passes from the individual to the state. Even without the ethology, though, this notion of growing state power and responsibility makes

---

[52] Steven Pinker, *The Better Angels of our Nature: The Decline of Violence and its Causes* (London, 2011).

[53] Sharpe, 'Revisiting', pp. 314–15, discussing Paul Langford, 'The Uses of Eighteenth-Century Politeness', *Transactions of the Royal Historical Society*, 6th ser., 12 (2002): pp. 311–31, and Spierenburg, *History of Murder*.

[54] See, e.g., Claude Gauvard, *'De Grace Especial': Crime, État et Société en France au fin du Moyen Age* (Paris, 1991), esp. pp. 705ff; Gerd Schwerhoff, 'Criminalized Violence and the Process of Civilization: A Reappraisal', *Crime, Histoire & Sociétés* 6.2 (2002): pp. 103–26; R.W. Kaeuper, 'Chivalry and the "Civilizing Process" ', in *Violence in Medieval Society*, edited by R.W. Kaeuper (Rochester, NY, 2000), pp. 21–35; Philippa Maddern, *Violence and Social Order: East Anglia, 1422–1442* (Oxford, 1992); and Daniel Lord Smail, *The Consumption of Justice: Emotions, Publicity, and Legal Culture in Marseille, 1264–1423* (London, 2003).

[55] See, e.g., Pinker, *Better Angels*, though he focuses on other, exogenous factors, and Hanlon, 'Decline'.

sense, especially if the state is, in Max Weber's formulation, something that 'exercises a monopoly on the legitimate use of force'. Theorists and historians who followed in Weber's wake recognized the utility of this definition, but had problems with both 'monopoly' and 'legitimate'; we might bear in mind, for example, the physical correction expected of husbands and masters. As our period draws to its end, laws authorized almost unlimited force and harm from slave owners, and only in 1891 did husbands lose the legal right to discipline their wives physically. Michael Braddick thus offered a useful refinement in describing the state as the 'ultimate *arbiter* of what constituted legitimate force'.[56] One might add that the state also laid claim to a monopoly on coercion resting on *deadly* force.

Pointing simply to state formation, though, can seem somewhat circular and unsatisfying. Can we get beyond this abstraction to see what the process looked like on the ground and to add more nuance to our understanding of the mechanisms by which it happened? Another way of restating and narrowing this that might provide additional traction is to talk of the rise of 'the public'—not 'the public sphere' so beloved of scholars following in the steps of Jürgen Habermas, but 'the public' and 'politics' as conceptualized in the early modern era with nods to classical roots, matters relating to *res publica* or the things of public, communal concern.[57] Phil Withington has already usefully infused the sociological literature on 'the state' with politics, arguing that 'early modern state formation is as much about the creation of citizens defined by their capacity for public activity as it is about the centralization of functions conventionally associated with modern politics'. In his works on urban life, he traces how 'citizens operating in corporate structures' developed an awareness of themselves as political actors in a public realm.[58] Or we might look further back, to early giants of legal history: F.W. Maitland and Frederick Pollock individually and together described the story of medieval law as the growth of 'the king's peace' out of and over the parcelized, dispersed powers of lords, with protections of particular places and people gradually becoming general. We might look back to efforts that began in the very late tenth century to assert 'the peace of God', or immunity from violence of certain people and places, that then fed into lordly protections and notions of a peace protected by kings. Notions of 'the Crown' as an entity that outlived and could be distinguished from any individual royal person developed by the early 1300s, at least.[59] Thereafter, as Maitland notes, the notion of 'the Crown' as a corporation sole emerged in the sixteenth

---

[56] Braddick, *State Formation*, p. 18. Emphasis added. Lockwood's recent examination in *The Conquest of Death* returns to the older language of the state having a 'monopoly on violence' in this period, but given the work of Amussen, Braddick, etc., I would continue to nuance this somewhat to note that the state claimed a monopoly on defining what constituted legitimate force and asserted a monopoly on *lethal* force.

[57] For a useful disambiguation, see Conal Condren, 'Public, Private, and the Idea of the Public Sphere in Early Modern England', *Intellectual History Review* 19.1 (2009): pp. 15–28. See also Jeff Weintraub's introductory essay in *Public and Private in Thought and Practice: Perspectives on a Grand Dichotomy*, edited by Jeff Weintraub and Krishnan Kumar (Chicago, 1997), pp. 1–42.

[58] Withington, 'Public Discourse, Corporate Citizenship, and State Formation', p. 1017; *The Politics of Commonwealth: Citizens and Freemen in Early Modern England* (Cambridge, 2005).

[59] See Jean Dunbabin, 'Government', in *The Cambridge History of Medieval Political Thought, c.350–c.1450*, edited by J.H. Burns (Cambridge, 1988), pp. 498–501.

century, to develop in time to be seen as a trusteeship for 'the Publick'.[60] Maitland points to the 1715 act which vested the estates forfeited by traitors in the Crown to the 'use of the Publick' as an important marker; we see this notion of trusteeship particularly strongly in William Blackstone's mid-1700s discussion of the king's peace and the pleas of the crown, 'so called, because the king, in whom centres the majesty of the whole community, is supposed by the law to be the person injured by every infraction of the public rights belonging to that community, and therefore is in all cases the proper prosecutor for every public offence'.[61] I want to suggest that in tacking back and forth between the history of homicide and the development of this sense of 'the Publick' or 'the public peace', we can discern previously unseen facets of both. We can begin by reintegrating social, legal, and political histories of homicide, and by attending to the distinction drawn between murder and manslaughter over the early modern era.

HOMICIDE LAW

We already see something of this rise of a 'public peace' when turning to the second significant shift in the history of homicide in early modern England: the emergence and then further refinement of a legal distinction between murder and manslaughter. Medieval law had demarcated some homicides as justifiable or excusable—killings in self-defence or by accident warranted guaranteed pardons—but made no formal distinction between different types of felonious homicide that

---

[60] Frederick Pollock, 'The King's Peace in the Middle Ages', in his *Oxford Lectures* (London, 1890), pp. 65–70; F.W. Maitland, 'The Crown as Corporation', *Law Quarterly Review* 17 (1901): pp. 131–46; Pollock and Maitland, *The History of English Law before the Time of Edward I*, 2nd edn (Cambridge, 1911). On the development of notions of 'the Crown' and Crown-as-corporation, see also Ernst Kantorowicz, *The King's Two Bodies: A Study in Medieval Political Theology* (Princeton, NJ, 1957). On the development of the notion of the 'king's peace', see also Tom Lambert, 'Protection, Feud and Royal Power: Violence and its Regulation in English Law, *c.*850–*c.*1250', PhD dissertation, Durham University, 2009, esp. ch. 5; Lambert, 'Introduction: Some Approaches to Peace and Protection in the Middle Ages', in *Peace and Protection in the Middle Ages*, edited by T.B. Lambert and David Rollason (Toronto, 2009), pp. 1–18; and more briefly, on the differences from Anglo-Saxon notions of *frið*, Lambert, *Law and Order in Anglo-Saxon England* (Oxford, 2017), pp. 207–15. As Lambert notes, Julius Goebel had expressed some reservations about Pollock's influential notion that the Anglo-Saxon kings' limited protections had grown into the single, general peace of the Anglo-Norman kings, preferring instead to focus on the Normans' control of procedure. Lambert convincingly demonstrates that the two arguments can be combined and argues that 'royal protections were expanded greatly in the Anglo-Norman period, but this was done primarily through tight control of, and innovation in, procedure'. [Goebel, *Felony and Misdemeanour: A Study in the History of English Criminal Procedure* (New York, 1937); Lambert, 'Protection, Feud and Royal Power', p. 198]. On the broader context of 'peace' movements in the high middle ages, and an argument that notions of the Peace or Truce of God developed into the king's peace in France in the twelfth century, see also Aryeh Grabois, 'De la Trêve de Dieu à la Paix du Roi: Étude sur les Transformations du Mouvement de la Paix au XIIe Siècle', in *Mélanges Offerts à René Crozet*, edited by Pierre Gallais and Yves-Jean Riou (Poitiers, 1966), pp. 585–96.

[61] 1 Geo. I, st. 2, c. 50; William Blackstone, *Commentaries on the Laws of England*, 4 vols. (Oxford, 1765–69), vol. 4, p. 2.

produced differences in punishment.[62] That changed in the sixteenth century, when the separation of murder from manslaughter allowed some killings to be punished with penalties less than death. The distinction persists in varied forms today and has come to seem natural; even so, it had a messy, protracted birth and called forth new legal fictions about 'constructive malice' or 'malice implied' as judges sought to reserve certain cases as acts of murder even though they seemed to fall on the other side of the newly drawn line. It reflected gendered assumptions about human nature, historically specific notions of legitimate force, and concerns about biblical injunctions to vengeance. More to the point, it made homicide more clearly criminal through higher conviction rates at the expense of more moderate punishment, and allowed the refinement of definitions of these crimes in ways that made homicide more fully public, an affront to 'public justice' more than a matter for private vengeance or composition.

The formal distinction between murder and manslaughter as such emerged in the sixteenth century, but grew from earlier roots. 'Murder', in English law, initially denoted secrecy or stealth; killings done openly and openly amended only slowly became matters of royal concern. In his work on early English law, Tom Lambert has offered a recent reminder that it took much longer for homicides than for thefts to be treated as capital pleas reserved to the king's courts alone. 'Killing someone was a very serious offence indeed in Anglo-Saxon England,' he notes, 'but it was an offence primarily against the victim and his family rather than against the king.'[63] Killers paid wergelds, or compensation, to the kin of the slain or risked the more violent side of feuding. Slowly, royal protections over particular people, places, or times expanded to become a more general 'king's peace' that killings of any sort and of any person offended. (In time, even serfs came to be included.) A key motor of this expansion, Lambert argues, was the Anglo-Saxons' royal sanction against *morð* and its Norman variant, the murder fine: the latter, initially a special protection for the French invaders, grew to cover nearly any free person killed secretly and without emendation.[64] In the background, canon law developments

---

[62] For the early history of using pardons to distinguish between different classes of homicide, see Naomi Hurnard, *The King's Pardon for Homicide before A.D. 1307* (Oxford, 1969). See Kesselring, *Mercy and Authority in the Tudor State* (Cambridge, 2003) for sixteenth-century changes to the laws and practices dealing with both types of excusable killings: in brief, in the late middle ages people charged with accidental death were, for a time, simply acquitted, but from 1498 they were once again to submit to trial, face forfeiture of their property, and need to pay the fee for the guaranteed pardon. In contrast, a statute of 1533 allowed that people killing in self-defence in very specific circumstances—that is, killing someone who was attempting murder or robbery on the highway or in one's own home—could be acquitted without need to await a pardon. See also T.A. Green, 'The Jury and the English Law of Homicide, 1200–1600', *Michigan Law Review* 74 (1976): pp. 414–99; J.G. Bellamy, *The Criminal Trial in Late Medieval England: Felony before the Courts from Edward I to the Sixteenth Century* (Toronto, 1998), pp. 57–69; and J.H. Baker, *Oxford History of the Laws of England, vol. 6: 1483–1558* (Oxford, 2003), pp. 553–62.

[63] Tom Lambert, 'Theft, Homicide and Crime in Late Anglo-Saxon Law', *P&P* 214 (2012): pp. 3–43, quote at 9.

[64] See Lambert, 'Protection, Feud and Royal Power', esp. pp. 71, 151, 179, 225, and now the monograph, *Law and Order in Anglo-Saxon England*, esp. pp. 225ff. Lambert is drawing in parts on arguments previously made by H.E. Yntema ['The *Lex Murdrorum*: An Episode in the History of English Criminal Law', *Harvard Law Review* 36 (1923): pp. 146–79] and countering arguments made

urged a greater focus on the intent of the actor and not just the consequences of the act, with more prodding of the distinctions between sin and crime and who suffered harm from wrongdoing.[65] By the reign of Henry II—possibly with the Assize of Clarendon in 1166, but certainly by the time the text known as *Glanvill* was composed in the 1180s—the king claimed all homicides as violations of his peace, or as criminal pleas that belong 'to the crown of the lord king', with a distinction persisting between murder and simple homicide.[66] 'Murder' was still reserved for dishonourable, secret slayings for which the killer did not claim responsibility.

By the mid-to-late 1300s, however, the word '*murdravit*' started to broaden in scope, not denoting secrecy so much as gravity, appearing in some indictments as a supplement to '*felonice interfecit*', or a charge of felonious slaying. However the indictment was phrased, capital sanctions applied. But as Susanne Jenks has observed, people charged with murder in addition to felonious homicide found themselves excluded from the jubilee pardon of 1377, and then after 1390 from pardons of 'all felonies' drawn up in general language. A simple felonious slaying could be forgiven under a general pardon, but a killing designated as murder had to be specifically named as such in a distinct pardon. Quite what distinguished one type of killing from another remained ill defined, but the older notions of secrecy had disappeared, and 'murder' seemed to be reserved for killings that involved some degree of prior malice or forethought: the Law French phrasing of the 1390 measure that barred some killers from general pardons of all felonies referred to '*murdre ou mort de homme occys par agayt, assaut, ou malice propense*'.[67]

We see no further development until the sixteenth century, when again the distinction became meaningful through mechanisms for mercy. True, the 1487 murder statute used phrasing that suggested a distinction—'murders and slaying', 'murderers and slayers', 'death or murder', etc.—but drew no differences in punishments or

---

most recently by Patrick Wormald for an earlier, Anglo-Saxon royal prohibition of homicide in *The Making of English Law: King Alfred to the Twelfth Century* (Oxford, 1999).

[65] See, e.g., Fraher, 'Theoretical Justification' and Heikki Pihlajamäki and Mia Korpiola, 'Medieval Canon Law: The Origins of Modern Criminal Law', in *The Oxford Handbook of Criminal Law*, edited by Markus Dirk Dubber and Tatjana Hörnle (Oxford, 2014), pp. 201–24.

[66] *The Treatise on the Laws and Customs of the Realm of England Commonly Called Glanvill*, edited by G.D.G. Hall (Oxford, 1965), pp. 3, 174–5 ['*placitorum criminalium aliud pertinent ad coronam domini regis*'.]

[67] Susanne Jenks, 'Exceptions in General Pardons', in *The Fifteenth Century XIII: Exploring the Evidence: Commemoration, Administration, and the Economy*, edited by Linda Clark (Woodbridge, 2014), pp. 153–82, quote at 160. For the relevant statutes, see 50 Edward III c. 1 and 13 Richard II St. 1 c. 1. For the early history of 'malice prepense' and the significance of the 1390 statute, see also F.W. Maitland, 'The Early History of Malice Aforethought,' in his *Collected Papers*, edited by H.A.L. Fisher, 3 vols. (Cambridge, 1911), vol. 1, pp. 304–28. As W.D.H. Sellar notes, a possible French influence might be seen in the Ordinance of 1356, which classified as more serious forms of homicide those '*perpetres de mauvaiz agait, par mauvaise volonte et par deliberacion*': 'Forethocht Felony, Malice Aforethought and the Classification of Homicide', in *Legal History in the Making*, edited by W.M. Gordon and T.D. Fergus (London, 1991), pp. 51–2. See also J.M Kaye, 'The Early History of Murder and Manslaughter', *Law Quarterly Review* 83 (1967): pp. 365–95 and 569–601, though now in parts superseded by Green (1976), Bellamy (1998), and Baker (2003).

procedures.[68] That changed over the early 1500s. Sanctuary, pardons, and above all, benefit of clergy—the exemption of men who claimed clerical status from some punishments in the king's courts—were put to new uses in giving substance to the sense that some homicides could be punished more lightly than others. A general pardon statute of 1523 once more exempted murder, but this time specifically *included* 'all felonies called Manslaughter not committed or done of malice prepensed'.[69] The drafters of later general pardon statutes drew similar distinctions. A statute of 1530 denied sanctuary for a second time to those who committed 'murder of malice prepensed' but allowed it to those who committed 'manslaughter by chance medley'.[70] The use of the term 'chance medley' would change in time, eventually to be reserved for misadventure, but early sixteenth-century writers typically treated it as either a synonym for, or a defining element of, manslaughter, a term that emphasized the sudden, unplanned nature of the fatal encounter.[71]

The most significant developments in giving the distinction between murder and manslaughter practical import were the enactments of those statutes that denied the evolving benefit of clergy to people who committed 'murder upon malice prepensed' while allowing it to other men who killed. A statute of 1512 first made this distinction, denying the privilege to people who killed on the king's highway or in the victim's home 'upon malice prepensed'.[72] While this statute expired after one year, members of parliament passed an act in 1532 that again removed the privilege from 'wilful murder of malice prepensed'.[73] A statute of 1547 set this distinction more lastingly, referring to both 'wilful murder' and 'murder of malice prepensed' as the type of killing that would be excluded from claims of clerical privilege.[74] By this time, sanctuary had effectively disappeared as a source and site of mitigation for felons, a victim of Henry VIII's attacks on the monasteries. As Shannon McSheffrey demonstrates, recourse to sanctuary had in fact increased over the late 1400s and early 1500s, and with royal support: even as they sought to tighten law enforcement, the early Tudor monarchs 'faced certain

---

[68] 3 Henry VII c. 2.

[69] 14 & 15 Henry VIII c. 17. A working draft of the pardon demonstrates that the labels given to the different forms of homicide were still somewhat new and unfamiliar: the list of offences to be pardoned included 'murders by way of defence and not prepensed'. 'Murders' was later struck through and 'manslaughter' written above. BL, Cotton MS Titus B.1, no. 44.

[70] 22 Henry VIII c. 14.

[71] See Green (1976), Bellamy (1998), and Baker (2003) for the early use of the term. It is largely avoided in the pages that follow, given the significant varieties of inflection it had from one writer to another. Coke would still equate the two words, noting that manslaughter was 'upon a sudden occasion, and therefore is called chance-medley'. Later he noted that 'killing of a man by chance-medley is killing of a man upon a sudden brawl or contention by chance'. [Edward Coke, *Third Part of the Institutes of the Laws of England* (London, 1669), pp. 55–6)] Pulton used it in much the same way. [Ferdinando Pulton, *De Pace Regis et Regni* (London, 1609), ff. 120, 123d.] Other writers came to equate it with killings *per infortuniam*, though, treating it as wholly involuntary. Matthew Hale offered as an example a death caused by the felling of a tree; the writer of a mid-seventeenth-century manual for coroners defined chance-medley as 'when one is slain casually and by misadventure, without the will of him that does the act' and used the example of a man throwing a stone at a bird that inadvertently killed a passer-by. See, e.g., Hale, *Historia Placitorum Coronae*, edited by Sollom Emlyn (Philadelphia, 1847), pp. 471–2 and DUL, MSP 49, p. 244.

[72] 4 Henry VIII c. 2.　　　　[73] 23 Henry VIII c. 1.　　　　[74] 1 Edward VI c. 12.

kinds of felons' they 'wanted or needed to prosecute but not to hang'—that is, men of the higher or lesser nobility.[75] Sanctuary had offered a useful way to make exceptions and had been implicated in the early drawing of distinctions between homicides that could be punished lightly and those that required death, but disappeared when struck by the 'asteroid' of the Reformation assault on the monasteries with which it was so closely related. Pardons and, above all, a reformulated benefit of clergy filled the space it had left behind.

Thus, in the early decades of the sixteenth century, two distinct labels attached to two categories of criminal homicide, and benefit of clergy served as the primary mechanism for making that distinction matter. Both murder and manslaughter remained felonies punishable by death; but those people who made and enforced the law adapted and secularized the medieval practice of providing clerics with immunity from the king's courts, to allow a lesser punishment for men convicted of manslaughter, together with some other offences. A statute of 1489 recognized the practice of extending this supposedly clerical privilege to literate laymen more generally, though limiting it to only a first offence.[76] Thereafter new statutes, including those mentioned above, took the privilege away from some offences, but they left it for this crime called manslaughter. The benefit of clergy allowed men who could pass a reading test to trade capital punishment for a branding, forfeiture of goods, and (after a 1576 statute) up to a year in gaol, in a process now supervised by royal officials rather than churchmen.[77] Maybe recalling how useful their criminous kin had found sanctuary, the lords made a point of ensuring that peers could claim their equivalent of the privilege without needing to read or be branded or risk their inheritance—but even they could not claim it for a second offence or for murder.[78] With the exception of the peerage, then, men who claimed clergy upon committing manslaughter faced some punishment even as they evaded death. In the reign of Charles I, for example, both Walter Donn and Montague Saunders lost all their personal property but not their lives upon conviction for manslaughter after their successful plea of clergy.[79]

The provision did have its limits, beyond applying only to a first offence and only for men who could pass the literacy test. It was not available to men convicted of homicide in the Admiralty Sessions, for killings at sea or on the rivers and waterways claimed for Admiralty jurisdiction. A statute of 1536 had brought aspects of this separate, civil law jurisdiction closer into conformity with the common law,

[75] Shannon McSheffrey, *Seeking Sanctuary: Crime, Mercy, and Politics in English Courts, 1400–1550* (Oxford, 2017), quote at p. 18.

[76] 4 Henry VII c. 13.

[77] For the 1576 statute, see 18 Elizabeth I c. 7. On benefit of clergy, see Lesley Skousen, 'Have Mercy upon Me O Lord: A History of Benefit of Clergy in Early Modern England', PhD dissertation, University of Wisconsin, 2013; J.G. Bellamy, *Criminal Law and Society in Late Medieval and Tudor England* (New York, 1984); and work forthcoming from Margaret McGlynn.

[78] 1 Edward VI c. 12, cl. 13.

[79] BL, Harley MS 1012, f. 42d, docquet book of patents, Charles I. The forfeiture of goods was long thought to have been a defunct penalty by the early modern period, but for further evidence that it was imposed in some manslaughter cases, see also Kesselring, 'Making Crime Pay: Felony Forfeiture and the Profits of Crime in Early Modern England', *Historical Journal* 53.2 (2010): pp. 271–88.

allowing that piracy and offences at sea would be punished 'as if' they were felonies, but they remained distinct. After some debate, common law judges decided that general pardons, benefit of clergy, and other forms of mitigation intended for felonies did not apply to crimes tried in these courts.[80] An even bigger limitation was that women who killed could not claim benefit of clergy until 1691, when a statute fully opened the privilege to women as well. A verdict of manslaughter might make it easier for a woman to obtain a pardon, and if the victim had been her husband, it meant that she just faced being hanged instead of burning at the stake as a petty traitor, but in the usual run of things, a manslaughter verdict was all but meaningless for women, as they could not claim clergy.[81] Of course, the very distinction between hot-blooded and cold-blooded killings reflected assumptions about male and female bodies and behaviours: not only did law deny clergy to women, but as Garthine Walker has demonstrated, it conceptualized manslaughter itself in masculine terms.[82] As the Elizabethan legal writer William Lambarde explained, the moderation for crimes committed in hot blood took into account 'the infirmity of man's nature', specifically the quick temper and ready violence associated with 'manhood'.[83] But even with these exceptions, for a good many of the people who committed killings in early modern England and Wales, benefit of clergy allowed a punishment less than death.

The development of the manslaughter verdict, tied to benefit of clergy, contributed to what John Bellamy has called a 'verdict revolution'. Few records of criminal court verdicts survive from the early sixteenth century in any systematic way, but when T.A. Green compared the verdicts rendered in late fourteenth-century records to those surviving from two counties between 1558 and 1603, he noted that the conviction rate had increased from about 20 to 25 per cent to over 50, though the percentage of defendants condemned to death remained about the same, at 20 to 25 per cent. Moreover, self-defence verdicts dropped off precipitously. 'Thus,' he observed, 'it appears that juries, recognizing that benefit of clergy provided an alternative sanction for homicide, felt free to convict in many cases that had formerly falsely been described as acts of self-defence [which came with a

---

[80] M.J. Prichard and D.E.C. Yale, eds., *Hale and Fleetwood on Admiralty Jurisdiction* (London, Selden Society, vol. 108, 1993), pp. ccviii–ccxx. For the relevant statutes, see 27 Henry VIII c. 4 and 28 Henry VIII c. 15. A debate in 1605 on whether King James's coronation pardon applied to offences triable in the Admiralty Sessions seemed to open the possibility of a distinction between offences on the high seas (for which it would not) and those on inland waterways (for which it might). Prichard and Yale note that Matthew Hale believed that a felony that was clergyable when committed on land would be so if committed on an inland waterway, but that this seems not to have been the practice of the Admiralty Sessions. Edward Coke flatly denied that clergy applied.

[81] For one example of such a pardon, see PSO 5/5, unpaginated but filed under June 1630, for Agnes ap Williams and Jane Thomas, whom judges noted had killed their victim in a 'sudden falling out'.

[82] Walker, *Crime, Gender and Social Order*, pp. 113–58. See also Davis, *Pardon Tales*, for the gendering of responses to homicide. The ways in which the very physiological notion on which the distinctions between hot-blooded manslaughter and cold-blooded murder mapped on to early modern notions of male and female difference is explored at more length in Kesselring, 'Bodies of Evidence', pp. 245–62. A statute of 1623/4 did allow women convicted of 'small felonies' (e.g. petty thefts) to be punished 'as if' they had claimed clergy (21 Jac I c. 6), but the privilege as such was only extended to women, and on a more equal basis with men, in 1691.

[83] William Lambarde, *Eirenarcha* (London, 1581), p. 244. See also Davis, *Pardon Tales*, e.g. pp. 36–7.

guaranteed pardon]'.[84] In his own study of late medieval and early modern criminal court practice, Bellamy notes a change in conviction rates from the middle years of the fifteenth century of about one in three to a rate of about two in three in the later years of the sixteenth century.[85] This change occurred across several types of felony, not just homicide, and drew upon a number of procedural changes. As argued elsewhere, the more creative use of pardons contributed.[86] Benefit of clergy played the biggest part in this development, though, not least in the distinction it allowed between murder and manslaughter. In our sample of homicide inquisitions and indictments from *c*.1480 to 1680, of a group of 1,348 men for whom a trial jury verdict is clear, juries found 67 per cent guilty of criminal homicide; when we break that down, they deemed 30 per cent guilty of murder, and 37 per cent guilty of manslaughter.

Jurors still sometimes showed mercy to killers by finding them guilty only of killing in self-defence, thus freeing them of all punishment whatsoever. In 1591, for example, when William Arnolde appeared in court to plead not guilty to a charge of 'the felonious killing called Manslaughter', the trial jury deemed his killing an act of self-defence.[87] At least fifty-three other men in this sample, originally charged with murder or manslaughter, benefitted from similar self-defence verdicts. But manslaughter now gave jurors an additional option, one that allowed some punishment, though likely short of death. Some killers went to trial on charges of manslaughter; many others started their trials on indictments for murder, which trial juries then downgraded to manslaughter. True, a verdict of manslaughter did not necessarily allow the killer to evade execution—that benefit of clergy was allowed only for a first offence was learned the hard way by one man in this sample who had previously claimed clergy after an arrest for stealing cloth, and who therefore faced the gallows upon his manslaughter conviction.[88] And a convict still needed to pass the reading test, a test that at least fourteen men in this sample were deemed to have failed. In some cases, it seems that judges disagreed with jurors' lenience and subjected the offenders to stringent testing, not allowing a mumbled, memorized bit of scripture to suffice.[89] So, a manslaughter verdict did not necessarily let a man avoid hanging; but in most cases, such a verdict freed the killer from the death sentence, subjecting him at most to branding, forfeiture of property, and perhaps some time in gaol. And the evidence indicates that jurors used this new verdict to convict killers in far greater numbers than had their medieval forebears.

---

[84] Green, 'The Jury and the English Law of Homicide', pp. 493–4.
[85] Bellamy, *Criminal Trial in Later Medieval England*, pp. 95–6.
[86] Kesselring, *Mercy and Authority.*   [87] *MCR* I. 205.
[88] *CAR* Kent (James), nos. 948, 916.
[89] See, for example, Arthur Turnour's notes on a Newgate case in 1616, in which a man convicted of manslaughter prayed his clergy and had it, but the judge intervened and selected several other biblical passages to be read and made him stand apart from potentially helpful bystanders; discussed in J.H. Baker, *The Legal Profession and the Common Law* (London, 1986), p. 333. On the other hand, Cockburn cites a story of Sergeant Daniel handing a felon his spectacles to make it easier for him to read the passage: J.S. Cockburn, *A History of English Assizes* (Cambridge, 1972), p. 126.

This increase in conviction rates—in the proportion of men identified as killers who faced *some* legal sanction—is the clearest way in which the formal legal distinction between more and less serious killings contributed to the criminalization of homicide, but we also see signs of this in the ways judges refined these two categories. As Green has argued, the formalization of a distinction between murder and manslaughter recognized a long-held popular belief that some killings were less deserving of death than others. Jurors in the past had simply acquitted those offenders who committed the less heinous homicides or crafted fictitious narratives that allowed them to convict the killer only of a self-defence slaying, which came with its guaranteed pardon. Now, with the verdict of manslaughter available, jurors did not need to do so.[90] What has perhaps not yet been recognized is that judges could thereafter exert more influence in determining into which category killings fell. Judicial decisions over the sixteenth and early seventeenth centuries refined the basic distinction that the one came upon 'malice aforethought' and the other upon a sudden surge of 'hot blood'. They did so in part with fictions of their own, with talk of constructive, transferred, or implied malice.

From the 1540s cases that tested the distinction between the two forms of killing began to appear in the law reports. On the one side, 'murder' broadened on the back of legal fictions as judges sought to bring killings that had no obvious signs of 'prepensed malice' against the victim under that heading. In what became known as the doctrine of constructive malice, judges decided that they could simply attribute malice to the defendant if death occurred during the commission of another felony. Lord Dacre's case in 1541 offered the first clear statement of this construction. While poaching game on a neighbouring estate, Dacre and his companions killed the gamekeeper who challenged them. As a nobleman, Dacre enjoyed the privilege of trial by his peers, some of whom reportedly baulked at a verdict of wilful murder. One eavesdropper on the conference among the king's council, chief justices, and the peers of the jury noted that 'they spoke so loud, some of them, that I might hear them notwithstanding two doors shut between us. Among the rest that could not agree to wilful murder, the Lord Cobham...was vehement and stiff.' But, 'suddenly and softly they agreed, I wot not how, and departed to the King's Bench together'.[91] Back in court, Dacre confessed to the killing, which the judges declared to be an act of murder. Another report noted that the judges wept when they sentenced him and begged the king to pardon him.[92] Whatever the politics of the moment that led King Henry VIII to the highly unusual decision to kill a peer for a crime short of treason, the judicial conclusion lived on as a key precedent: most narrowly conceived, the case was held to show that all parties in a group gathered to some illicit end could be held guilty of the crime of any one member without needing to demonstrate the malicious intent of all individually.[93]

[90] Green, 'The Jury and the English Law of Homicide', p. 493, and *Verdict According to Conscience: Perspectives on the English Criminal Trial Jury, 1200–1800* (Chicago, 1985).

[91] SP 1/166, f. 73.

[92] *Letters and Papers, Foreign and Domestic, of the Reign of Henry VIII*, edited by J.S. Brewer (London, 1862–1932), vol. 16, no. 954, Chapuys to the Queen of Hungary.

[93] For later references to the Dacre case as precedent, see 84 *ER* 1094, 88 *ER* 1565, and also Matthew Hale, *Historia Placitorum Coronae*, p. 465. Hale also cited the Drayton Bassett case to

The Dacre case also fed into arguments that even in the absence of 'prepensed malice', if someone killed during the commission of another felony, malice could be taken as implied. Here the Salisbury and Herbert homicide trials of the 1550s produced key statements.[94] In the first, Richard, George, and John Vane Salisbury, together with two other men, engaged in an affray that resulted in the death of a servant of one Dr Ellis. The judges informed the jurors that if they deemed the accused to have acted upon malice against Dr Ellis, even if the killers had no ill will against the actual victim, they could nonetheless find the killing murder. A second issue arose: John Vane Salisbury had not been part of the initial group that set out to attack Ellis, but had happened along midway through the affray and joined suddenly. In his case, the jurors decided upon a verdict of manslaughter.[95] A few years later, Sir George Herbert led a group of some forty men to attack Sir Robert Mansfield; Anne Maxwell, a woman who came out of Mansfield's home to try to talk the men down, died after a stone that one of Herbert's men threw in the direction of Mansfield's crew struck her instead. Was this murder, or simply an accident? All the judges met on this case, and divided: a minority said that 'no malice was intended against the woman, and murder cannot be extended beyond what was intended'. Ultimately, though—and after citing Dacre's case—the court concluded that they could deem such a killing, however accidental, an act of murder if it happened in the midst of a premeditated attack or criminal activity.[96]

Similarly, sixteenth-century judges decided that if an individual planned to kill one person but inadvertently killed another, the act constituted murder despite the lack of 'malice prepensed' against the victim. After some earlier indications of such a view developing, the key case came in 1573: John Saunders sought to kill his wife with a poisoned apple, but for fear of discovery did not intervene when he saw her give part of the apple to their young daughter, with fatal consequences for the girl. As one law reporter noted, 'whether or no this was murder in John Saunders the father was somewhat doubted, for he had no intent to poison his daughter, nor had he any malice against her, but on the contrary he had a great affection for her, and he did not give her the poison'. After some deliberation, the judges ultimately decided, however, that he was the 'original cause of the death, and if such death should not be punished in him, it would go unpunished'. Saunders intended to kill someone, and 'it is every man's business to foresee what wrong or mischief may happen from that which he does with an ill intention, and it shall be no excuse for him to say that he intended to kill another, and not the person killed... The end of

support this point. In 1578, after a great riot over disputed possession of the manor, one claimant and over two dozen of his men were indicted on charges of murder for the death of one of the men on the other side. Ultimately, four of them were convicted, though only for manslaughter. Hale cited this case to show that 'if many come to commit a riotous unlawful act, if in the pursuit of that action one of them commit murder or manslaughter, they are all guilty' (pp. 440–2). On this case, see also STAC 5/A30/27 and John Baker, 'R v Saunders and Archer (1573)', *Landmark Cases in Criminal Law*, edited by Philip Handler et al. (London, 2017), pp. 51–4.

[94] For Salisbury's Case (1552), see Plowden, *Les Commentaries, ou Reports de Edmund Plowden* (London, 1816), vol. 1, p. 100a; and for Herbert's Case (1558), see BL, Harley MS 5141, ff. 40–1. See also Jeremy Horder, *Provocation and Responsibility* (Oxford, 1992), pp. 16–19, and Luke Wilson, *Theaters of Intention: Drama and the Law in Early Modern England* (Stanford, CA, 2000), pp. 43–7.

[95] Plowden, *Commentaries*, vol. 1, pp. 100–1.

[96] 73 *ER* 279 and BL, Harley MS 5141, ff. 40–1, Lansdowne MS 639, p. 120.

the act shall be construed by the beginning of it, and the last part shall taste of the first, and as the beginning of the act had malice prepense in it, and consequently imported murder, so the end of the act, viz., the killing of another, shall be in the same degree, and therefore it shall be murder and not homicide only.'[97] And so notions of transferred malice broadened the scope of murder.

Significantly, judges also decided that killing officers of the law in the course of their duties implied malice as well, however sudden or unplanned the attack may have been. Here, the link to developing notions of 'public justice' became especially evident. That the courts could deem killings committed by people acting on behalf of the law justifiable was settled well before the sixteenth century; the reverse only unfolded over the late sixteenth and early seventeenth centuries.[98] A royal proclamation issued in 1538, and reissued in 1547, sought to deny sanctuary, benefit of clergy, or other sources of remission to those who assaulted or killed 'officers having authority under the king's majesty...in contempt of the laws, power, and jurisdiction royal of the king our sovereign lord'—but it seemed largely admonitory in purpose and left uncertain what should happen when such killings might appear accidental.[99] In 1586, judges who conferred on a case in which a constable's assistant died in an affray determined that such a killing constituted murder in law, even if the killer did not know the party killed and if the affray began suddenly and without planning. The report of their deliberations noted that despite the absence of the usual markers of malice aforethought, the 'law will adjudge it murder, and that the murderer had malice prepense, because he set himself against the justice of the realm'.[100] In a case from 1611, a London sergeant of the mace was killed while trying to arrest someone at night, rather than in daylight hours as he ought to have done. All the justices convened at King James's command to determine how best to respond. They opined that even if the arrest warrant or process had deficiencies, or if the warrant was not shown, no matter how sudden or unplanned the act may have been, the killing of an officer of the law while doing his duty constituted murder.[101]

Despite the various objections in this case that might incline a judge towards a verdict of manslaughter, the justices determined 'to make this offence murder by construction of law upon the special matter without any malice prepense'. They decided that 'when the officer or king's minister by process of law (be it erroneous or not) arrests one in the king's name, or requires the breakers of the peace to keep the peace in the king's name, and they notwithstanding disobey...and kill the

---

[97] Plowden, *Commentaries*, 474a. Note that they had more difficulty deciding what to do with the man charged as an accessory, for helping to procure the poison. Ultimately, after several years and repeated discussions, they decided that he should not die for this, but remained sufficiently torn about their decision that they did not want to make a precedent of it, and so reprieved him from one term to another until he could obtain a pardon. For a detailed examination of this case, see Baker, 'R *v* Saunders and Archer (1573)', pp. 29–57.

[98] For killings by officers of the Crown, see Anthony Fitzherbert, *La Graunde Abridgement* (London, 1516), Corone 261, 288, 328, referencing late fourteenth-century cases.

[99] *TRP*, vol. 1, nos. 179 and 288.

[100] Yong's Case, 28 Eliz., 4 *Coke's Reports* 40a (76 *ER* 984).

[101] Mackalley's Case, 9 Jac. I, 77 *ER* 824.

officers or the king's minister, reason requires that this killing and slaying shall be an offence in the highest degree of any offence of this nature: and that is voluntary, felonious, and murder of malice prepense'. While considerations of the life of the killer might carry some weight, above all, 'the life of the law itself (which protects all in peace and safety) ought to be more favoured'. Chief Justice Sir Edward Coke drew an even broader lesson from this decision, observing not just that 'in this case, the law implies malice prepense', but that it did so 'for by the law of God everyone ought to be in love and charity with all men, and therefore when he kills one without provocation, the law implies malice'.[102]

Coke's commentary here is significant in two ways. One, we see a bold articulation of the protections owed to those acting on behalf of the courts. These were not police officers or salaried officials in any modern sense, but largely volunteer laymen, being given some special status because of the master they served: the law. Two, we also see here this assertion that when someone kills without provocation, 'the law implies malice'.

Judges and lawmakers in these years also ensured that especially brutal, though not evidently premeditated, killings could be deemed murder. In the 1580s jurists opined that 'there are two kinds of malice, implied and express...implied malice is when a man kills another suddenly but without the latter making any defence'.[103] The so-called 'Statute of Stabbing' of 1604 sought to make a similar distinction: properly titled 'An Acte to take away the Benefit of Clergy from some kind of Manslaughter', it stipulated that anyone who fatally stabbed a person who had not drawn a weapon or previously struck the offender would be denied clergy and thus suffer death as in cases of wilful murder, 'although no malice be proved'.[104] Provocation began to supplement 'hot-bloodedness' as a marker of manslaughter.

A key decision came in 1600, after Widow Watts launched an appeal against her husband's killer. True, the victim had made rude and mocking gestures to the man who then killed him, but the judges decided that these insults did not offer enough provocation to mitigate a charge of murder. They directed the jury that 'it shall be presumed to be malice precedent, and that such a slight provocation was not sufficient ground or pretence for a quarrel; and so delivered the law to the jury, that it was murder'. The jurors, however, had other thoughts. Eight agreed to find the defendant not guilty of murder and talked the others around to their point of view. The court, 'much misliking' the verdict, examined the jurors closely, ultimately fining them for collusion and securing a new verdict more to their tastes; the killer hanged. Thereafter, as J.H. Baker has noted, the nature of the provocation came to matter more than the heat of the blood, for judges at least.[105] Hot blood was necessary but not sufficient.

Judges made a number of clarifications, outlining the sorts of provocation that could serve to reduce murder to manslaughter and those that could not. In his work as a commissioner charged with reforming contemporary homicide law,

---

[102] Ibid.
[103] Quote from Richard Crompton, *Loffice et auctoritie de iustices de peace* (London, 1587), f. 19v. See also Lambarde, *Eirenarcha*, p. 255.
[104] 1 Jac I c. 8.   [105] *Watts v Brains* (1600), 78 *ER* 1009; Baker, *Introduction*, p. 530.

Jeremy Horder has traced the development of the 'modern doctrine of provocation' in the seventeenth century, a doctrine only recently challenged for its gendered and outmoded medical bases. In brief, judges outlined four key provocations that could serve to reduce murder to manslaughter: seeing a friend or family member attacked (from two cases in 1612); grossly insulting though not dangerous physical assaults such as tweaks of the nose or boxes on the ear (from a number of early seventeenth-century cases); seeing an English person unlawfully deprived of his or her liberty (from a 1666 case); and lastly, seeing a man committing adultery with one's wife. Notably, given the difference from law elsewhere, this last provocation defence only applied to the killing of the other man, not the wife, and only from 1671. These four defences came together in the report on Mawgridge's Case in 1707, which served thereafter as the defining statement on what counted as provocation.[106] Offering a deadly response to any of these affronts could not be legally excused, but did not necessarily merit death. Acting immediately upon certain provocations, in the 'continuing heat of the blood', could make a killing manslaughter rather than murder, but judges patrolled the edges of what provocations would suffice, insisting that private vengeance for a variety of affronts could indeed count as murder.

In practice, of course, much ambiguity and flexibility remained. In 1599, for example, after two sailors fell to blows and agreed to meet later that night to fight with rapiers, one killed the other. Inquest jurors did not know how to label the killing. Their verdict? 'Whether this be murder or manslaughter we refer it to the law and as it shall be adjudged, so we find.' Ultimately, a grand jury indicted the killer for murder but the trial jury decided upon manslaughter. The culprit pleaded his clergy, was branded, entered a bond for his future good behaviour, and then went free.[107] John Turner, a fencing master, killed his partner in a public entertainment in 1603, despite both using blunted foils. As one commentator observed, 'The case is and will be much argued by lawyers, whether it will prove chaunce medley, manslaughter, or murder by reason of malice, as many challenges passed between them before.'[108] Turner, the killer, went free, but soon fell prey to another man he had bested in a fight. In another ostensibly friendly fencing match, Turner blinded one Robert Crichton, lord Sanquhar. Sanquhar thereafter plotted his revenge, ultimately deciding that the safest way to kill a fencing master was with a gun and hired help: the two men he hired shot Turner over drinks one evening in 1612.

---

[106] Perhaps because the classic works delineating the distinction between murder and manslaughter typically ended *c*.1600, the subsequent development of provocation defences has gone underappreciated. Here, Jeremy Horder's work, though geared towards modern reform of such defences, is invaluable. See 'The Duel and the English Law of Homicide', *Oxford Journal of Legal Studies* 12 (1992): pp. 419–30, and *Provocation and Responsibility*, esp. pp. 23–42, where Horder traces the development of the four-pronged definition of provocation over the seventeenth century. Note, however, that Horder mistakenly dates the adultery case to 1617, not 1671. For the re-dating and its significance, see Kesselring, 'No Greater Provocation? Adultery and the Mitigation of Murder in English Law', *Law and History Review* 34 (2016): pp. 199–225. On the role of anger and the pre-history of provocation in the middle ages, see now Elizabeth Papp Kamali, 'The Devil's Daughter of Hell Fire: Anger's Role in Medieval English Felony Cases', *Law and History Review* 35 (2017): pp. 155–200.

[107] Hunnisett, *Sussex Inquests, 1558–1603*, no. 527.

[108] *The Letters of John Chamberlain*, edited by Norman McClure, 2 vols. (Philadelphia, 1939), vol. 1, p. 184.

The ensuing trial of this Scottish lord as an accessory to wilful murder became a political event for all sorts of reasons. But it also allowed Sir Francis Bacon, acting as solicitor general, to opine on the varieties of homicide, and quickly to disabuse Sanquhar of any notion that his offence might be deemed less serious because of the 'indignity [he] received from so mean a man'. 'I agree,' Bacon said, 'that even in extreme evils there are degrees.' Yet, he argued forcefully, vengeance was for the law alone, and Sanquhar's crime constituted murder. Despite what Sanquhar saw as grave provocation (and despite his noble status), he died on a London gallows for his crime.[109]

Some people—Bacon included—registered their distaste for drawing a differ-ence between more and less serious killings in a way that allowed some killers to live: the Bible, after all, enjoined that blood be shed for blood.[110] Notably and most simply, though, the emergence and refinement of a distinction between mur-der and manslaughter shifted decision-making from *whether* a killing would be punished to *how* it would be punished, and brought such decisions into the open. Judges and lawmakers often despaired that jurors so often found duellists or those engaged in even-handed fights guilty only of manslaughter, insisting that any vengeance belonged to the Crown or to 'public Justice'.[111] Differences of opinion over what counted as sufficiently provocative to make a killing manslaughter rather than murder sometimes became heated—the Commons heard complaints against Chief Justice Kelyng in 1667 when he fined, imprisoned, and berated jurors who deemed a killing manslaughter that he thought should be punished as murder.[112] But such disputes were now being heard in the king's courts and the killings sub-jected to at least some criminal sanction. And judges had more of a role than before in refining distinctions between more and less serious forms of homicide. Thomas Green observed that, with the emergence of a formal distinction between murder and manslaughter, 'common law adapted to social views'.[113] True, and in bringing that distinction openly into the courts, those 'social views' could be challenged and refined. Sir Edward Coke's influential early seventeenth-century definition of murder left much scope for such interventions:

> Murder is when a man of sound memory, and of the age of discretion, unlawfully killeth within any county of the realm any reasonable creature *in rerum natura* under the king's peace, with malice forethought, either expressed by the party or supplied by law, so as the party wounded or hurt, etc., die of the wound or hurt, etc., within a year and a day after the same.[114]

---

[109] Howell, *State Trials*, vol. 2, c. 751. For the broader legal context of this killing and trial, see Kesselring, 'Marks of Division: Cross-Border Remand after 1603 and the Case of Lord Sanquhar', in *Crossing Borders: Boundaries and Margins in Medieval and Early Modern Britain*, edited by Sara M. Butler and K.J. Kesselring (Leiden, 2018), pp. 258–79.

[110] Genesis 9:6. Bacon, *The Charge of Sir Francis Bacon…touching Duells* (London, 1614), pp. 19–22. He called the distinction 'a monstrous child of this later age' with 'no shadow of it in any law divine or human', p. 21.

[111] See, e.g., 'A discourse touching the unlawfulness of private combats, written by Sir Edward Cook, Lord Chief Justice of England, at the request of the Earl of Northampton', in *Collectanea Curiosa*, edited by J. Gutch, 2 vols. (Oxford, 1781), vol. 1, p. 10, and chapter four, this volume.

[112] Howell, *State Trials*, vol. 6, cc. 992–6.

[113] Green, 'The Jury and the English Law of Homicide', p. 498.

[114] Coke, *Third Part*, p. 47.

Malice defined murder; but malice could be implied by law.

We have long recognized the eighteenth-century extension of penal sanctions to include punishments other than death—most notably transportation and imprisonment—as a key factor in extending the law's reach.[115] The emergence of a meaningful distinction between murder and manslaughter in the sixteenth century had similar effects. It made homicide more clearly criminal through higher conviction rates at the expense of more moderate punishments. It also allowed judges to refine the lines between killings that warranted death and those that did not: they employed their own fictions in ways that privileged agents acting on behalf of law and allowed less room for private vengeance by narrowing the miti-gating effects of 'hot blood' or provocation. It also offered a safety valve for dealing with elite offenders, much as sanctuary had done. While Lords Dacre and Sanquhar died for their parts in killings deemed murder, other powerful men could at least be brought to court on charges of manslaughter. In a variety of ways, then, the distinction between murder and manslaughter that developed in the period under study made homicide more fully public, a matter less often for private settlements or vengeance and increasingly for the king's courts and public justice. The crimin-alization of homicide in these years continued developments begun long before, but also saw them intensified and reshaped, thanks partly to the advent of the manslaughter verdict and the uses to which people put it. The chapters that follow address a few more of these changes and uses.

CRIMINALIZING HOMICIDE: CHAPTER OUTLINE

These two changes, to the incidence and to the definitions of homicide, provide both the context and the motivation for the pages that follow, which explore other ways in which homicide became more fully 'public' in these years. Two things that the chapters collected here do *not* address, it should be noted, are suicide and 'violence' in general, the latter for very good reasons, but the former perhaps less defensibly.

These chapters do not engage directly with the subject of 'self-murder'. While I have tried throughout to avoid imposing modern definitions of murder upon the past—not automatically excluding slayings of infants or by means of weapons such as witchcraft, for example—the exclusion of what early modern authors called self-murder is certainly anachronistic. Every legal writer's cataloguing of types of criminal homicide included the killing of one's self, often as one of the most heinous and reprehensible of offences against God, king, and commonwealth. As John Wilkinson put it in his guide for coroners, simply and bluntly: 'there is another kind of homicide, which is a kind of murder called *felo de se* [a felon of oneself], and that is where one hangs, or kills, or drowns himself for lack of grace: for as it is murder and felony for one man willingly and wilfully to kill another, so likewise it is murder and felony for a man to kill or drown himself willingly and

---

[115] See especially Beattie, *Crime*.

wilfully'.[116] Self-murder or *felo de se*: the neologism 'suicide' likely only originated in the 1630s, to distinguish the neoclassical belief in the permissibility of killing oneself (in some circumstances) from the then-dominant belief in its sinful criminality.[117] Juries decided whether people who had killed themselves had done so willingly and intentionally, and if so, found them guilty of felony, with their property forfeit much like that of other felons. While people had long believed that some people who killed themselves did so when *non compos mentis*, perhaps suffering the effects of illness, only in the late seventeenth and eighteenth centuries did such verdicts come to dominate and the characterization of self-slaughter as a crime equivalent to murder weaken. Indeed, Michael MacDonald and Terence Murphy have argued that the offence was punished more frequently and perhaps more severely over the sixteenth century than it had been before, the intensifying opprobrium a by-product of political and religious change.[118] In some ways, the history of the 'rise and fall' of hostility to self-slaughter is very much linked to the story being told here. My interest here is primarily in explaining *interpersonal* homicides, which may offer sufficient justification for setting suicide to the side; but perhaps not, if one is also interested in explaining the political and cultural meanings of acts understood as murder in early modern England.

Another subject that this book does not address is 'violence' in general. Amongst other reasons to avoid conflating violence and homicide, some of which have already been mentioned above, one must bear in mind the striking fact that assault and battery were simply not felonies in these years. Unlike so many property offences and other sins against one's fellow man, inflicting even serious physical harm on another person typically did not prompt the penalty of death. Assault and battery incurred relatively minor sanctions, usually small fines. Triable as a trespass or misdemeanour in the king's courts, such offences might also appear in manorial and other low-level courts. Whether minor or grievous, assaults remained open to private settlements throughout this period and were treated much more like civil than criminal matters. Not yet understood to constitute matters of serious royal or public concern on a par with felonies, assaults only came to receive such treatment in the eighteenth and especially the nineteenth centuries.[119]

---

[116] Wilkinson, *Treatise... Concerning the Offices and Authorities of Coroners*, p. 10.

[117] Michael MacDonald and Terence R. Murphy, *Sleepless Souls: Suicide in Early Modern England* (Oxford, 1990), p. 145. As a further justification for not including a study of suicide here, one might point to the excellent work already done on the subject. In addition to MacDonald and Murphy's book (and related articles), see R.A. Houston, *Punishing the Dead? Suicide, Lordship, and Community in Britain, 1500–1830* (Oxford, 2010).

[118] MacDonald and Murphy, *Sleepless Souls*. But note that Houston disputes the notion that attitudes shifted from harshness to lenience over the period, seeing them as ambivalent from beginning to end (p. 372), and see also Sara M. Butler, 'Degrees of Culpability: Suicide Verdicts, Mercy, and the Jury in Medieval England', *Journal of Medieval and Early Modern Studies* 36.2 (2006): pp. 263–90 for a more detailed examination of the medieval background to the changes posited by MacDonald and Murphy.

[119] On assault, see, e.g., Greg Smith, 'Violent Crime and the Public Weal in England', in *Crime, Law and Popular Culture in Europe, 1500–1900*, edited by Richard McMahon (Cullompton, 2008), pp. 190–218; Phil Handler, 'The Law of Felonious Assault in England, 1803–61', *Journal of Legal History* 28 (2007): pp. 183–206; Drew D. Gray, 'The Regulation of Violence in the Metropolis: The Prosecution of Assault in the Summary Courts, c.1780–1820', *London Journal* 32 (2007): pp. 75–87;

Mayhem, or maiming, was subject to an individual appeal of felony, though it was not punishable by death, either. It could only be prosecuted in the specific case of someone intentionally, maliciously destroying a limb such that the victim could no longer 'serve the common weal by his weapons in the time of war or by his labour in the time of peace': removing eyes or an arm counted, but not a nose or even ears.[120] Statutes added to this traditional common law crime, but in very limited circumstances: a statute of Henry IV's had made it felony to cut out eyes or tongues, and a statute passed in response to the maiming of MP Sir John Coventry in 1671 made it a felony to slit someone's nose or to maim a person in one of a few specific ways, of 'malice forethought, and by laying in wait'.[121]

More generally, though, while some people might see menaces and assaults as the 'natural fountains and spring heads' of great offences against the king and kingdom, they did not treat these affronts as capital crimes on par with theft, seditious speech, or other such sins. Even cases of attempted murder bypassed felony trials in the king's courts; the Court of Star Chamber was pressed into service to punish would-be killers, and we read of borough courts imposing whippings and other corporal but not fatal punishments upon those who had tried but failed to kill. London diarist Henry Machyn tells of a woman who had tried to poison her husband, for example: in January of 1553 she was whipped through the streets of London, naked from the waist up, and then pilloried. This may seem harsh, true, but had she succeeded and been caught, she would have burnt at the stake, as a wife's wilful slaying of her husband constituted an act not just of murder but of petty treason.[122] What was at issue in the discussions and punishments of homicide really was the *killing* of another person, the taking of a life, and not violence in some more general sense.

What the following chapters *do* cover are, in brief: coroners' inquests; private settlements arranged through feuds and appeals; private revenge as sought through duels; and print, punishment, and publicity. They do not attempt to cover all aspects of homicide's early modern history, but focus on a few key subjects that speak to the politics of homicide and its criminalization. Making murder public was largely a matter of making it of general concern, an offence to the community at large, but that happened in part by making it 'public' in another sense of the word, too: making instances of it openly visible or manifest. Chapter two thus

and Peter King, 'Punishing Assault: The Transformation of Attitudes in the English Courts', *Journal of Interdisciplinary History* 27 (1996): pp. 43–74. Treatment of more offences against the person as felonies would await Lord Ellenborough's Act of 1803, an act of 1828, etc.

[120] Pulton, *De Pace Regis et Regni*, ff. 15d–16.

[121] 3 Hen IV c. 5 and 22 & 23 Car II, c. 1. See Baker, *History of the Laws*, p. 553. Some other statutes created specific punishments short of death for some other kinds of assault, sometimes based on the nature of the space being protected. See esp. 33 Henry VIII c. 12 for an act that made the drawing of blood in the king's palace punishable by loss of a hand and perpetual imprisonment.

[122] *The Diary of Henry Machyn, Citizen and Merchant-Taylor of London, from A.D. 1550 to A.D. 1563*, edited by John Gough Nichols (London, Camden Society, vol. 42, 1848), pp. 29–30. For other examples, see ibid., pp. 31 and 197. For the law re attempted murder, see e.g., Pulton, *De Pace Regis et Regni*, f. 125. For attempts being triable in Star Chamber, see William Hudson, 'Treatise on the Star Chamber', *in Collectanea Juridica*, edited by F. Hargrave, 2 vols. (London, 1742), vol. 2, p. 108.

examines the coroner's inquest. How did individual homicides become known and categorized? Coroners and their juries of laymen did much of this work. Coroners held an office that dated from the late twelfth century, but one freshly charged and refocused from around 1487, when King Henry VII and parliament sought to press the coroners to action through fees and fines. The coroners' determinations of the nature of a sudden death, in early years, focused on the financial incidents owed to the king. Over time, financial interests in a killing became more diffuse and the king's interests became more expansively understood. The active intervention of the Privy Council, constituted as such from the 1540s, and especially of the councillors acting as judges in the Court of Star Chamber, helped police and channel the efforts of inquests. The mix of lay participation and central oversight gave the early modern inquest a special flavour. Slowly, fitfully, something unexpected began to happen: the coroners' inquests came to be seen as serving not just the king's interest and the king's peace but something conceived as public justice, or even a public interest that might in some ways become distinguishable from that of the monarch.

Chapter three turns to private settlements for slayings, attending to the broader history of private satisfaction-seeking, or feuding, and focusing on the history of compensation for homicide. Compensation for homicide prevailed in many other European jurisdictions, well into the early modern era, but had ostensibly disappeared from England centuries before. As this chapter shows, payments continued longer than we might have thought, but largely in a distinctive guise as harnessed to the appeal. When such compensation served as composition, or a means of bypassing legal sanctions altogether, it hindered the successful imposition of the king's peace, let alone any emerging notion of a public peace. Mediated through the ancient mechanism of the appeal, however, as a complement rather than a competitor to royal justice, compensation continued into the sixteenth century and beyond, thanks in part to the needs and actions of the widows of slain men. But these appeals did decline over the early modern period. Here, too, a statute of 1487 played a part, as did the uses judges made of the new manslaughter verdict. Judges and others derided appeals as 'suits of revenge', tainted by association with the feud and an approach to peace-making and satisfaction-seeking that had less and less legitimacy as public justice came to supersede private interests.

In time, those illegitimate 'private interests' could come to be imagined as encompassing those of the person wearing the crown, too. In the interim, though, some of the loudest and most insistent attacks on private interests focused on private vengeance, especially as sought through the personal combats coming to be known as duels. This notion of the duel, as an inherently private, unauthorized quest for revenge fought by elite men, is the subject of chapter four. Born in the late sixteenth century, the duel became a special focus of King James VI and I as he moved south from Scotland to assume the English throne in the early seventeenth. He drew upon his Scottish experiences with feuds and single combats when characterizing the duel and its special threat to royal justice. (If the early legislation of Henry VII's reign was one inflection point in this story, so, too, was the accession of James I, with all its attendant effects.) Although common law judges insisted that existing laws and courts could deal with this thing coming to be known as the duel, James sought special measures to deal with it—whether through special acts of parliament, special proclamations, or actions in the courts of Star Chamber and Chivalry, the latter specially reconstituted specifically to deal with this threat. And yet, despite the fevered rhetoric about the dangers of the duel, James repeatedly pardoned duellists and jurors repeatedly found them guilty only of manslaughter or even self-defence, saving them from the gallows. This chapter argues that the abstraction of the duel as a special kind of fight by men of special status helped in the creation of stronger statements of the supremacy of the king's peace and public justice over private interests, in part by doing so in ways that many elite men found useful or at least not unduly threatening.

The final chapter explores the ways in which individual homicides and conversations about criminal killings more generally became 'public' in the most basic sense of that word. If we want to see what was genuinely new about homicide in these years, one thing we must include on our list is the advent of print. Pamphlets that detailed particularly gruesome or tragic killings and described the providentially ensured punishments of the killers began to proliferate from the final decades of the sixteenth century. Punishments themselves seemed to become more numerous and more intensely visible at about the same time. Playwrights, too, began to put recreations of real-life murders on stage, and to craft plays that put revenge and domestic tragedies before ever broader audiences. All this was accompanied by the spread of legal printing more generally—statutes, law reports, manuals for legal professionals and amateurs, and more. In this profusion of print we see some signs of disquiet with the distinction between murder and manslaughter that we have traced in this introductory chapter, but also another mechanism, by which murder became more completely criminalized in these years. Certainly, in the print of the day we see more evidence of the process of criminalization at work. It helped inculcate the message that vengeance ought to be left to public justice rather than private action. Throughout the period, and indeed into the present, Sir Edward Coke's definition of murder continued to enshrine 'the king's peace' as the thing a killing violated, but as these chapters show, that king's peace slowly came to be equated with, and then partially superseded by, something conceptualized as 'the public peace' and 'public justice'.

2

'In *Corona Populi*'

Early Modern Coroners and their Inquests

Called together by coroners, townsmen and male villagers of all sorts shared responsibility for deciding which corpses to treat as victims of homicide and which individuals to try for the crime.[1] If they thought a killing criminal, they were the first to try to determine whether it constituted murder or manslaughter. Although participants in the coroners' inquests did not have the final word, they did much to shape the narrative in most cases of homicide. Convened to view the bodies of the dead—often the remains of people they had known—inquest jurors had to determine how the person died and, if necessary and if possible, at whose hands. True, not all homicide trials began with a coroner's inquest: individuals who suspected a criminal killing could go directly to a grand jury to try to obtain an indictment, and indeed had to do so in cases without a corpse. The nearest relations of people who died in suspicious circumstances could launch a criminal appeal of death with or without an inquest, bypassing an indictment altogether if they wished. Most cases of suspected homicide that came to trial passed through the hands of a coroner and his jury, however.[2] Why, one might ask, and to what ends? In whose interests did the inquest function and what purposes did it serve? While the inquest was an ages-old feature of English law, one that continues today, this chapter suggests that

[1] The foundational work of R.F. Hunnisett should be noted at the outset. In addition to his monograph on the medieval coroners, Hunnisett did much of the work of excavating and laying foundations for a study of their early modern successors with his calendar of Nottinghamshire inquisitions and his subsequent series of calendars of Sussex coroners' records. The contribution of Jeremy Gibson and Colin Rogers in surveying the territory with their guide to coroners' records throughout the country is also particularly valuable. See: R.F. Hunnisett, *The Medieval Coroner* (Cambridge, 1961); *Calendar of Nottinghamshire Coroners' Inquests, 1485–1558* (Nottingham, 1969); *Sussex Coroners' Inquests, 1485–1558* (Lewes, 1985); *Sussex Coroners' Inquests, 1558–1603* (London, 1996); *Sussex Coroners' Inquests, 1603–1688* (London, 1998); *East Sussex Coroners' Records, 1688–1838* (Lewes, 2005); Jeremy Gibson and Colin Rogers, *Coroners' Records in England and Wales* (Birmingham, 1988).

[2] Based on homicide cases with a recorded verdict in J.S. Cockburn's calendars of Sussex assize records from 1558–1625, Carol Loar has calculated that 68 per cent (119 of 176) of the prosecutions were based on an inquest alone or on an inquest followed by a grand jury indictment, whereas only 32 per cent had no accompanying inquest. (Moreover, those prosecutions following an inquest had a higher rate of conviction than those based only on an indictment, with 66 per cent of the former and 47 per cent of the latter resulting in guilty verdicts.) See Loar, '"Go and Seek the Crowner": Coroners' Inquests and the Pursuit of Justice in Early Modern England', Ph.D. dissertation, Northwestern University, 1998, pp. 43, 102–4. Another exception that should be noted is deaths in waterways, which were investigated by inquests convened at the behest of Admiralty officials, but apparently without a coroner. See, e.g., the voluminous stacks of inquisitions on bodies found in the Thames, overwhelmingly the products of accidental drownings, in HCA 1/78–81.

its justifications and practices changed in the early modern period in ways that both reflected and contributed to the more complete criminalization of homicide. Coroners and their jurors helped make murder public in more ways than one.

Studies of the early modern coroner's inquest have thus far focused, broadly speaking, on the coroners' competence and jurors' independence. The medico-legal, investigative nature of modern inquests prompted a few specialists in forensic medicine to look back at early origins, for example, and to be alarmed by what they found.[3] Many an early modern inquest went no further than to declare that an individual had died 'by the visitation of God', or some other similarly laconic ascription of cause. Jurors sometimes contented themselves with such investigative techniques as testing whether a corpse bled when touched by the suspected killer. Clearly, these inquests did not meet modern standards of forensic medicine. They also seemed deficient when compared to contemporaneous practices elsewhere, in which professional judges and physicians dominated investigations. More recently, Carol Loar has sought to show that early modern inquest jurors proved more diligent in their investigations than some modern readers might have thought, and that they regularly relied upon medical knowledge and medical professionals in their deliberations. Her conclusions are now strengthened by Sara Butler's examination of the medico-legal work of the medieval coroners.[4] Matthew Lockwood's study echoes Loar and others in finding evidence of investigatory techniques of some sophistication, but also disputes their importance, observing 'that, as in modern times, forensic medicine was not necessarily a pre-requisite for effective criminal detection'.[5] In a different vein, Malcolm Gaskill has demonstrated the value in examining the inquest within its early modern context, rather than judging it by modern criteria, explaining how its techniques and assumptions fit within a broader *mentalité* that privileged divine providence and the divine revelation of wrongdoing.[6] One thing these studies all show, at least implicitly, is that the purposes of inquests and the standards by which they might be judged were not always and everywhere the same.

The jurors on early modern coroners' inquests have also figured, sometimes indirectly, in the examinations focused on their counterparts on the grand and petty juries that sat at criminal trial. Scholars have debated the degree to which jurors might have embodied and acted upon notions of justice that differed from

---

[3] J.D.J. Havard, *The Detection of Secret Homicide* (London, 1960); T.R. Forbes, *Surgeons at the Bailey: English Forensic Medicine to 1878* (New Haven, CT, 1985).

[4] Carol Loar, 'Medical Knowledge and the Early Modern English Coroner's Inquest', *Social History of Medicine* 23.3 (2010): pp. 475–91. For a briefer, earlier discussion of these points, see also Kesselring, 'Detecting 'Death Disguised',' *History Today* 56.4 (2006): pp. 20–7. Sara Butler's recent book also endeavours to rehabilitate the reputations of pre-medical coroners and their medical knowledge: *Forensic Medicine and Death Investigation in Medieval England* (New York, 2015). For a helpful overview of the subject more generally, see Katherine D. Watson, *Forensic Medicine in Western Society: A History* (New York, 2010). While he focuses on the distinctive Scottish variant, R.A. Houston also devotes some attention to the medico-legal functions of the English coroner in his study *The Coroners of Northern Britain, c.1300–1700* (Basingstoke, 2014).

[5] Lockwood, *Conquest*, p. 325 and ch. 3.

[6] Malcolm Gaskill, 'The Displacement of Providence: Policing and Prosecution in Seventeenth- and Eighteenth-Century England', *Continuity and Change* 11.3 (1996): pp. 341–79.

formal legal norms, and their independence from judicial intervention when doing so. T.A. Green saw the discrepancies between inquest findings and those at the eventual criminal trials as evidence of 'jury nullification', a practice in which jurors used their discretion in crafting verdicts either to repudiate a given law or to deem it inapplicable in a given case. Jurors gave voice to community or lay perceptions of good order that did not always accord with the law as written. Furthermore, their *potential* for independence also conditioned judicial attitudes, he argues.[7] Historians of suicide have also looked to discrepancies between 'the facts', the determinations of coroners' inquests, and the verdicts of trial juries as evidence of popular discretion and popular sentiments about self-slaying.[8] In her study of crime and the courts in early modern Sussex, Cynthia Herrup portrayed trial jurors as agents of community decision-making who sought to promote a consensual 'common peace' in offering verdicts sometimes at odds with the law or the facts.[9] In contrast, some have questioned the commonality of interests among propertied trial jurors and their unpropertied neighbours, while others have questioned the autonomy of jurors from those with greater wealth and power.[10] Such moderations of assessments of jurors' independence are useful, but Lockwood goes further in dismissing what he calls a 'romantic notion' of juror agency. In his formulation, 'the early modern jury was not so much a venue for the articulation of communal conceptions of justice as it was a state-controlled tool for extracting information and implementing central and elite judicial priorities'.[11]

Coroners' jurors have received less attention than trial jurors, however, perhaps in part because the nature of surviving documentation complicates evaluations of their status and wealth. Nonetheless, both James Sharpe and Carol Loar have pointed to the significance of the inquest's immediacy: unlike the trial jurors' decisions, mediated by time and distance, coroners' juries typically deliberated much more closely to the events in question and may thus have better reflected community concerns.[12] One might add that unlike their counterparts at trials, jurors on coroners' inquests had no property qualification to meet. Moreover, coroners, unlike justices, were often elected to their posts. Their juries met publicly and deliberated openly. Making blanket statements about the independence of jurors, from either coroners or judges, seems difficult in the absence of better indicators than levels of wealth—a measure borrowed from the subjects under study, who used it to justify excluding the poor from trial juries by equating wealth with integrity. It is clear, though, that

---

[7] Green, *Verdict According to Conscience.*

[8] MacDonald and Murphy, *Sleepless Souls*; Loar, 'Go and Seek the Crowner'; S.J. Stevenson, 'The Rise of Suicide Verdicts in South-East England, 1530–1590: The Legal Process', *Continuity and Change* 2 (1987): pp. 37–75; Houston, *Punishing the Dead.* For studies of medieval jury nullification, focused on suicide, see also Butler, 'Degrees of Culpability', pp. 263–90, and 'Local Concerns: Suicide and Jury Behaviour in Medieval England', *History Compass* 4.5 (2006): pp. 820–35.

[9] Herrup, *Common Peace.*

[10] See, e.g., some of the essays collected in *Twelve Good Men and True: The English Criminal Trial Jury, 1200–1800*, edited by J.S. Cockburn and T.A. Green (Princeton, NJ, 1988).

[11] Lockwood, *Conquest*, pp. 147, 195.

[12] Loar, 'Go and Seek the Crowner'; J.A. Sharpe and J.R. Dickinson, 'Coroners' Inquests in an English County, 1600–1800: A Preliminary Survey', *Northern History* 48.2 (2011): pp. 253–69.

inquest jurors, much like trial jurors, could and did sometimes interpret the law selectively. Good grounds exist for seeing in the coroner's inquest possibilities for popular participation and discretionary decision-making in the law's operation, even though one must acknowledge the very real constraints upon this participation. We might at least concur with James Masschaele's verdict, in his study of the wide range of medieval inquests into legal and administrative matters well beyond the criminal law, in which he characterizes the jury as a 'relationship between people and state'.[13]

The discussion that follows endeavours to add to these previous studies, in part by expanding on their observations about the distinctiveness of coroners' inquests, and also by examining inquests through a political rather than mainly medical or legal lens. Early modern coroners' inquests differed from medieval and from modern inquests, and from the deliberations of contemporaneous trial juries, in a variety of ways. They differed, too, from the responses to suspicious deaths mandated in other jurisdictions: the Scots, the French, the Spanish, and others relied on professional judges and medical experts, with nothing comparable to this popular, public inquiry.[14] Being attentive to these differences may help us better understand the functions and significance of the early modern coroners' inquests in their own time and place, and how that changed over time.

Thinking of the political aspects of the coroners' juries might call to mind studies of the modern inquest that have highlighted its use as a tool to hold authorities to account. Picking up on the encomiums of nineteenth-century radicals and reformers who spoke of the coroner's jury as a bulwark of civil liberties, Ian Burney has examined the ways in which inquests into the deaths of paupers, prisoners, and political protesters sometimes exposed and critiqued abuses of power.[15] Pamela Fisher has presented evidence that this political use of the inquest dates back even earlier than Burney suggested, tracing it to at least the 1760s.[16] Do we see signs of something similar in the sixteenth and seventeenth centuries? That inquests were political in the broad sense of being shaped by struggles for power between competing interests becomes immediately apparent, but does a close examination show a more narrowly political element to the inquest, in which coroners and jurors were believed to be acting in the 'public interest'? As this chapter demonstrates, we see only faint signs of any notion that inquests could serve a 'public interest' understood as distinct from the interests of the king, but stronger evidence that they were thought to serve the interests of something described as 'public justice'. Importantly, too, the notion of the inquest serving the interests of public justice developed not just or even primarily through oppositional uses so much as it did

---

[13] James Masschaele, *Jury, State and Society in Medieval England* (Basingstoke, 2008), p. 1.

[14] Scotland had 'crowners', true, but with different functions. See Houston, *Coroners of Northern Britain*.

[15] Ian A. Burney, *Bodies of Evidence: Medicine and the Politics of the English Inquest, 1830–1926* (Baltimore, 2000). See also J. Sim and T. Ward, 'The Magistrate of the Poor? Coroners and Deaths in Custody in Nineteenth-Century England', in *Legal Medicine in History*, edited by M. Clark and C. Crawford (Cambridge, 1994), pp. 245–67.

[16] Pamela Jane Fisher, 'The Politics of Sudden Death: The Office and Role of the Coroner in England and Wales, 1726–1888', PhD. dissertation, University of Leicester, 2007.

through Crown efforts to police the inquest. Law as an impartial public good needed to be defended against arbitrary corruptions of all sorts.

In brief, then, this chapter examines the politics of the early modern coroner's inquest. It begins by discussing the status, duties, and experience of coroners and their jurors, noting as well the broader public experience with such inquests and positing a shift from the coroner's focus on revenue to public order. The discussion then turns to the procedures and problems that shaped inquests as well as the variety of reasons why their findings might not match 'the facts'. It then highlights the constraints within which inquest participants acted. Authorities recognized the political potential of the inquest and sometimes sought to harness it. Significantly, in the sixteenth century, coroners' inquests operated under the supervision of two newly reconstituted institutions, the Privy Council and its sibling, the Court of Star Chamber. The interaction of jurors' actions and official oversight reveals a sense of the inquest as serving the needs of 'public justice', a public justice that might just at times be somewhat separate or separable from that of the monarch.

CORONERS AND THEIR JURIES

The coroners held an ancient office, but the nature of their duties and the purposes of their inquests changed over time. Coroners first appeared in 1194, holding an office created by the king to assist and to oversee sheriffs in the collection of royal revenues. They had as their special charge the collection of fees due from holding the *'placitorum coronae regis'*—the major offences deemed to be against the king as much as against an individual, those that were coming to be seen as 'criminal' rather than civil.[17] Coroners who answered partly to boroughs and lords of semi-autonomous franchises began to appear soon after. J.D.J. Havard and R.F. Hunnisett have speculated that the office emerged from efforts to collect the *murdrum*, or murder fine. Meant initially to protect the Danish, then Norman, invaders from violent attacks by the colonized, the fine applied to all the inhabitants of an area in which a body was found, unless they produced the killer or proved that the victim was English. Coroners thus heard 'presentments of Englishry' and collected fines for default, in what seems to have degenerated over time into little more than a tax until abolished in 1340.[18] Beyond the murder fine, coroners also collected the other financial incidents of death. People found guilty of killing themselves or others stood to forfeit their possessions, as did those who fled upon suspicion of

[17] For the foundational eyre article of 1194, see William Stubbs, *Select Charters* (Oxford, 1888), pp. 259–60.

[18] Havard, *Detection of Secret Homicide*, pp. 11–12; Hunnisett, *The Medieval Coroner*, pp. 27–34. For the murder fine, see F.C. Hamil, 'Presentment of Englishry and the Murder Fine', *Speculum* 12.3 (1937): pp. 285–98, and Bruce O'Brien, 'From Morðor to Murdrum: The Preconquest Origin and Norman Revival of the Murder Fine', *Speculum* 71.2 (1996): pp. 321–57. On the early history of homicide and murder, see also Lambert, 'Theft, Homicide and Crime in Late Anglo-Saxon Law', pp. 3–43.

wrongdoing and became outlaws.[19] Even in cases of accidental homicide, coroners collected something for the royal coffers. Objects or animals that contributed to the death—perhaps a horse or a cart that had crushed a bystander—passed to the royal treasury as 'deodands'.[20] Havard's assertion that the medieval inquest 'was concerned solely with the opportunities it afforded for fines and amerciaments' is too strong, but certainly, revenue collection represented the early coroners' main purpose.[21]

Both Hunnisett and Havard have written of the inquest's late medieval zenith and subsequent decline. By their standards, one might see the decline continuing into the sixteenth century; but we can better describe that early modern history as a repurposing and refocusing away from the king's finances towards public order. Concern with royal finances and with 'justice', or order, had always appeared entirely compatible; the one did not preclude the other, and in some ways, they had been synonymous. But as the one diminished in importance, the other grew and changed in subtle yet significant ways. Over the fourteenth century, coroners lost some of their responsibilities to the newly created justices of the peace. Escheators took over some of the financial duties.[22] The abjurations of the realm that they had once supervised disappeared in the reign of Henry VIII. The criminal appeals they heard became increasingly rare. Over the sixteenth century, coroners continued to pronounce outlawries, but otherwise focused on homicides. They had as their first and foremost duty the supervision of inquests into suspicious and sudden deaths, as well as deaths in gaols. They retained a role in appraising forfeitures or deodands from such fatalities, though they seem to have done so more often with suicides and accidental deaths than with homicides, leaving forfeitures from the latter to be collected more often by sheriffs, escheators, and others.[23] The former more often went to almoners, at least in theory to be put to

---

[19] Perpetrators of both suicide and homicide stood to forfeit their chattels; homicides also faced escheat of their real property. For medieval coroners' collection of forfeitures, see Hunnisett in particular; for forfeiture more generally, see Kesselring, 'Felony Forfeiture in England, c.1170–1870', *Journal of Legal History* 30.3 (2009): pp. 201–26.

[20] On deodands, see Teresa Sutton, 'The Deodand and Responsibility for Death', *Journal of Legal History* 18 (1997): pp. 44–55; and 'The Nature of the Early Law of Deodand', *Cambrian Law Review* 9 (1999): pp. 9–20; J.J. Finkelstein, 'The Goring Ox: Some Historical Perspectives on Deodands, Forfeiture, Wrongful Death, and the Western Notion of Sovereignty', *Temple Law Quarterly* 46 (1973): pp. 169–290.

[21] Havard, *Secret Homicide*, p. 27; see also Hunnisett, *Medieval Coroner*, esp. pp. 2–3, 27–34, 109–11.

[22] Hunnisett, *Medieval Coroner*, pp. 190–200.

[23] Some confusion seems to exist about a statute of 1483 (1 Richard III c. 3): it mandated that the goods of suspects no longer be seized before conviction, but they were still to be appraised. That coroners and their juries were more assiduous in their financial obligations regarding self-inflicted deaths emerges from Hunnisett's calendars of the Sussex records. Of the 243 inquisitions (on 244 deaths) surviving from 1485–1558, 58 per cent (34/59) of the inquests into suicides mentioned goods to be forfeited, whereas only 14 per cent (12/86) of the inquisitions dealing with murder, manslaughter, or self-defence mentioned goods to be forfeited. (Moreover, most of those were by franchisal rather than county coroners, men reporting to a lord of a liberty rather than to the Crown.) Similarly, among the 520 Sussex inquisitions surviving from 1603 to 1688, 45 per cent (33/73) of the records dealing with suicides mentioned goods to be forfeited, while only 11.5 per cent (11/96) of those dealing with felonious death did the same. As I have discussed elsewhere, this does not indicate that these other killers faced

charitable uses, and the latter were increasingly dispersed as gifts to suitors or grant-holders.

For their work they received no salary, but early Tudor measures sought to encourage coroners' efforts with first a carrot and then sticks: an important statute of 1487, early in the reign of Henry VII, offered coroners 13s 4d for any inquest held on a death deemed felonious, to be paid either from the forfeited goods of the killer or from fines levied upon the township. They received no fee for inquests into other types of death, but lest that discourage their activity, a proclamation issued in 1493 reiterated the promise of payment and also threatened a fine of 100s for every default. A statute passed in 1509 mandated fines of 40s if coroners failed to hold inquests into deaths by simple misadventure.[24] A pair of statutes at mid-century broadened the scope of their responsibilities, and also added more incentive with another threat of fines: in what John Langbein depicted as important steps towards a public prosecutorial function for justices of the peace, Queen Mary's 'bail and committal' statutes of 1554–55 gave JPs powers to record examinations and prepare evidence for trial. The acts gave similar powers to coroners. They were to take down in writing the core of the evidence brought before them at inquests into felonious deaths to aid in prosecution; for failure to do so, justices of gaol delivery could fine them as they 'shall think meet'.[25]

Writing in the 1560s, Sir Thomas Smith observed that coroners typically ranked among 'the meaner sort of gentlemen'.[26] Modern commentators concur that most coroners seem to have been of somewhat lower status than the men who served as justices of the peace and sheriffs, but still firmly within the gentry.[27] In earlier centuries, coroners had to be knights, but early modern legal writers agreed that this rule no longer applied. To serve as a coroner, an individual faced no requirements other than having sufficient wealth within the county of his appointment to cover the costs of office and any fines he might incur.[28] He needed no legal or medical training: he learned what to do informally, through conversations or service with a senior coroner and perhaps with the help of one of the guidebooks that began to appear in the sixteenth century.[29] He would have found knowledge of Latin useful,

no forfeiture, but if they did, officials other than the coroner handled the matter. See Kesselring, 'Felony Forfeiture', p. 274.

[24] Statutes: 3 Henry VII c. 2 and 1 Henry VIII c. 7. For the proclamation, see *TRP*, vol. 1, no. 30. Only from 1752 did they stand to receive a standard £1 fee for each inquest 'duly taken', as well as compensation for their travel expenses.

[25] 1&2 Philip & Mary c. 13 and 2&3 Philip & Mary c. 10. See John Langbein, *Prosecuting Crime in the Renaissance* (Cambridge, MA, 1974), pp. 13–15. For evidence of this prosecutorial function being assumed by JPs well in advance of the legislation, see William B. Robison, 'Murder at Crowhurst: A Case Study in Early Tudor Law Enforcement', *Criminal Justice History* 9 (1988): pp. 31–62.

[26] Thomas Smith, *De Republica Anglorum* (London, 1583), p. 72.

[27] Hunnisett, *Sussex Inquests, 1558–1603*, p. xxxi; Loar, 'Go and Seek the Crowner', p. 44.

[28] See Wilkinson, *Treatise… Concerning the Office and Authorities of Coroners*, pp. 9, 2–4; Edward Coke, *Second Part of the Institutes of the Laws of England* (London, 1797), p. 175.

[29] See Edward Umfreville, *Lex Coronatoria: Or, the Office and Duty of Coroners* (London, 1761), who describes his own initiation to the job at the hands of a coroner who had served for twenty-five years, who in turned learned from another who had previously served for forty years. For one surviving manuscript guidebook and formulary, *temp.* Elizabeth, see Nottinghamshire Record Office, DDE 67/1. Another, in Durham Cathedral Library, RAI 126, dates from *c.*1625, collating materials produced

but not absolutely necessary: coroners typically had clerks who prepared the inquest documentation for them.[30]

Significantly, many coroners—including those who dealt with the majority of homicides, that is, the county coroners—obtained their positions through election rather than through appointment. Unlike other key royal officials in the counties, such as sheriffs and justices of the peace, county coroners were elected by the 'county community', male freeholders meeting at the quarter sessions. Moreover, they could then serve until death or debility made them unable to continue, unlike officers who had finite terms or who found their authority terminated upon the death of the sovereign.[31]

The elections sometimes provoked heated contests, suggesting the seriousness with which some people treated this choice. In 1593, for example, the Privy Council intervened after reports that three JPs in Brecon had gathered an 'unlawful assembly of people armed and weaponed in warlike manner' to ensure the election of their preferred candidate for the coronership.[32] An intense dispute in 1570 saw an assize judge secure writs for the election of two new coroners for Glamorgan, upon report that the current ones had both been convicted for various offences and had failed to hold inquests when they ought to have done. A majority of the near one thousand freeholders who reportedly showed up endorsed two new men, only to have the sheriff refuse to swear them into office and to prepare for a new election, even as he continued to back the existing coroners. At that point, the Privy Council reprimanded the sheriff, but also decided to seek certification from local JPs about the purported problems with the original coroners, on report that the assize judge might have acted precipitously. The surviving records unfortunately do not clarify how this dispute ended, but leave no doubt that the choice of coroner mattered.[33]

The earl of Shrewsbury's papers include mentions of three such elections—the 1570–71 dispute in Glamorgan and also two others, in 1583 and in 1592—which give a sense of the significance of the position in county politics and its potential attractions. In the scramble after one coroner's death, a candidate observed that the place 'will be sought for with speed'. Despite the support of some colleagues, he ultimately recused himself, having considered 'the service and travail that that officer shall be bound unto from time to time, and upon the sudden to be called off and then no remedy but ride he must'. He preferred peace and quiet, he said, over 'the profit thereof, although the office is both of worship and credit'.[34] Another man stepped forward to express his interest, noting that the office 'will be to me both a credit and a commodity'.[35] After another coroner's death, the earl solicited

from 1547 forward. Works published in 1538 and 1577 offered some commentary on the office, but the first published guide with extensive practical instructions seems to be Wilkinson's treatise of 1618 (see note above).

[30] See, e.g., STAC 2/29/145.   [31] See writs ordering such elections in C 242.

[32] *APC*, vol. 24, pp. 333–4.

[33] *A Calendar of the Register of the Queen's Majesty's Council in the Dominion and Principality of Wales and the Marches of the Same (1535) 1569–1591*, edited by Ralph Flenley (London, Cymmrodorion Record Series, no. 8, 1916), pp. 85–92.

[34] Lambeth Palace Archives, MS 3199, f. 371.

[35] Lambeth Palace Archives, MS 3199, f. 369.

help in securing the election of his own favoured candidate, and in defeating a group who 'confederate together... to elect and place a new coroner, such a one as them best liked'.[36]

Interestingly, an opponent in this dispute wrote to urge the earl to back down, insisting that 'the election of the coroner should be made by the commons of the said county, even as the election of the knight of the shire for parliament ought to be, in both which cases all honourable estates, being excluded from the commons... have no voice therein'. He urged the earl to 'leave the election of this office free to the country', though perhaps opening the door to a compromise candidate by noting that 'for mine own part, and so I think I may say for the rest of the gentlemen that deal in this action, if it be to a man fit for his sufficiency and honest behaviour and for his dwelling to serve their part of the country in any reasonable manner, they would willing yield'.[37] For some people, then—at least in these examples from Wales and the borders—the ability to choose the coroner and the character of the man selected clearly mattered.

Over the preceding centuries, kings (and more recently, queens) had given various boroughs and lords the privilege of having their own coroners. The methods by which these men gained and lost their positions varied. In some boroughs, the mayor served as coroner *ex officio*, while in others a coroner was elected by the freemen or chosen by elected bodies.[38] One assumes that the lord himself picked the coroner in those franchises with the right to have their own, but here, too, a broader input may sometimes have prevailed. William Morgan, from Newport in south Wales, described a local custom in which the tenants of the lord each year elected three 'of the most honest and substantial' of their fellows, from which group the high steward selected one to serve as coroner.[39]

To hold an inquest, a coroner needed at least twelve men on his jury. Since he needed twelve men to agree to a finding, however, he usually chose more. Jurors on coroners' inquests had to meet no requirements save for being men of the vicinity in which the death occurred, typically from the four neighbouring townships.[40] Notably, inquests into prison deaths might well include up to six prisoners.[41] Thus, unlike those called to serve on grand and petty juries at trial, these men had no

---

[36] Derbyshire Record Office, D 258/36/1/20.

[37] Lambeth Palace Archives, MS 710, ff. 5–5v, and MS 699, f. 21. For the other two disputes, see MS 3199, ff. 369, 371; MS 3206, f. 581; and MS 3197, f. 21.

[38] Based on nineteenth-century parliamentary inquiries, Fisher notes that in 1835, some 142 boroughs had the right to their own coroner, with selection methods split nearly evenly between an official elected to some other office serving *ex officio* and elections on a variety of franchises. Fisher, 'Office and Role of the Coroner', pp. 76–7.

[39] SP 46/3/5, f. 30. (See also STAC 2/24/436.) Fisher calculates that in 1726, some eighty franchise jurisdictions had their own coroners. This practice ended only in 1926. 'Office and Role of the Coroner', p. 65.

[40] Hunnisett, *Medieval Coroner*, p. 32.

[41] Umfreville describes the mixed jury, with six prisoners, as the standard for prison deaths in his 1761 treatise on the coroner's office, citing fourteenth- and seventeenth-century precedents: *Lex Coronatoria*, p. 213. While the inquisitions typically do not specify whether any of the jurors were prisoners, Shannon McSheffrey has identified a few early sixteenth-century inquisitions that do: KB 9/975, mm. 235–8. For other examples, see also: KB 9/539, mm. 60, 62 (1538).

minimum property qualification to meet. In practice, they ranged in status from labourers through to gentlemen, with the bulk coming from what we might term the lower middling and lower ranks—yeomen and men that Elizabethan social commentator William Harrison classified as 'the fourth and last sort', including husbandmen and artificers such as tailors, shoemakers, and carpenters. Harrison observed that typically, this 'fourth and last sort... have neither voice nor authority in the commonwealth', but 'in cities and corporate towns, for default of yeomen, they are fain to make up their inquests of such manner of people'.[42]

The documentation from coroners' inquests rarely lists the jurors' occupations or status designations. When such information does appear, however, it overwhelmingly identifies trades and craftsmen in towns, and husbandmen and yeomen in rural areas. Records from a set of twenty-two inquests held in Chester between 1592 and 1595 name the occupations of 277 men. They list five yeomen and one husbandman, but otherwise identify trades and craftsmen of various sorts, including dyers, joiners, bricklayers, and more. Numerically, tailors and shoemakers dominated, with forty-two appearances of men with the former designation and thirty-four of the latter on these juries.[43] A smaller batch of five inquisitions from Newcastle upon Tyne in 1610 tells a similar story, including one gentleman, several yeomen, four merchants, and similar numbers of shipwrights, tailors, glovers, and cordwainers. Others on the lists included barbers, rope makers, skinners, blacksmiths, and slaters. A carpenter, a cutler, and a chapman joined them, as did a spurrier, a miller, and a draper.[44] Outside the towns, juries such as that which sat on the death of Richard Harris at Lydley, Shropshire, which included fifteen husbandmen and one yeoman, seem not to be unusual.[45] If such small samples reflected practices more generally, the men on coroners' juries were typically of a slightly lower status than those on trial juries, and thus somewhat more representative of the broader population.

What we can discern of jurors' ability to write matches this snapshot of social origins. A person's ability to sign his or her name can serve as a rough and ready indicator of literacy skills and of social status. In his pioneering study of illiteracy in early modern England, David Cressy argued that signing ability 'may be taken, with some misgivings, to signify a cut-off point in the middle range, somewhere between a rude ability to read and actual fluency in writing'. He also noted that the acquisition of literacy skills among men replicated socio-economic hierarchies.[46] A set of early seventeenth-century inquest records from County Durham includes ten with the signatures or marks of the jurors themselves. In these inquisitions, produced between 1606 and 1610, fifty-two of the 154 jurors signed their names; 102, or 66 per cent, provided marks instead. In only one of the ten inquisitions did jurors signing their names dominate. In all the others, those leaving marks constituted

[42] Harrison, *The Description of England*, p. 118.
[43] Chester Archives and Local Studies, QCI/6/1–13 and QCI/7/1–10. Some of the names and occupations on these inquisitions were illegible. Some of the individuals identified appeared on more than one inquest; these counts make no distinction between men who appeared once or more than once.
[44] KB 9/730, mm. 595–600.   [45] KB 9/517, m. 80.
[46] David Cressy, 'Levels of Illiteracy in England, 1530–1730', *Historical Journal* 20.1 (1977): p. 2.

the majority.[47] In a set of ten such inquest documents from Bury St. Edmunds, produced from 1621 through to 1626, the jurors divided almost evenly between men who signed their names and those who did not, with seventy-three of the 145 jurors signing and seventy-two providing marks.[48] The records produced by six inquests held in Chester between 1610 and 1635 have a higher proportion of men able to sign, with only thirty-two of the eighty-three jurors providing marks.

These three small early seventeenth-century data sets thus show 54 per cent of the coroners' jurors making marks, and presumably thus being unable to write with any ease, though they may well have had some reading ability. It also accords with the data indicating a lower middling status for the typical inquest juror. For comparison, Cressy had no data for the 1620s in his study of thousands of Norwich documents, but for the decades immediately before and after found that 32 to 38 per cent of yeomen, 44 to 49 per cent of craftsmen and tradesmen, and 77 to 86 per cent of husbandmen did not sign their names.[49] Records from a later set of inquests—twenty-eight, held in Lincolnshire from 1669 to 1699—suggest increasing literacy rates, with at most 33 per cent of the jurors providing marks.[50] This need not indicate rising status levels among jurors, but rather slow increases in literacy in the population more generally. Again, it tracks with Cressy's data for men of lower middling status: he found that in the 1660s, some 24 per cent of yeomen, 33 per cent of tradesmen, and 71 per cent of husbandmen did not sign their names, whereas in the 1690s, the percentages were 18, 30, and 82 respectively.

Evidence suggests, then, that the people charged with responding to homicides constituted a broad cross-section of early modern society: the coroners were gentlemen, though typically of the lesser sort, and their jurors came from all social backgrounds, though with men of lower middling and lower status numerically dominant. J.S. Cockburn's calendars of the Kent assize records, which cover the years from 1559 to 1688, allow a bit more flesh to be put on these bones, in particular by adding information on the amount of experience both coroners and jurors might have. The Kent assize records list thirty-six men who served as county coroners, besides passing mention of others who served as the coroners of boroughs and liberties. Of the twenty-one whose status is indicated, all were noted as 'gentlemen', save for one who appeared variously as 'esquire' and 'gentleman'. Some seem to have had legal training.[51] They ranged in number from two to five in office at any one time. As men moved in and out of the position, overlap always existed,

---

[47] DUL, CCB 8/218/4/1–5, 7, 8, 12, 15, 19. [Deaths: four suicides by hanging; three deemed to be the results of illnesses; two accidents; one murder.]

[48] Suffolk Record Office, Bury St. Edmunds, D 11/11/1.   [49] Cressy, 'Illiteracy', p. 5.

[50] BL, Add MS 31028, *passim*. Lockwood used this set of inquests as his sample for literacy rates as well, suggesting that just slightly over 23 per cent of the jurors used a mark (*Conquest*, pp. 152–3); my tally excludes those inquests which had no marks at all when names were written in a common hand, for which it seems possible that a clerk transcribed the names, and ends at 1699/1700.

[51] Some shared names with people registered at one of the Inns of Court, at least. While some of these names are too common to be certain that we are dealing with the same individuals, we can be more confident of others (e.g. Christopher Mockett, Kentish coroner and registered at the Inner Temple, http://www.innertemplearchives.org.uk/search.asp#name). Of course, not everyone with legal training was registered with one of the great Inns for which some records survive, and not everyone registered at the Inns was training in law.

with at least one experienced coroner remaining in office as new men replaced the old. Counting only those twenty-eight men for whom we have both a beginning and likely end date to their time in office, they served anywhere from a low of four to a high of thirty-nine years as coroners, with an average time in service of just under seventeen years. Notable stalwarts included William Webbe (1560–93), Martin Coates (1569–1605), Nicholas Dering (1603–41), and Robert Heath (1653–85).

The assize files do not include documentation of all the inquests a given coroner supervised, but they most likely include the bulk of the inquisitions into deaths deemed the result of the felonious killing of one person by another. Coroners were to hand their inquest files over to the assize judges who visited most counties twice a year. Those dealing with deaths that the coroner's jury deemed felonious and for which the accused awaited trial remained among the assize files to serve as indictments to initiate criminal proceedings. Coroners were to forward the rest, including those for suicides and other felonious killings in which no accused stood ready to face trial, to King's Bench. There clerks would review them for errors or for indications of forfeitures or deodands due to the Crown. The inquisitions among the assize files calendared by Cockburn, then, probably include most of those produced by inquests on felonious, non-suicidal deaths for which trials occurred, but a smaller proportion of the others. They can, nonetheless, give us a few details about coroners' careers and their jurors.

William Webbe, listed as a coroner from 1560 to 1593, had forty-one inquisitions surviving among the assize files, almost all of which dealt with felonious deaths. These inquests took him to thirty-five different towns and villages. With usually only one or two inquests into felonious deaths a year, in 1584 he supervised six investigations that produced accusations of criminal homicide. His juries ranged in size from twelve to twenty, although groups of about sixteen proved most common. Roughly 610 men sat on these juries, with perhaps thirty who served more than once. John Wagstaffe, Edward Wilcock, John Ingelden, and John Mannings, for example, were among the fifteen jurors who convened to discuss the death of 12-year-old Thomas Jones at Biddenden in 1583, and a year later sat on another inquest in the same parish.[52]

Robert Heath served as a county coroner from 1653 to 1685. Sixty-seven of his inquest reports survive among the assize files for Kent, enough to make a few observations. Findings of suicide and accidental death are all but absent from this collection. While the trial juries often came to different conclusions, fifty-eight of these inquests identified killings as murder (including eighteen deaths of infants), eight as felonious homicide, and only one as misadventure. In those years for which records of his inquests survive, Heath supervised anywhere from two to six investigations into deaths deemed felonious per year, with five being a fairly standard number. These sixty-seven inquests took him to some forty-six different towns and villages.

---

[52] *CAR* Kent, Elizabeth I, nos. 1228 and 1424.

Among these inquests, Heath's juries ranged in size from thirteen to twenty-one jurors, while most had nearer to seventeen members. Given the imprecision imposed by common surnames, vagaries of spelling, and the occasionally illegible or torn list of names, we cannot find precise numbers, but it seems that at least 928 different men served on these juries. Perhaps eighty-three men appeared on more than one of these juries—and these records, again, are just a subset of all of the inquests Heath would have supervised as coroner. Abraham Ashdowne, John Mercer, William Harvey, and Hugh Nethersole, for example, served together on two inquests, both in 1657. The first sat at Wouldham and the other at nearby Barham. In the first, they identified John Polley as a murderer for having struck neighbour Edward Travers with a stone, though a trial jury later found Polley guilty only of manslaughter. In the second, they and their fellows deemed William Boghurst guilty of murder for his son Thomas's slow death by starvation, while the trial jury found that Thomas died by the providence of God.[53]

A reasonably sizable group of men, then, had experience on at least two of Heath's juries. A few served on more than two, with at least thirteen men having this dubious distinction in this subset of inquest reports. Thomas Hickmote sat on three inquests at Cranbrook from 1662 to 1669: in the first he sat with a jury that deemed David Morgan the unfortunate victim of a badly hit cricket ball, in the second with a jury which decided that John Voutrell had killed a man by maliciously throwing a pot at his head, and in the third with a jury that declared Robert Morrys the victim of a brutal beating. This same Thomas Hickmote may also have served on a fourth of Heath's juries, one that helped indict Bridget Caffinch of Frittenden for the murder of her infant in 1661. (In these four cases, incidentally, only Bridget Caffinch ended up being sentenced to hang.)[54] Francis Phipp, Thomas Paine, and Edward Smyth served on the jury which met at Strood on 1 September 1656 and decided that Joan Batt had strangled her illegitimate infant daughter, a crime for which a trial jury in due course found Batt guilty.[55] Two years later, Paine and Smyth served on another jury at Higham, on the body of Elizabeth Borne, deemed to have been beaten to death by another woman.[56] Three years later, Phipp, Paine, and Smyth sat on one of Heath's juries at Strood, this time over the body of a man named in the record as Albertus Casimir Pollonnoes. In a determination with which a trial jury eventually agreed, Phipp and his companions decided that Isaac Jacob and Casimir Kersegey had set upon the wealthy traveller in the highway near Gravesend, stealing from him goods of extraordinary value and fatally wounding him with a cutlass.[57] Phipp, Paine, and Smyth, like other men of Kent, thus shared much experience with homicide and the collective responsibilities of responding to it.

---

[53] *CAR* Kent, 1649–1659, nos. 1560 and 1562.
[54] *CAR* Kent, 1660–1675, nos. 33, 402, 639, and 1131.
[55] *CAR* Kent, 1649–1659, no. 1365.   [56] *CAR* Kent, 1649–1659, no. 1627.
[57] *CAR* Kent, 1660–1675, no. 195. None of these men is recorded as having served on other coroners' juries. Paine later served as a trial juror (nos. 1521, 1528); Smyth may have, too, but given the commonness of his surname, this is uncertain.

THE PUBLICITY AND POLITICS OF THE INQUEST

Quite a few men evidently served on coroners' juries, sometimes on more than one, ensuring a broad familiarity with the inquest. Even more people would at least have witnessed one in action. Inquests occurred throughout the county, and they took place in public. The older, medieval injunction that all males in the four neighbouring vills over age 12 attend an inquest may no longer have been enforced, but the events clearly remained well attended.[58] As Thomas Smith observed, writing in the 1560s, 'The empanelling of this inquest, and the view of the body, and the giving of the verdict, is commonly in the street in an open place, and in *Corona populi*'. The collective, open viewing of the body constituted a necessary element of any inquest: all needed to be done expressly '*super visum corporis*'. Furthermore, Smith wrote, jurors were 'not enclosed into a straight place (as I told before of other inquests) but are suffered to go at large, and take a day, sometime of twenty or thirty days, more or less, as the fact is more evident or more kept close'.[59] That is, unlike trial juries, which had little time and space in which to come to a decision, the men on coroners' juries had more freedom to investigate at large.

Inquisitions and records produced by disputed cases bear Smith out in noting the openness of the proceedings. Jurors typically first viewed the body wherever the victim had died, then gathered in a church porch, a town or guild hall, an inn, or some other such place to hear and discuss further evidence.[60] They had audiences for their doings, too, beyond the witnesses and family members who had a direct interest in the proceedings. Agnes Beaumont reported that the jurors who investigated her father's death viewed the corpse where it lay in the house she had shared with him, then convened in the parlour of her brother's house, which was 'very full of people'. Despite being in a private home, this inquest allowed 'great observation' by many neighbours.[61] In one case, an observer with no obvious tie to the incident was recorded as having interjected some legal advice. In another, a man accused of trying to sway the jury maintained that he had merely taken a seat in one of the church pews to rest himself, together with 'divers other lookers on, being none of the jury'.[62] Of another, on the beating death of Anne Stirope, inquest jurors later affirmed that the body had been brought out to the 'common view' or the 'open view of the coroner, coroner's inquest, and the standers-by, and there sufficiently viewed and to their satisfaction and contentment'. One of those standers-by, a 70-year-old man, testified that he had attended simply 'for his own pleasure and for company'.[63] One Nantwich homicide eventually prompted an unusually well-documented case in which 116 people testified; most noted having observed the body, but some also complained that the coroner had tried to keep them from the

---

[58] Statute of Marlborough, 52 Henry III c. 24 (1267).

[59] Smith, *De Republica Anglorum*, p. 73.

[60] For some held in a guildhall, see, e.g., Hunnisett, *Nottingham Inquests*, nos. 156, 161, 170, 173, 174, 308.

[61] *The Narrative of the Persecutions of Agnes Beaumont*, edited by Vera J. Camden (East Lansing, MI, 1992), pp. 72–81. Thanks to Cynthia Herrup for this reference.

[62] STAC 8/18/13; STAC 8/3/37.   [63] STAC 5/B8/32.

inquest, which they implied was unusual or improper in some fashion.[64] Carol Loar has suggested that the openness and publicity of the inquests may have helped disseminate knowledge of forensic medicine to people who might later have served as jurors themselves.[65] The same openness, publicity, and sense of shared interest may also have made the inquests forums for political action and education.

That politics pervaded inquests emerges most clearly from records of disputed cases. Of the legal disputes relating to coroners' inquests, those most readily found relate to suicide and deaths by misadventure: the royal almoners had the right to collect the goods of suicides and deodands, and frequently complained that coroners or their juries had somehow infringed upon their dues. Cases relating to homicide more generally were also launched by royal officials as well as a range of private complainants. The varied financial interests in homicides and other fatalities ensured a robust level of oversight.[66] The records produced by these cases provide a multifaceted view of the politics of the inquest, with an abundance of detail about procedures and norms and their alleged violations. Charges in individual cases cannot be treated as being any more 'true' than a coroner's or trial jury's verdict, nor can they be seen as typical of investigations that usually proceeded without formal complaint; they do nonetheless suggest some of the many ways in which politics infused the inquest. The discussion that follows mines a number of such complaints, to trace both the procedures of the inquest and the possibilities for corruption, influence, and error—and maybe even principled interventions—that they afforded.

---

[64] Cheshire Archives and Local Studies, DDx. 196, discussed in Steve Hindle, ' "Bleedinge Afreshe"? The Affray and Murder at Nantwich, 19 December 1572', in *The Extraordinary and the Everyday in Early Modern England*, edited by Garthine Walker and Angela McShane (Basingstoke, 2010), pp. 224–45.

[65] Loar, 'Medical Knowledge', p. 486. See STAC 5/H61/32 for a related example, in which a witness at an inquest offered testimony based on his experience on an earlier inquest.

[66] For the effects of forfeitures and the financial incidents of death on law enforcement, see Kesselring, 'Making Crime Pay: Felony Forfeiture and the Profits of Crime'. Lockwood now offers a longer and more detailed examination of one facet of this practice, arguing that 'overlapping individual financial interests created a system of surveillance that monitored the investigation of death by means of self-interested central court litigation', *Conquest*, esp. ch. 5. I agree with the general thrust of some of Lockwood's arguments, but have reservations on a few points. He suggests that 'the creation of a system of forfeiture that punished illegitimate violence through the seizure of property was the first step in regulating culpable death' (p. 203), but forfeitures of felons' goods developed centuries before what he sees as the key 'regulatory moment' beginning in the 1530s. Nor was the monitoring of this 'system' placed in the hands of the almoner, as he describes (pp. 202–4). The almoner did indeed have rights to the forfeited goods of suicides and to deodands, unless otherwise given away by grants to towns or lords, but *not* to forfeitures of felons or murderers more generally. Nor is there any evidence—or at least none cited by Lockwood and none that I have found—that the 'decision' to allow almoners to sue in Star Chamber was a conscious choice by the Crown to tighten the surveillance over culpable homicide, as he describes. (He cites a line in MacDonald and Murphy, *Sleepless Souls*, pp. 25–6, who in turn cite a line in Guy, *Court of Star Chamber*, p. 37, but neither offers clear support for such a claim. He also cites Houston, *Punishing the Dead*, pp. 279–313; any support there for this claim is not immediately evident.) But yes, the almoners' policing of coroners' inquests to look for deodands and the goods of suicides likely had many of the effects that he suggests, and thus contributed to the developments outlined in this chapter.

Indeed, the problems could begin at the beginning. Someone had first to call the coroner. In the first instance, the determination that a death merited investigation depended upon the insight and initiative of family, neighbours, or bystanders. This public responsibility was expected not of a particular official, but shared by the community more generally. The sextons asked to arrange burials for the recently deceased may have played some role here. So, too, might the pauper widows appointed in some cities from the late sixteenth century to serve as 'searchers of the dead' have helped to identify bodies meriting an inquest, as did women preparing bodies for burial more generally.[67] With no central registry of deaths, no modern police force, and no modern medical examiners, the identification and reporting of suspicious deaths depended largely on lay initiative. Members of the community were supposed to call the coroner not just for obviously felonious homicides, but also for all deaths caused in any way by another person, no matter how accidental. In theory, someone should have reported any sudden, violent, or unexplained death to a coroner.[68]

The sheer number of deaths that coroners' juries deemed to have resulted from the 'visitation of God' and purely natural causes suggests that people often erred on the side of caution when deciding whether to call a coroner. On the other hand, cases sometimes emerged in which the original determination that a death did not merit a coroner proved wrong or subsequently came into question: in 1569, for example, Elizabeth Evette's body was already in the ground before rumours that she had died from her master's 'unreasonable correction' prompted the coroner to order an exhumation.[69] When William Ryce died, his master sent for the searchers of the dead and the barber surgeon who had treated Ryce for a recent illness. All readily agreed that Ryce's burned and ulcerated 'privy member', part of which the surgeon had recently removed, led to his death and so they called no coroner; only years later did accusations of poisoning prompt an investigation.[70]

Sometimes, too, people who clearly should have notified a coroner may have failed to do so, either to avoid expenses or to hide a murder. One such case happened at the Abbey of Combermere in 1520. As a card game turned ugly, a household servant stabbed and killed one of the monks who had tried to separate him from the other combatant. When some of the brothers hastened to seize the killer and call the coroner, the prior intervened. He feared that news of the killing would

---

[67] See, for example, Richelle Munkoff, 'Searchers of the Dead: Authority, Marginality, and the Interpretation of Plague in England, 1574–1665', *Gender & History* 11.1 (1999): pp. 1–29; Malcolm Gaskill, 'Reporting Murder: Fiction in the Archives in Early Modern England', *Social History* 23 (1998): pp. 18–19; and Craig Spence, *Accidents and Violent Death in Early Modern London, 1650–1750* (Woodbridge, 2016), pp. 43–50. For one interesting case, see Hereford County Record Office, BG 11/8/4, the depositions dealing with the death of Joan Blackeweye, in which Sybill Myllward noted that she and Eleanor Reignolls had been sworn by the mayor of the city to view the body.

[68] 'Sudden' and 'unnatural' were open to interpretation. Sir Matthew Hale seems to have restricted 'sudden' to deaths not following an illness. See Havard, *Secret Homicide*, pp. 39–42. Sara Butler's work on the medieval coroners' jury includes a stimulating discussion of the determination of '(un)natural' deaths: *Forensic Medicine*, pp. 177–84.

[69] London Metropolitan Archives, Repertories of the Court of Aldermen, COL/CA/01/01/018, f. 520d.

[70] In this case, judges ultimately concurred with the original evaluation: STAC 8/41/3.

endanger the house, which already had a reputation for gambling and 'evil rule kept at undue times'. He and the abbot reportedly made everyone present swear oaths to keep the killing quiet. John Janyns, the killer, moaned that he had been 'born to be hanged' and worried that too many people knew of his deed. In the event, he remained in service at the abbey for another year, and it seems that three years passed before rumours of the monk's unnatural death prompted an investigation.[71]

An even more remarkable case of collusion to avoid an inquest happened in Wiltshire in 1551. Working their fields on the Wednesday before Easter, Willie Nott and his brother John saw two men ride by and enter Birchwood forest. Shortly thereafter they heard noises that they believed to be from a great fight between the men, then a cry, then silence. Subsequent depositions differ on details, but on either the Friday or the Saturday following, Willie Nott went for a walk in the woods and found a man's body that showed signs of serious physical trauma. Nott told his neighbours, several of whom came to view the corpse. Then, in theory, someone should have fetched the coroner. Instead, several of them went to the nearby JP, John Byer. They asked if they might forego the coroner, pleading that they were too poor a group to pay the fees the coroner would demand. They said, moreover, that the body simply stank too badly and too dangerously to remain unburied any longer. Byer agreed. By his own admission, he told them to do their own informal inquest, essentially: 'Take honest men with you and view him well and so bury him.' A neighbouring family, with a member who had gone missing about the same time, later heard rumours of the illicit burial and insisted on exhuming the body for proper examination. They charged that the proceedings had been done not to avoid noxious fumes and onerous fees, but to cover up a murder.[72]

While these incidents eventually came to light, one suspects that other instances of obviously suspicious deaths remained hidden from official view—and from the historical record—for similar reasons. And then, of course, there would have been some unnatural deaths that observers may well have honestly mistaken for natural and that never came to light or appeared in the record. The people who had first to decide whether to call a coroner clearly played a key role in the process that produced the records on which histories of homicide rely, and that resulted in deaths being deemed criminal and killers being brought to justice.

Deciding *which* coroner to call might also constitute a decision with political implications. Inquests presented opportunities to challenge claims to jurisdiction. When Frideswide Taylor was found dead on the manor of George Owen, near Oxford, Owen's other tenants sent word to the county coroner to come view the body. The aldermen of Oxford had recently claimed that Owen's manor lay within their jurisdiction, however. They now showed up with the mayor, the town's own two coroners, and a sizeable group of armed men. The town's mace bearer proved that the device he carried retained purposes beyond the ceremonial, as he broke it in the ensuing melee. The townsmen maintained that Owen's people had attacked their coroners and 'hurled them clean out of the doors of the same house and

[71] STAC 2/19/158 and STAC 2/26/18.
[72] STAC 2/26/448, STAC 3/10/64, STAC 2/18/148.

threatened to beat them if they meddled any further'. The combatants reportedly upended the table on which Frideswide's body lay, before one group ran off with the corpse.[73] In other cases, coroners ordered the exhumation of bodies already examined by agents of another jurisdiction. In 1607, for example, the coroner of the king's household prompted complaints when he demanded to view the body of one Jerome Trollope, then seven days buried after already having been the subject of an inquest by the Dean of Westminster's coroner.[74]

When a coroner was called in, he usually arrived within two or three days, but might take substantially longer. He then met with a jury, typically no more than five days after the first finding of a body.[75] Whenever the coroner did appear, he called upon a constable or other such official to gather jurors. The two coroners of Maldon, for example, wrote to the borough's sergeant of the mace, asking him to have brought 'before us this present Saturday within this town at the hour of four afternoon, four and twenty sufficient and lawful men of the said township to inquire in the court before us to be holden (for our sovereign lord the king) upon the view of the dead body of James Remington how, after what manner, and by what means the said James came unto his death'.[76] They sometimes had trouble finding enough men. Then, as now, jury duty could be unwelcome. Accordingly, men called upon to serve on an inquest could be fined for refusing to attend, and it seems that sergeants sometimes corralled rather than summoned potential jurors in an effort to get the required numbers.[77] The jury was an important associational forum, but not a purely voluntary one.

The constable or other official who gathered potential jurors thus presumably had some ability to influence outcomes through his selections. Complaints about jury-rigging usually focused on the coroner, however, as he had the final say in which of the men so gathered became jurors. Chester coroner Emmet Warburton, for example, was accused of bypassing a number of the 'honest and substantial' men who had appeared to serve on the jury in favour of men who had borrowed from, or worked for, the deceased, in hopes that they would deem the death accidental rather than suicide and thus avoid the forfeiture of his property.[78]

Unlike trial juries, no formal mechanism allowed challenges to the men who sat on coroners' inquests. Coroner Henry Hockenhell faced accusations in Star Chamber that he had empanelled as jurors only servants and friends of the suspected murderer and his kinsmen, out of special favour to the killer. When William Clayton, 'one of the king's servants in those quarters', tried to challenge the choice

---

[73] STAC 4/7/14.   [74] BL, Cecil Papers 120/161.

[75] Hunnisett, *Sussex Inquests, 1603–1688*, p. xxiv. In *Sussex Inquests, 1558–1603*, p. xxxviii, Hunnisett suggests an average delay between date of death and inquest of about eight days for the west of the county and seventeen for the east, but notes that both averages are thrown off by a small number of exceptionally long delays, usually in cases of drowning and infanticide, when 'date of death' and the date on which the body was found could be far apart. The median delay between date of death and inquest seems to be shorter.

[76] Essex Record Office, D/B 3/3/210, no. 2.

[77] For reference to fines, see KB 9/866, m. 97. For an account of the compulsion of one potential inquest juror, see John Foxe, *Acts and Monuments* (London, 1570), book 12, p. 2319.

[78] STAC 5/A1/2.

of jurors, Hockenhell reportedly said that 'it had not been seen aforetime that any such challenge should be made or had at a coroner's inquest and would put thereupon whom it pleaseth him'. When preparing to pronounce the verdict, Hockenhell ordered the church doors locked and the complainant barred from entry.[79] Hockenhell, naturally, denied that he had empanelled friends and allies of the putative killer. He insisted that he followed usual procedure in asking the constables of the four towns nearest the killing to send jurors, but allowed that when not enough men appeared, he also sent to two other towns, too. He said, moreover, that while he had responded to Clayton's objections to his jurors with a statement that he knew of no precedents for such challenges, he had nonetheless removed two men that Clayton identified as particularly compromised.[80]

The coroner thus had a good deal of power in shaping the composition of his jury. Once gathered and sworn, however, the jurors did not always do his bidding. Those coroners hoping to influence their juries' findings might try to use procedural rules to their advantage. According to one accusation, Sussex coroner Magnus Fowle wanted a finding of manslaughter but faced a jury leaning towards a verdict of murder. As their first meeting on 1 September threatened to end in an outcome not to his liking, he suspended the proceedings and asked the jurors to reconvene on 12 November. In the interim he reportedly devised plans to have some of the jurors called away from the locality on the day in question, so he could then replace them with other, more amenable men.[81]

According to another accusation, coroner John Nashe used everything from mockery to intimidation to get the verdict he wanted. He was called upon to view the body of one William Banwell, a Prittlewell yeoman, who died after gentleman Edward Sharpe took to him with a cudgel. Nashe called a jury together, and reportedly said that Banwell's bruised body was 'the ugliest corpse' he had ever seen. Moreover, he observed, the evidence seemed strong enough that he would not change places with the suspected killer for £1,000. He then set a date for the jurors to resume their work. In the meantime, however, friends of the accused reportedly laboured and bribed Nashe to ensure that Sharpe avoid indictment. When the jurors did meet again, they proved obstreperously independent. Jurors expressed fear of the friends who had accompanied Sharpe to the inquest and pointed out that they had not yet heard evidence from some people they wanted to examine. When they imputed some partiality to the coroner, Nashe reportedly flew into a rage. They 'were base fellows to meddle with his office', and 'very idiots and fools to stand up it so stiffly', he said. He dismissed the jurors, giving them a new date to reconvene. When they did, Nashe pulled out a ready-prepared verdict reporting that the victim had died after having been gored by a bull. When the jurors refused to sign, he threatened that he would call them to meet and meet again in all the remotest places in the county. He implied that he could put them to such expense and bother that they might as well bend to his will sooner rather than later. Yet they proved obstinate still. He appeared to soften, setting the location of their next meeting at Maldon. According to the accusation, however, Nashe then found a

---

[79] STAC 2/18/222.   [80] STAC 2/29/145.   [81] STAC 5/C18/26.

way around his unhelpful jurors: he personally went before the grand jury at the next assize session to secure an indictment for Sharpe, but provided such weak evidence that the grand jury necessarily deemed it insufficient to go to trial and thus allowed Sharpe to go free.[82]

Coroners could clearly influence an inquest's outcome, particularly in determining juror selection and both the timing and location of meetings. Yet just as clearly, jurors sometimes went their own way. Perhaps some of their confidence and independence came from their active roles in the process. Inquest jurors were not a passive lot who simply digested the evidence put before them. A general call went out asking anyone with relevant information to appear at the inquest, but jurors could also request specific witnesses. They sometimes called upon 'expert' testimony— from physicians, surgeons, and women thought to have better knowledge of things corporeal—but also used their own experiences as guides. While evidence of participation by medical professionals is generally absent from the laconic inquisitions, stray references in the proceedings on cases that became contested and other ancillary documents indicate that jurors freely called upon surgeons' testimony.[83] A surgeon's manual published in 1652 treated such reports as routine elements of a surgeon's practice; one publication on a notable killing came from Abraham Jennings, who identified himself as both a physician and the foreman of the inquest.[84] While forensic autopsies only became common from the 1670s, at least a few happened by the late sixteenth century.[85] But such testimony and techniques did not yet dominate the inquest. They remained a supplement to the actions and opinions of the jurors themselves. Jurors evaluated signs of swelling, festering,

---

[82] STAC 8/18/13.

[83] See, e.g., STAC 5/H53/37, with references to two surgeons and an apothecary. DUL, MSP 53, p. 32, records a coroner's summons to a surgeon to appear at an inquest in 1640.

[84] Thomas Brugis, *Vade Mecum, or, a Companion for a Chyrurgion* (London, 1652) and Abraham Jennings, *Digitus Dei, or, An Horrid Murther Strangely Detected* (London, 1664). For additional references, see also Loar, 'Medical Knowledge'. For a particularly unusual one, see SP 16/230, f. 172, for a certificate signed by a midwife and a surgeon, as well as the coroner and jury foreman, documenting the natural death of a Newgate prisoner's baby. In *Forensic Medicine and Death Investigation*, Butler argues similarly that medieval coroners' juries sometimes called before them medical experts, and shows that a good many such juries already included in their number barbers, surgeons, or other such trained individuals.

[85] For reference to an autopsy in one such case, see STAC 5/33/19. See, too, Hunnisett, *Sussex Inquests, 1603–1688*, nos. 127 and 542, for references to autopsies held in 1613 and 1618; notably, records of both inquests come from the Rye borough registers, not from the brief fair copy inquisitions that show up in KB or ASSI files. For discussion of other early forensic autopsies, hidden if one relies on inquisitions alone, see also David Harley, 'Political Post-mortems and Morbid Anatomy in Seventeenth-Century England', *Social History of Medicine* 7 (1994): pp. 1–28; Loar, 'Medical Knowledge'; and Kesselring, 'Detecting Death Disguised', for a 1594 forensic autopsy into a suspicious death. For a seminal work on early legal medicine, see also Catherine Crawford's essays in *Legal Medicine in History*, edited by Crawford and Michael Clark (Cambridge, 1994). Interestingly, the testimony of surgeons and even the autopsies we treat as harbingers of modern forensic medicine sometimes appear in the exact same cases as those involving cruentation, the practice in which a suspect was made to touch the body to see if blood appears and which is sometimes today depicted as the epitome of superstition—perhaps we ought to take notice of the witness who explained that cruentation was in accord with both 'the opinion of Aristotle and the common experiment'. For the quote, see Cheshire Archives and Local Studies, DDx.196, f. 10; for other cases involving both surgeons and cruentation, see STAC 5/H53/37, STAC 5/H61/32, and STAC 8/33/19.

and rotting based on their own knowledge. They themselves measured the depth of wounds. They frequently tramped off to muddy riverbanks, fetid privies, and open fields to learn what they could of the circumstances of a death.

A well-documented case from East Yorkshire in the mid-1500s shows the degree of activity and initiative jurors might take. One Roger Barnes was indisputably found to be dead. The cause, of course, constituted the key question: his death followed a longstanding illness, but also a brutal beating by servants of local grandee Sir John Constable. The jurors convened for this potentially sensitive case included husbandmen and a few yeomen gathered from the neighbouring parishes, men who ranged in age from 36 to 70. They viewed Barnes's body two days after his death. He had a wound on his leg, but being clean and uncorrupted, it did not seem to them of a sort likely to kill him. Having heard a woman report that the leg was broken so badly that the foot might be laid flat on the thigh, two of the jurors tried for themselves. Robert Clerk and Walter Donne, husbandmen of Great Holden and both about 60 years old, reported having manipulated Barnes's leg to judge the severity of the injury. The jurors then turned to examining the nature of his illness, calling in the Scarborough surgeon Nicholas Carr, who had previously treated him. He avowed that Barnes died of his problems with the 'collick and the stone'. The jurors subsequently visited a physician in Beverley who confirmed the same. He, and other witnesses, talked of Barnes's longstanding difficulties urinating. Indeed, jurors could see for themselves that the 'privy members of the lower part of his body was black and swollen'. Barnes's son continued to insist that the beating had killed his father; though he would not swear to it, the jurors considered his charge carefully. They met together several times and had announcements made in local churches that anyone who knew any matter of relevance should appear before them. They waited the better part of a year before finally delivering their verdict that Barnes had died of his illness rather than the beating.[86]

Whether the men involved in this particular case came to the 'right' conclusion, jurors could clearly be strikingly independent and do their duty assiduously. Yet disputed cases, taken collectively if not individually, leave no doubt that both jurors and coroners sometimes crafted verdicts at odds with the 'facts'. Assize records, too, show trial jurors frequently narrating the same events in very different ways than had the coroners' juries. Whether on their own or in collusion with their colleagues on the inquest, coroners and jurors often pronounced verdicts with which others disagreed.

Sometimes they may simply have erred, whether from a lack of evidence or by evaluating evidence within now discarded intellectual frameworks. After deliberating over Alice Lanway's body in April 1605, for example, a coroner's jury decided that she had killed herself. She had already been buried in unconsecrated ground with a stake driven through her heart—customary in some parts of the country for people who killed themselves—before someone noticed one of her rings in a neighbour's possession and had the case reopened. While interested parties found

---

[86] The voluminous and unusually revealing depositions in this case survive in the East Riding of Yorkshire Archive Service, DDCC/139/65. See also STAC 4/10/11.

an abundance of things to complain about in the subsequent homicide proceedings, no one argued that the coroner's jury had done anything amiss in the circumstances.[87] Evidence did not always permit an indisputable verdict: the jurors sitting on the death of Anne Marshall in 1695 never resolved their differences, with six insisting that she died from a beating by a person unknown and fifteen recording their belief that she died of natural causes.[88] So, too, might many of the determinations of murder by witchcraft have constituted 'honest' errors, given the strength of belief in the existence of occult powers.

Beyond simple errors, coroners and their jurors might decide a case against the facts based upon motivations that ranged from intimidation and hope of reward to favour and friendship. The problems elite men posed for the criminalization of homicide extended beyond their own violence to the efforts they sometimes made to protect themselves and their dependants. So, too, might coroners and their juries act upon their own notions of the merits of a particular case, deciding that a legally mandated punishment did not suit the offence or offender in question. They might, for example, deem a case of murder to be manslaughter, even though the facts of the case might not warrant it, to allow a man to claim benefit of clergy, or to ease a request for a pardon. Or they might deem a killing to be an act of self-defence, which ensured the offender a guaranteed pardon, though they knew the killer had not strictly satisfied the legal requirements for excusable homicide. They might describe a self-slaying as the result of natural causes or misadventure, or deem the person mad at the moment of the killing, in order to preserve the family's possessions from forfeiture. The claims and counterclaims in disputed cases make it hard to determine which motive prevailed in any given instance, but as others have shown, the records leave no doubt that such impulses sometimes shaped inquest verdicts.[89]

Disputes over verdicts were sometimes political in nature. Local power struggles obviously affected some—for example, when jurors avoided implicating the servants of one magnate or another from favour, fear, or bribery. Inquests sometimes identified people whose abuse led to their children's or servants' deaths as culpable killers, even though trial juries almost always moderated the judgement; we might see such cases as political, in a sense, perhaps reflecting principles of good household governance and hierarchical social structures. But what of politics in the more specific sense of a concern for the 'public interest'? Did coroners' jurors ever use their position to critique abuses of power or to promote a public good in ways that foreshadowed later encomiums of the inquest as a protector of civil liberties, and were their actions ever interpreted as such in their own time?

One might expect to see this sort of political action most readily in inquests on prison deaths. Jurors sat on such cases throughout the period, in numbers that reflect the harrowing conditions in early modern gaols.[90] Yet in almost all these inquests, jurors concluded simply that the individuals had died of natural causes,

---

[87] BL, Royal MS 17B XLII.   [88] BL, Add MS 31028, f. 82.

[89] See, e.g., Green, *Verdict According to Conscience*, and Loar, 'Go and Seek the Crowner', ch. 3.

[90] Based on coroners' inquisitions returned to King's Bench, J.S. Cockburn notes that at least 1,291 prisoners died in gaol in the five counties of the Home Circuit between 1558 and 1625; Cockburn, *Introduction*, pp. 38–9, 145–71.

at God's hands rather than those of the gaoler. The jurors who viewed the bodies of two women who died on successive December days in the Lincoln gaol, for example, observed merely that they had died at the 'visitation of God'.[91] Another jury, sitting on the deaths of ten prisoners in the Colchester gaol over the space of only fifteen days, deemed them victims of 'the sickness of the house'.[92] Some such inquest reports seem fraudulent, noting that a jury had convened 'on view of the body' of someone the parish register recorded as having been buried days before.[93] But might we perhaps see hints of a critique in the verdict of one Northampton jury that sat in 1546 on the deaths of six prisoners in little more than a month? They described the dead as 'prisoners of the king in his gaol', and victims not of the visitation of God but of '*frigore & fame*': cold and hunger.[94] Or what of the two inquests, weeks apart in 1544, held by two juries that specifically included prisoners—four on one, two on the other—that alluded to natural deaths from serious illnesses, but which also attributed the deaths to the 'squalor of the gaol'?[95] In 1573, one Norwich inquest did deem the death of prisoner Edmund Cole at the hands of the gaoler and a warder a felonious homicide, noting that the men had clubbed Cole to death with a cudgel. But this sort of verdict was extremely rare; and the warder, at least, soon received a royal pardon.[96]

One particularly famous case—that of Richard Hunne—does suggest the possibility of a more explicit critique and its import for contemporaries. A wealthy merchant tailor and freeman of the city of London, Hunne had pursued a lengthy conflict with members of the London clerical establishment before his death in prison in December 1514. In 1511, he refused to pay the mortuary, or fee for burial, expected by the cleric who had interred his young son. Suit and countersuit followed. Hunne's charges of slander against one of the priests prompted his own excommunication, which he followed with a potentially devastating and dangerous charge of praemunire against not only the clerics immediately involved in his earlier suits, but also the Archbishop of Canterbury (and Lord Chancellor) William Warham. All this took place against the backdrop of disputes between some Londoners and their clergy over mortuaries, tithes, and other such payments, imputations of heresy among some of those same Londoners, and a parliamentary attack on clerical immunities such as benefit of clergy. Hunne found himself arrested on charges of heresy in October 1514 and imprisoned in the Lollards' Tower adjoining St. Paul's Cathedral. There he was found dead on the morning of 4 December. The bishop's officials announced that Hunne had hanged himself, but many of Hunne's friends and others who had followed his disputes with the clergy suspected murder.[97]

---

[91] KB 9/565, mm. 36, 37.   [92] KB 9/486, m. 58.

[93] See, e.g., Hunnisett, *Sussex Inquests, 1558–1603*, no. 410, *Sussex Inquests, 1603–1688*, no. 139, and *The Parish Register of Horsham in the County of Sussex, 1541–1635*, edited by R. Garraway Rice (London, Sussex Record Society, vol. 21, 1915), pp. 350, 379.

[94] KB 9/567, m. 171.   [95] KB 9/558, mm. 49, 55 ('*squalore carceris*').

[96] C 66/1108, m. 35.

[97] On Hunne, see, e.g., Thomas More, 'A Dialogue Concerning Heresies', in *The Complete Works of St Thomas More*, edited by T.M.C. Lawler (New Haven, CT, 1981), vol. 6, p. 326; Edward Hall, *Hall's Chronicle*, edited by Henry Ellis (London, 1809), pp. 572–80; John Foxe, *Acts and Monuments*

London coroner Thomas Barnwell, accompanied by two sheriffs, gathered a full jury of twenty-four men to meet in the Lollards' Tower the following day. They meticulously examined the body and its surroundings and called witnesses before them. They identified William Horsey, the bishop's chancellor, together with the summoner and the bell-ringer as the culprits in a foul murder designed to look like suicide.[98] Called to explain themselves before the king's councillors and justices, with Henry VIII himself present at some of the meetings, the jurors nonetheless stuck by their verdict. Desperate letters went from the bishop of London to the king, who ultimately intervened with a directive that the justices of King's Bench disregard the inquest verdict and acquit Horsey of the murder. Justice was not ultimately done, then, if the coroner's verdict is to be believed. And many people at the time did believe the verdict, ensuring it a political salience in the ongoing disputes that shaped the nature and reception of the eventual break from Rome. The case received mention in a wide variety of publications, including works by such men as Sir Thomas More, William Tyndale, Simon Fish, and chronicler Edward Hall, and in one dedicated anonymous tract that might be considered the first of a new genre of murder pamphlets.[99] John Foxe's later history preserved a place for Hunne among the early martyrs of the Reformation, and a place among its heroes for this particular coroner's jury, a group of men Foxe described as bravely standing for truth against the 'devilish malice' of the 'murdering papists'.[100]

'PUBLIC' OVERSIGHT

The Hunne case suggests the possibilities for oppositional uses of the inquest, but also the limits upon such use. Jurors might have been able to discomfit the suspected killers; they might have exposed the killers' actions to public view; but they could not have their verdict hold. All inquest findings of criminal homicide were subject to trial, of course. And inquests also remained subject to interventions and actions from the authorities.[101] In other high-profile gaol deaths, authorities intervened quickly to ensure a jury of 'substantial' men: their substance was meant to indicate integrity, but might as easily denote men who would accept that the 'right' verdict did not always match the facts. Rumours of dark deeds spread quickly when Henry

---

(London, 1570), book. 7, pp. 969–78. For modern commentators, see, e.g., A.G. Dickens, *The English Reformation* (University Park, PA, 1989, 2nd edn), pp. 112–15; John Bellamy, *Strange, Inhuman Deaths: Murder in Tudor England* (Stroud, 2005), pp. 3–8; and G.W. Bernard, *The Late Medieval English Church* (New Haven, CT, 2012), pp. 1–16.

[98] For the inquisition itself, see KB 9/468, m. 14.

[99] A point made by Bellamy, *Strange, Inhuman Deaths*, p. 8. For the tract, the basis of Hall and Foxe's later accounts, see *The Enquirie and Verdite of the Quest Panneld of the Death of Richard Hune* (Antwerp, 1537?).

[100] See Foxe, *Acts and Monuments*, book 7, 969–78 and also his account of a coroner's inquest into the later death of William Wyseman in the Lollards' Tower (book 11, 1999), though in that case the jurors were unable to find firm proof of any nefarious deed.

[101] When Francis Norris, earl of Berkshire, killed himself, for example, the coroner was ordered to suppress the verdict of suicide, presumably to avoid having the earl's daughter and heir become a less attractive marriage prospect through the forfeiture of his property. SP 14/127, f. 139.

Percy died in the Tower in 1585. The eighth earl of Northumberland and brother of the executed Catholic rebel and seventh earl, Percy had been incarcerated on suspicion of treason but was now found shot through the heart. The queen's councillors had a pamphlet published that sought to counter sceptical responses to the inquest's verdict of self-murder with assurances that it was 'found by a very substantial jury chosen among the best commoners of the City, empanelled by the Crowner upon the view of the body, and diligent enquiry by all due means had according to the law'. It also reported on the special public inquiry into the death and the inquest that had been held in the Star Chamber, meant to indicate that all had been done as it ought to have been.[102] When authorities saw a need to placate public opinion, they could intervene to shape the outcome of potentially troubling inquests in an effort to ensure that an inquest served rather than undermined their interests.

Central authorities oversaw and often restrained the independence of both coroners and jurors in a variety of ways, and to a variety of ends. They acquired more ways of doing so over the early modern period. The statute of 1487 that ordered the submission of inquests to King's Bench was itself a step towards greater oversight. The justices of King's Bench often called upon coroners to explain deficiencies and errors in the inquisitions that they submitted, and imposed penalties for failures to account properly for the financial proceeds of justice.[103] These same justices, when travelling the counties on their assize circuits, also occasionally questioned the actions of coroners and their juries. Or, in some cases, they questioned coroners' inaction: two Kent coroners, for example, faced charges at the assizes for failing to hold inquests that they should have held.[104] The common law judges also agreed in a 1616 case that inquest jurors who refused to give a verdict ought to be fined.[105]

The king or queen's councillors exercised a good deal of oversight, too, both to pre-empt and to punish—and seem to have been more able and inclined to do so in the sixteenth century than before, with the growth of conciliar government and its attendant courts of justice. The same parliament that passed the 1487 act mandating fees, fines, and new record-keeping responsibilities for coroners in an effort to deal with the 'daily increase' in murders also gave members of the king's council

---

[102] Anon., *A True and Summarie Reporte of the Declaration of some Part of the Earle of Northumberlands treasons delivered publicly in the Court at the Starrechamber...by her Maiesties special commandement...touching the maner of his most wicked & violent murder committed upon himselfe* (London, 1585), p. 13. Discussions about the nature of the earl's death also had foreign audiences: Anon., *Crudelitatis Calvinianae Exempla duo Recentissima ex Anglia...exhibet indignissimam mortem Illustrissimi viri comitis Northumbriae* (Rheims, 1585). For political uses of inquests and autopsies to shape public opinion, see also Harley, 'Political Postmortems'. For publications on other contentious prison deaths that include reports on the coroners' inquests, see Anon., *A True and Lamentable Relation of the Most Desperate Death of James Parnel, Quaker, who wilfully starved himself in the prison of Colchester* (London, 1656), and Anon., *The Whole Business of Sindercome* (London, 1657), on the Tower death of a man who sought to assassinate Cromwell.

[103] See Hunnisett's volumes, which collate the inquests with other King's Bench documentation to show when such intervention occurred.

[104] *CAR* Kent, Charles I, no. 2243; *CAR* Kent, 1676–1688, no. 776.

[105] Taverner's Case, 81 *ER* 144.

a new charge to intervene in local law enforcement.[106] From the time in 1540 when the royal council was reconstituted as the Privy Council, a body with its own clerk and registers, we see frequent notes in those registers of councillors sending letters to prevent problems or responding to reports of unfolding troubles with directives urging coroners to show all due care and 'indifferency' in their dealings.[107] The Privy Council's offshoots, the councils in the Marches and in the North, have left fewer records, but seem to have engaged in similar activities. In one case, indeed, privy councillors at Westminster asked their counterparts in the Marches to appoint 'assistants' to ensure that a coroner do his duty properly.[108] In another, privy councillors ordered a sheriff to be sure that the coroner empanelled a suitable jury 'of such persons as without any respect shall deal therein uprightly and according to justice'.[109] In a third, they told the justices of assize to call a coroner and jury before them to explain the reasons for their delay in giving a verdict.[110] Perhaps most significantly, members of the council also sat as judges in the court of Star Chamber: with earlier roots, Star Chamber developed as a public court of justice under Henry VIII's chancellor, Thomas Wolsey, and gained some institutional distinction when the council was reconstituted in 1540, but the two remained closely linked until the court's abolition in 1641.[111] Indeed, known more properly if less succinctly as the 'Lords of the Council Sitting in the Star Chamber', in this capacity the monarch's councillors exerted a good deal of punitive control over inquest participants.

The councillors did not just admonish and warn, but also overturned the decisions of coroners and their juries and sometimes imposed heavy penalties on them, in cases launched either by a royal official or by an aggrieved party. Most of the contested cases discussed thus far are known from the files produced by Star Chamber. Unfortunately, the formal records of decisions made about complaints heard in Star Chamber, and of the punishments imposed, are now missing. A reader can thus easily mine the Star Chamber files for accounts of disputed inquests while forgetting that these might well have resulted in serious sanctions. Barrister John Hawarde's report of the results of one such case, however, indicates just how

---

[106] 3 Henry VII c. 1. This is the Act 'Pro Camera Stellata' that was long seen (mistakenly) to have created the Court of Star Chamber. To deal with maintenance, embracery, and other subversions of inquests and juries, the act authorized the Chancellor, Treasurer, and Keeper of the Privy Seal (or any two of them) to call before them a bishop and a temporal lord and the two chief justices of King's Bench and Common Pleas, to investigate any charges of subversion of justice.

[107] See, for example, *APC*, vol. 8, p. 348; vol. 20, p. 300.

[108] *APC*, vol. 10, p. 158.   [109] *APC*, vol. 10, p. 424.   [110] *APC*, vol. 11, p. 409.

[111] In 1540, with the formalization of the Privy Council, Council and Court acquired separate registers. See J.A. Guy, *The Cardinal's Court: The Impact of Thomas Wolsey in Star Chamber* (Hassocks, 1977), pp. 14 and 63, and A.J. Pollard, 'Council, Star Chamber, and Privy Council under the Tudors: II. The Star Chamber', *English Historical Review* 37 (1922): pp. 516–39. On Star Chamber and its records, see also: Guy, *The Court of Star Chamber and its Records to the Reign of Elizabeth I* (London, 1985), and the works of T.G. Barnes, including 'The Archives and Archival Problems of the Elizabethan and Early Stuart Star Chamber', in *Prisca Munimenta: Studies in Archival and Administrative History*, edited by F. Ranger (London, 1973), pp. 130–49, and Barnes, 'Star Chamber and the Sophistication of the Criminal Law', *Criminal Law Review* (June 1977): pp. 316–20. See, too, Steve Hindle's discussion in *The State and Social Change*, esp. pp. 71–2, which also addresses the use of Star Chamber to control juries, and now Lockwood's study.

onerous the punishments could be: in October 1596, one Mathewe, a coroner in Wiltshire and also in the employ of Sir Walter Longe, stood accused of 'subtle carriage' in a case that involved another of Longe's servants as the suspected killer. Mathewe held the inquest some five weeks after the death and without viewing the body itself. Moreover, he empanelled jurors only from areas in which Longe held sway and none from the area in which the killing had happened. Under his guidance, the jury found a verdict of self-defence rather than felonious homicide. For this wrongdoing, the queen's councillors and justices sentenced Mathewe to a variety of punishments that included loss of all offices, a fine of £500, imprisonment, and the pillory at both Westminster and at the next Wiltshire county assizes.[112]

Jurors might also find themselves forced to defend their decisions to privy councillors sitting in Star Chamber. A one-time clerk then counsel in the court, William Hudson, took an interest in recording notable cases, and showed a particular interest in those that dealt with negligent or obstreperous juries.[113] Most of the cases he noted involved grand and petty juries at trial: the early Elizabethan grand jurors from Derbyshire, for example, who had to pay heavy fines and parade about Westminster Hall and the next county assizes wearing papers that explained their offence in quashing an indictment for murder, were only some of many.[114] Hudson also recorded the decision, again early in Elizabeth's reign, which saw eleven coroners' jurors from Staffordshire fined for perjury after finding a case that the judges thought to have been manslaughter merely a matter of self-defence.[115] They had sat upon the death of John Palmer, who died from wounds suffered in an affray between his master, William Robinson, and a party of men led by Walter Horton. Even before Palmer drew his last breath, friends of Horton visited the county coroner, who in turn made sure that his jurors had enough of a gap between their first sitting and the delivery of their verdict to allow them to be laboured and bribed. But the jurors in time divided. It seems that they had agreed on a verdict of 'chance medley', by then an imprecise label. Some had been surprised to hear that later interpreted by the coroner as self-defence, when they had thought it a term for manslaughter. The jurors subsequently brought before Star Chamber insisted that they had done their duty. They had viewed the scene of the affray, examined the body, heard witnesses, and called upon the services of a surgeon. Nonetheless, those who had backed the verdict's subsequent redefinition as self-defence found themselves punished for doing so.[116]

---

[112] John Hawarde, *Les Reportes del Cases in Camera Stellata*, edited by W.P. Baildon (London, 1894), pp. 61–2. The case is also mentioned, though with less detail, in BL, Harley MS 2143, f. 67. For the interrogatories and depositions in the case, see STAC 5/D17/14.

[113] See T.G. Barnes, 'Mr. Hudson's Star Chamber', in *Tudor Rule and Revolution*, edited by DeLloyd J. Guth and J.W. McKenna (Cambridge, 1982), pp. 283–308.

[114] Hudson, 'A Treatise on the Court of Star Chamber'; BL, Lansdowne 639, p. 142. See also Richard Crompton, *Star Chamber Cases* (London, 1630), pp. 8 and 25. Charles Hamilton, 'Star Chamber and Juries: Some Observations', *Albion* 5.3 (1973): pp. 237–42 traces a number of such cases, but somewhat perplexingly echoes G.R. Elton in seeing such interventions into the decisions of 'such inconsequential individuals... [as] a striking commentary on the limitations of the government's power' (p. 241).

[115] BL, Lansdowne 639, p. 143.   [116] STAC 5/R23/27; STAC 5/R9/9.

Such oversight and intervention suggest both the political potential of the inquest and the constraints upon its oppositional uses. But they also indicate some of the means by which inquests came to be refocused from the largely financial to a broader concern with public order and public justice, one that initially conflated the interests of sovereign and subjects, but that came in time to admit distinctions between the two. From the 1530s, the king's almoners launched cases to ensure that the forfeitures of suicides went to the 'right' hands, but more generally, royal officers also oversaw the inquests in order to root out corruption and favour, and to ensure that offenders more often answered to the law. They heard charges of partiality and special dealing, but also intervened in those sorts of cases historians sometimes view as (perhaps laudable) instances of jury nullification and communal self-regulation. Coroners who delayed verdicts to allow parties to reconcile and reach a private settlement faced the court right alongside those who took bribes. While the manslaughter verdict gave coroners' juries a new option in responding to violent deaths, they had some supervision in applying it.

Interestingly, even as Star Chamber and Privy Council did much to ensure that inquests operated in the interests of the 'king's peace', that peace was being slowly redefined as 'public', in ways that would in time give the inquest a new salience. In these years, a sense of a 'public interest' separate or separable from that of the person wearing the crown was only slowly emerging. Legal writers still saw the coroner as first and foremost a servant of the Crown, as his name implied. But the Crown could mean more than the monarch alone, and according to late sixteenth- and early seventeenth-century writers, the coroner was no longer understood or intended to be so strongly focused on royal revenue as his medieval predecessor had been. The monarch's own 'interests' had changed in ways that called forth and were described as corresponding more readily with those of a 'public'. When Sir Thomas Smith had observed that the inquest happened in front of an open audience, 'in *Corona populi*', he then opined, 'but I take rather that this name commeth because that the death of every subject by violence is accounted to touch the crown of the Prince and to be a detriment unto it, the Prince accounting that his strength, power, and crown doth stand and consist in the force of his people, and the maintenance of them in security and peace'.[117] The sovereign's interest in the inquest was not primarily financial, in Smith's estimation, but included also the obligation to use it to quell private vengeance and entrench the law.

Sir Edward Coke's later discussion of the coroner and his jury suggests a further, subtle broadening of this sense of the inquest's purpose. In line with his 'ancient constitutionalism', an effort to root the common law in ancient customs and precedents that gave it priority over the will of a king, Coke maintained that the office originated well before the Conquest, at least as early as the days of King Alfred. The coroners were elected, he wrote, 'for that both the king and the county had a great interest and benefit in the due execution of his office'. Since the coroner was chosen by the people, moreover, his authority did not end with the death of

---

[117] Smith, *De Republica Anglorum*, p. 73.

the king, as happened with most other officials concerned with justice.[118] Elsewhere, Coke explained that coroners were elected, as sheriffs used to be, 'because the people had a great interest and safety in the due execution of their offices'.[119] This notion of the ancient, pre-Norman status of the coroner, and his election by freeholders in the county court, was echoed by John Selden and other legal writers, too, becoming orthodoxy until challenged in the late nineteenth century and finally put to rest by R.F. Hunnisett in the mid-twentieth.[120] Rather than simply observing Coke's error, we might also reflect on the significance of that misdating of the office's origins.

John Wilkinson's guide for coroners, first published in 1618, included the oath that all new coroners were to swear. After taking the oath of supremacy, the coroner was to pledge to serve 'both for the king's profit and the good of the inhabitants within the said county'. When instructing jurors, Wilkinson informed them that they worked 'to the end the king, and his immediate officer, may be truly certified how and by what means he hath lost his subject'.[121] They, too, had to swear oaths to discharge their duty properly. The edition of 1657, published after the abolition of monarchy, reflected a shift from king to commonwealth as the authority for which these sworn inquests acted: coroners pledged to work 'both for the Commonwealth's profit and the good of the inhabitants within the said county'. The jurors were sworn 'to the end that the Keepers of the Liberty of England... may be truly certified how and by what means a member of this Commonwealth is lost'.[122]

With the return of monarchy in 1660, the oaths and charges once again privileged the king. But some things had changed. For one, Star Chamber had disappeared for good. Members of parliament had ended the ability of the king's councillors to exercise judicial authority in Star Chamber in 1641, even before the civil wars began, depicting the court as an agent of arbitrary impulses. They did not now restore it. Royal officials could still find other ways to intervene and intermeddle in the law's operation, of course, but the abolition of and refusal to recreate the highest prerogative court speak to an emerging sense of a public interest that might at times diverge from that of the people wearing and attending upon the crown.[123]

To end with an admittedly wholly atypical tale: the case of Arthur Capel, earl of Essex, hints at the difficulties that the late seventeenth-century authorities could face when trying to use an inquest for their own particular purposes. Quite aside from the loss of Star Chamber and its pre-revolutionary sticks, the emergence of party politics and the profusion of print further complicated matters for royal

---

[118] Coke, *Second Part*, pp. 31, 174–5.

[119] Edward Coke, *Fourth Part of the Institutes of the Laws of England* (London, 1797), p. 271.

[120] See, e.g., Nathaniel Bacon, *An Historical and Political Discourse of the Law and Government of England from the First Time to the End of the Reign of Elizabeth... Collected from Some Manuscript Notes of John Selden* (London, 1689), p. 41; R.F. Hunnisett, 'The Origins of the Office of Coroner', *Transactions of the Royal Historical Society* 8 (1958): pp. 85–104.

[121] Wilkinson, *Treatise... Concerning the Office and Authorities of Coroners*, pp. 4 and 6.

[122] Ibid., pp. 5–8.

[123] On the efforts of common law judges to control trial juries after the demise of Star Chamber, including Justice Kelyng's fining of jurors in homicide cases, see, e.g., James Q. Whitman, *The Origins of Reasonable Doubt: Theological Roots of the Criminal Trial* (New Haven, CT, 2008), p. 173ff.

agents. Essex was found dead in the Tower in 1683 after having been incarcerated on charges of treason for his part in the Rye House Plot to assassinate King Charles II and his brother, James. A carefully selected jury of twenty-three men of substance deemed the deed self-murder. A good many others, however, refused to believe the verdict. As some detractors pointed out, the inquest jurors acted in unorthodox circumstances, for someone had moved and cleaned the body before they viewed it. Men who promoted the murder theory found themselves arrested. Laurence Braddon languished in prison for years after launching his own investigation. In a set of pamphlets first published overseas, he, Robert Ferguson, Henry Danvers, and others cited inquest irregularities and the authorities' interventions as reasons for suspicion. One commented on the force of the inquest verdict in making up people's minds, noting that when he spoke of murder, others pointed to the inquest and said that should suffice. In contrast, he argued that 'the many and gross irregular practices with respect to the coroner's inquisition are further proofs of my lord's being murdered'.[124] Jurors had reportedly been denied when they asked to see the clothes in which Essex had died, for example, and when they requested an adjournment to seek more evidence they were told that the king himself wanted their verdict immediately. Only with the Revolution of 1688/9 were the critics released from prison and the case reopened, though in the event, a plea from Essex's widow to be left in peace brought that to an inconclusive close. Laurence Braddon could nonetheless now publish on London's presses the results of his investigation, as well as his claims that what authorities had once deemed an act of disaffection towards the government was in fact an effort on his part to serve the king and 'a Common Good'.[125]

CONCLUSION

In declaring that a person had legitimately killed another, or that she or he had killed someone in a manner that in turn merited death, inquest jurors participated in actions near the centre of political power. If sovereignty lay, at root, in the ability to take life, then inquest jurors had an awesome responsibility. Their participation helped to legitimize judicial homicides; they became agents through which the Crown claimed to monopolize the legitimate use of deadly violence. Through their mediation, responses to slayings moved from the hands of kin to that of the king,

---

[124] Henry Danvers, *Murder will out, or a clear and full discovery that the Earl of Essex did not murder himself, but was murdered by others* (London, 1689; first published 1684), pp. 2–3, 8.

[125] See Michael MacDonald, 'The Strange Death of the Earl of Essex, 1683', *History Today* 41 (1991): pp. 13–18; Melinda Zook, *Radical Whigs and Conspiratorial Politics in Late Stuart England* (University Park, PA, 1999), pp. 116–19; Howell, ed., *State Trials*, vol. 9, cc. 1127–331, for the trial of Speke and Braddon. For a sampling of contemporary tracts, see the authorized *Account of How the Earl of Essex Killed Himself in the Tower of London, the 13th of July 1683, as it appears by the Coroners Inquest, and the several informations following* (London, 1683); Laurence Braddon, *Murther Will Out* (London, 1692); and Robert Ferguson, *Enquiry into and detection of the barbarous murther of the late earl of Essex* (London?, 1684), which went further in not just deeming the death a murder, but blaming it on the soon-to-be James II.

and then slowly to that of the '*Corona populi*'. Certainly, they did not act alone or have the final say. Final outcomes did not always accord with their verdicts. And that is as it 'ought' to have been: according to legal writers, at least, jurors acted on the king's behalf, and any sense of a broader public interest that might be separable from the interests of the authorities remained in its infancy. But the accumulated actions of these juries contributed to the process by which 'public justice' came to complement then subsume that of the person wearing the crown. While the coroner's inquest manifested striking continuities over its long history, its functions and meaning—indeed, its authorization—shifted over time. In the cumulative actions of these jurors, as policed and directed from above, we see one of the ways in which the state both grew and slowly changed shape, and one of the ways in which homicide became more fully public.

3

'An Image of Deadly Feud'
Recompense, Revenge, and the
Appeal of Homicide

Early in September 1628, John Dean died after Daniel Cotton struck him with a pitchfork. A coroner's jury deemed the killing murder. Early in the following year, however, King Charles pardoned Cotton for his crime, saving him from the gallows and restoring to him his forfeited goods and land. What may well have mattered most in securing this remission was that Cotton had worked in the king's service. But the warrants for Cotton's pardon took care to depict the killing as having been, in fact, the product of a sudden quarrel and not longstanding malice. Moreover, with this exception aside, Cotton had long behaved himself 'religiously, modestly, and honestly'. He had a wife and nine children who depended upon him for their livelihood. And his wife would not be the only woman helped by this arrangement: the documents note that 'the wife of the said Dean, being satisfied therein, hath freely released the said Cotton of all appeals for the fact'.[1] What was this appeal, and what role did 'satisfaction' still have in early modern responses to homicide?

In 1487, as we have seen, parliament imposed new obligations on coroners and empowered members of the king's council to deal with the maintenance and embracery that purportedly allowed murders to multiply. The same session also took steps that, for the first time, privileged the king's suit against a slayer over that of the victim's kin.[2] While the coroner's inquest was the most common way to bring a killer to court, it was not the only one: individuals could launch their own cases, called 'appeals', to try to secure justice as they saw it, be that death or damages. To be clear, these appeals were not a means to query a court's judgement (at least not in the usual sense), but a way to initiate a trial by private accusation. And now, after 1487, the king's suit no longer had to wait for a year and a day to allow any private appeal to proceed first. Yet, remarkably, while a king could pardon a killer

---

[1] PSO 5/5, no foliation but entered under January 1628/9 (my thanks to Cynthia Herrup for this reference), as well as C 82/2038, no. 548 and SP 16/123, f. 47. The volume of privy seal warrants notes more than forty pardons for homicide (usually specified as manslaughter) from April 1626 to November 1631, but only one akin to Cotton's, for a killing in Ireland for which 'satisfaction is undertaken to be given to the widow', entered under April 1629.

[2] 3 Henry VII c. 2. Unfortunately, little parliamentary material for this session survives to explain the context or impetus for this legislation. See R.E. Horrox, 'Henry VII: Parliament of November 1487, Introduction', in *The Parliament Rolls of Medieval England*, edited by C. Given-Wilson et al. Internet version. Scholarly Digital Editions, Leicester, 2005, and below at note 49. Note that in some printed editions, the murderers/coroners statute is recorded as if part of c. 1.

from royal penalties, he could still not remit an individual's suit—that survived even a royal gift of grace—and the appeal itself lived on in an attenuated form throughout this period, only disappearing fully and finally in the early nineteenth century.[3] Even as homicide became more fully criminalized, more fully an offence against the king's justice and then eventually the justice of a public more broadly conceived, traces of this individual, private connection persisted.

In response to a killing, individuals who had an interest in the victim's life and death could seek satisfaction in the form of either vengeance or compensation, and could do this either illicitly on their own or through the courts. 'Feud' is the name we give to wholly private satisfaction-seeking. The appeal, in contrast, was a legal device that from the twelfth century had helped channel satisfaction-seeking through the king's courts in a way that conflated the private and 'public'. An ancient mode of initiating criminal proceedings and a personal right of victims or their heirs or widows, an appeal was launched and prosecuted by an individual accuser, in contrast to a 'public' accusation of felony through an indictment mediated by a jury.[4] An aggrieved party could use an appeal to secure an execution or, informally, to prompt an out of court settlement. Their heyday done by the late thirteenth century, appeals had occasional revivals but generally declined in number as charges filtered through juries became more common. Their decline accelerated over the sixteenth century, thanks in part to the changes introduced in 1487 and also, as this chapter demonstrates, to the impact of manslaughter verdicts. Somewhat surprisingly, though, they did not disappear. Daniel Ernst has demonstrated that the appeal survived as something more than a fossil or forgotten anachronism, as historians had previously suggested, noting its use by justices unsatisfied with a verdict to allow a new trial.[5] As this chapter shows, compensation payments for homicide continued longer than had previously been thought, too, and so provided a continued role for the appeal.

This chapter examines the history of extra-judicial settlements in an effort better to explain the triumph of 'public justice' and the criminalization of homicide. First attending to the broader context of private satisfaction-seeking, or feuding, it then focuses on the appeal, asking why the appeal declined but also how and why it survived. While private vengeance posed an obvious threat to the monopolistic claims of royal justice over homicide, so too did private settlements. Authorities saw both private vengeance and private composition as antithetical to justice,

---

[3] See *The Trial of Abraham Thornton* (1817), edited by John Hall (Glasgow, 1926), esp. pp. 32–5 and 115ff, which offers the best account of the final appeal of murder—and wager of battle—which prompted the legislation to abolish this ancient procedure.

[4] On the appeal, see in particular: William Holdsworth, *A History of English Law*, 4th edn, 17 vols. (London, 1936), vol. 2, pp. 197–8, 256–7, 341, 360–2, 461; Daniel R. Ernst, 'The Moribund Appeal of Death: Compensating Survivors and Controlling Jurors in Early Modern England', *American Journal of Legal History* 28.2 (1984): pp. 164–88; Margaret H. Kerr, 'Angevin Reform of the Appeal of Felony', *Law and History Review* 13 (1995): pp. 351–91; Daniel Klerman, 'Settlement and the Decline of Private Prosecution in Thirteenth-Century England', *Law and History Review* 19.1 (2001): pp. 1–65; Klerman, 'Women Prosecutors in Thirteenth-Century England', *Yale Journal of Law and Humanities* 14 (2002): pp. 271–318.

[5] Ernst, 'Moribund Appeal'.

whether defined as royal or, more broadly, public justice. They sought to stamp out the former, but left some space for the latter after bringing it under tighter judicial control: while composition that allowed the evasion of legal action had no place, compensation paid in addition to punishment or as secured through the courts might yet be tolerated in some cases. Even as the parties thought to have an interest in a victim's life and death broadened from immediate kith and kin to the king and then to the public more generally, the private appeal was retained in somewhat reimagined and repurposed roles. A recognition of the needs of widows, in particular—forced upon observers not least by the actions of widows themselves—left some space for compensation, though more clearly as a complement than as a competitor to public justice.

FEUD

Talk of compensation and satisfaction often calls to mind that vexed concept of the feud, and indeed, people over the early modern era castigated the appeal as a remnant or echo of the feuds of more 'barbarous' times and places. Historians generally agree that England ceased being a feuding society long before its neighbours. In the twelfth century, Henry II laid claim to all homicides as pleas to be determined in his own courts. Then, over the thirteenth century, royal justice superimposed itself on disputes that had previously been settled by self-help with (generally) more success, though feud-like behaviour did not disappear entirely and could quickly reassert itself when need or opportunity arose. Victims increasingly sought satisfaction through the king's courts, opting for judicial punishment of their opponents rather than their own more dangerous attempts to seek revenge. Fines and forfeitures were to go to the king rather than be paid as satisfaction to victims, and would be supplemented by penalties inflicted upon the bodies of offenders. Historians of medieval violence have drawn upon anthropology to demonstrate the 'peace in the feud', noting that feuding can be seen as a means of limiting violence and bringing peace, a form of justice-seeking or conflict resolution with its own conventions.[6] They soften the demarcation between king and kin, or between law and feud, and adopt functionalist perspectives to note that the two were by no means wholly distinct or antithetical. Royal officials arbitrated out of court settlements; disputants used legal action to further their tit-for-tat revenge. And, of course, unambiguously bloody, wholly extra-judicial reprisals did not disappear, and provided a rough justice of their own. But the consensus generally holds that while some feuding behaviour continued in and alongside royal justice, the English moved away from being a feuding society far sooner than did others in western Europe.[7]

---

[6] A key early influence on the re-envisioning of feud was Max Gluckman, 'The Peace in the Feud', *P&P* 8 (1955): pp. 1–14.

[7] See Jenny Wormald, 'Bloodfeud, Kindred, and Government in Early Modern Scotland', *P&P* 87 (1980): pp. 54–97; Keith M. Brown, *Bloodfeud in Scotland, 1573–1625* (Edinburgh, 2003); *Vengeance in the Middle Ages*, edited by Susanna Throop and Paul Hyams (Farnham, 2010); Paul Hyams, *Rancor and Reconciliation in Medieval England* (Ithaca, NY, 2003); Edward Muir, *Mad Blood Stirring: Vendetta*

As the foremost historian of feuding in medieval England warns, however, if we try to be too precise about what feuding was, we end up chasing our own tails. 'Feud is a much overused term,' Paul Hyams notes, 'a notion in real peril of collapsing and losing all precision and utility.' He prefers to avoid essentialist definitions of an 'institution' that never existed as such, and instead to look at patterns of behaviour. When we see satisfaction (whether in blood or money) secured by self-help, we are seeing behaviour that we might label feud. If we see vengeance-seeking done in ways that might channel or limit violence, within a range of rough equivalence to the original injury, done openly and with a sense of legitimacy, and especially if accompanied by ceremonies or rituals of treaty-making, perhaps ones that address the honour of family members beyond the immediate principals, then we might feel even more comfortable labelling this part of feuding culture. If there is a characteristic hue to the band within the spectrum of methods for resolving conflict that we call feud, Hyams suggests that we might find it in a 'particular concept of wrong' as yet undifferentiated from legal notions of 'crime' as acts offending a king or entity beyond victim and kin.[8] Over the thirteenth century, he notes, all this became much less common. Concepts of 'wrong' became differentiated between crime and tort; kings sought to have these crimes understood as offences against themselves and only secondarily, if at all, against victims and their kin; and individuals increasingly turned to law as a safer way to seek satisfaction.

Some historians, however, seem to use the term 'feud' simply to mean long-lasting violent enmity. If that is our definition, then of course we continue to find examples of it in England throughout the early modern period, though in what seem to be diminishing numbers.[9] Aristocratic animosities continued to play out in street battles between great men's retainers (very often on the way to or from court), the occasional ambush in an empty landscape, and somewhat less violently (towards their fellow man, at least) in poaching forays on each others' estates. One might point to instances such as the near-fatal affray between the young earl of Northumberland's retinue and a party of Archbishop Savage's men in 1504, which emerged from both the short tempers of servants on a bad day and longer-term struggles for regional

---

in Renaissance Italy (Baltimore, 1998); Howard Kaminsky, 'The Noble Feud in the Later Middle Ages', *P&P* 177 (2002): pp. 55–83; Richard Fletcher, *Bloodfeud: Murder and Revenge in Anglo-Saxon England* (Oxford, 2003); *Feud in Medieval and Early Modern Europe*, edited by Jeppe Büchert Netterstrøm and Bjørn Poulsen (Aarhus, 2009); Tom Lambert, 'Protection, Feud, and Royal Power: Violence and its Regulation in English Law, *c.*850–*c.*1250', PhD dissertation, Durham University, 2009', and *Law and Order in Anglo-Saxon England* (Oxford, 2017); Mark Godfrey, 'Rethinking the Justice of the Feud in Sixteenth-Century Scotland' and Alexander Grant, 'Murder Will Out: Kingship, Kinship and Killing in Medieval Scotland', in *Kings, Lords and Men in Scotland and Britain, 1300–1625: Essays in Honour of Jenny Wormald*, edited by Stephen Boardman and Julian Goodare (Edinburgh, 2014), pp. 136–54 and 193–226.

[8] See Hyams, 'Was There Really Such a Thing as Feud in the High Middle Ages?', in *Vengeance in the Middle Ages*, pp. 152, 157, and 'Does It Matter When the English Began to Distinguish between Crime and Tort?', in *Violence in Medieval Society*, edited by Richard W. Kaeuper (Woodbridge, 2000), pp. 107–28. On the difficulties with the term and the concept, see also John Hudson, 'Faide, Vengeance, et Violence en Angleterre (ca 900–1200)', in *La Vengeance, 400–1200*, edited by B. Barthélemy et al. (Rome, 2006), pp. 341–82.

[9] See, e.g., Lawrence Stone, *The Crisis of the Aristocracy, 1558–1641* (Oxford, 1965); Steven Gunn, *Early Tudor Government, 1485–1558* (Houndmills, 1995).

hegemony.[10] Some such conflicts look very much like private warfare between lords with sizeable private armies, a phenomenon that diminished in time with the Tudors' efforts to limit the retaining of large numbers of servants uniformed in the livery of their masters. Or, perhaps, one might look to relationships such as the thirty-year rivalry between Sir John Danvers and his allies on the one hand and Walter Long and his friends on the other for political control of Wiltshire, which typically manifested itself in lawsuits but ultimately saw two of the Danvers kill Henry Long in an inn in 1594, to widespread criticism and dismay.[11] 'Gentlemanly' disputes of this sort can be found throughout the period, though generally without the homicidal violence.

The Tudors sometimes brought such disputes to an end through judicial intervention, with indictments in the common law courts or compelled appearances in Star Chamber followed by pardons upon due submission or, occasionally, by letting law run its course. Under Queen Mary, famously, Lord Charles Stourton was executed for murder, a highly unusual outcome for a titled nobleman. He had, however, ignored many warnings of various sorts in his longstanding conflict with William Hartgill, and had used the law far too nakedly and crassly to his own ends.[12]

Both Stourton and Hartgill were of the class of men who served as JPs, sheriffs, and local leaders, though Stourton was of a rank above his foe. They fell out in 1549: in a property dispute that followed the death of Charles Stourton's father, Hartgill, then the family steward, supported the widow against the son. A long litany of assaults, poaching forays, seizures of corn, and other such affronts ensued. Stourton rebuffed local offers of mediation. The Courts of Queen's Bench and Star Chamber both ordered that Stourton pay damages; the Privy Council repeatedly enjoined better behaviour. Indeed, Stourton invoked Star Chamber and compliance with council directives in a ruse to get the Hartgills into his power. He sent William and his son John messengers to say that he was ready to pay the damages Star Chamber had ordered and 'to commune with them also for a further ending and quieting of all matters between them'.[13] They met at Kilmington church, 11 January 1557. Stourton showed up with a sizeable entourage, lured William and John out of the church to accept their payment, and then had his men 'arrest' them, ostensibly on charges of felony. Bound and beaten, the Hartgills were kept without food for two days. JPs came to examine them and ordered Stourton to free his prisoners, but then left. Stourton had them clubbed nearly to death, then brought them to his home. There, he ordered their throats slit and their bodies buried. In time, investigations ordered by the council found the corpses. Stourton and a group of his men were arrested; as a lord, Stourton then faced a trial from his peers. They found him

[10] R.W. Hoyle, 'The Earl, the Archbishop and the Council: The Affray at Fulford, May 1504', in *Rulers and Ruled in Late Medieval England*, edited by Rowena Archer and Simon Walker (London, 1995), pp. 239–56.

[11] For this dispute, see Alison Wall, 'For Love, Money, or Politics? A Clandestine Marriage and the Elizabethan Court of Arches', *Historical Journal* 38.3 (1995): 511–33, esp. pp. 517, 519.

[12] John Bellamy provides a good account of the Stourton case in *Strange and Inhuman Deaths*, pp. 141–67. For the earlier appearances in Star Chamber and before the council, see BL, Harley MS 2143, ff. 1, 2, 4, and 5; for the trial record, see KB 8/36, m. 11.

[13] BL, Lansdowne MS 3, f. 102.

guilty, the queen refused to pardon him, and Stourton became one of two lords in sixteenth-century England to be executed for his part in a homicide—in this case, a particularly gruesome one emerging from a longstanding conflict that defied standard efforts at mediation and that had, indeed, subverted them to deadly effect.

On other occasions the Privy Council arbitrated disputes. Notes of arbitrations pepper the Privy Council registers, most often for disagreements over property or commercial transactions, but sometimes for conflicts that threatened or had already seen violent encounters.[14] At its meeting on 22 November 1540, for example, the council summoned before it two men involved in a long-running feud that had resulted in a homicide. The council had John Done and Thomas Holcroft 'set at one and made friends by arbitrement', requiring Done to pay amends of 100 marks to Holcroft.[15] In March 1551, Lord Dacre and Lord Wharton's dispute came before the councillors, who treated with the men to 'remit one to another all hatred, ill will, and displeasure' and to promise to bring any future quarrels to the council. Their long enmity included accusations that the men of one had been fishing in the river of the other or hunting their game, but also that Wharton had sought to conceal the murder of some of Dacre's servants. Nor did the dispute end quickly or easily: a few years later, the participants came again before the council, 'having good exhortation given them to remit all former grudges, rancours, and displeasures, and to continue in unfeigned amity and friendship'. Upon their promises to do so, they took each other by the hand in the presence of the queen's advisors.[16] Lord Wharton and the earl of Cumberland had a long list of complaints about each other, too, that resulted in at least one armed standoff between rival groups of retainers, and which the council also sought to mediate at various points—though, as R.W. Hoyle notes, it took the brokering of marriages between the rival factions before the disputes came firmly to an end.[17]

With the queen's chief servants variously acting as privy councillors or Star Chamber judges depending on the time of day, the line between judicial and extra-judicial intervention became especially blurred in some such settlements. In June 1586, the councillors sitting as judges in Star Chamber sought to settle a local dispute that had resulted in assaults and legal actions before it worsened: Henry and Hercules Foljambe as well as Henry Leeke, all of Derbyshire, were brought from the Marshalsea prison where they had been put for their 'disorderly behaviour' towards Sir Francis Leeke. They came before the council with a written submission that acknowledged their errors, their plans to amend, and their hope for favour. With Francis Leeke subsequently called in as well, 'both parties were moved to be contented that all former contentions, quarrels, and strife might be friendly taken up

---

[14] Norman Jones touches on the role of conciliar government in the Elizabethan era in taking on arbitration as a somewhat more formal and open way of resolving disputes than purely private mediation: *Governing by Virtue*, pp. 126ff.

[15] *Proceedings and Ordinances of the Privy Council of England*, VI (1540–42), p. 87. On conciliar attempts to intervene in aristocratic feuding, see also McSheffrey, *Seeking Sanctuary*.

[16] *APC*, vol. 3, pp. 499–500 and vol. 5, pp. 86–7. For this dispute, see R.W. Hoyle, 'Faction, Feud and Reconciliation amongst the Northern English Nobility, 1525–1569', *History* 84 (1999): pp. 590–613.

[17] See Hoyle, 'Faction, Feud and Reconciliation'.

and ended between them without any further complaint or strife of law, and that hereafter they would behave themselves peaceably towards each other'. In token of a 'true and unfeigned atonement and reconciliation' they gave their hands to each other in the councillors' presence. The councillors in turn warned that they planned to deal severely with any party who broke the agreement, with a minimum of a year's imprisonment.[18]

We can, then, find examples of violent, long-term enmities throughout the sixteenth century (and beyond), and also signs of arbitration and treaty-making that continued at least somewhat independently of judicial processes though clearly under royal direction. Depending on one's definition of feud, one can find behaviours to match. But if we are looking for things called 'feuds' in this period, we need to look to the north. The only place where such conflicts seemed to go openly by that name and with any sense of legitimacy (though local and contested) was in the borders against Scotland.

Scholars of the feud repeatedly insist that it was not necessarily in opposition to law and was often treated as a legitimate alternative to it. They are right, but only to a point. Of course, one might argue that if by 'feud' we mean securing satisfaction (either in blood or compensation) directly and without use of royal justice or public law, then we are in fact defining it in ways that set it up necessarily as distinct from or in opposition to law. More pertinently, if we look at how people in the sixteenth and seventeenth centuries used the word 'feud', we see people who saw it as something distinct from and in opposition to law, even as they themselves might at times participate in a range of behaviours we might see as feud-like. The view that feuding was antithetical to law is not simply an anachronistic modern definition that a previous generation of historians imposed on the past; it is a product of the period under study.

The word 'feud' itself makes little appearance in English until the late sixteenth century, and then very often in reference to events in the north or in Scotland. It is occasionally preceded by 'barbarous' and typically by 'deadly'.[19] It is 'deadly feud' that appears in the 1601 'Act for the More Peaceable Government of the Parts of Cumberland, Northumberland, Westmoreland, and Bishopric of Durham', for example.[20] Likewise in many other texts of the period, though John Leslie offered a nice variant in his *Treatise of Treasons* (1572), referring to 'fatal feud and deadly malice'.[21]

Anglo-Scottish border commissioners late in Elizabeth's reign sought measures for 'avoiding of the most bloody and ungodly ceremony maliciously upholden by the name of deadly feado'. When someone killed a person from the other side of

---

[18] *APC*, vol. 14, pp. 157–8. The *APC*'s editor notes that the paper, though tucked into a Privy Council register, seems to be a record of a meeting of the court of Star Chamber, given the attendance list.

[19] Based on a text search of *EBBO*, though such a search cannot be comprehensive, given that not all early modern texts survive and that not all that are included in *EEBO* are yet fully text-searchable. See, too, the *Oxford English Dictionary*, which also notes the frequency of the phrasing 'to be at (deadly) feud'. *The Dictionary of the Older Scottish Tongue*, now searchable online at http://www.dsl. ac.uk/, offers histories of 'fede' and 'feid', noting that they frequently appear with 'dedely or mortall'.

[20] 43 Elizabeth I c. 13.   [21] John Leslie, *A Treatise of Treasons* (Louvain, 1572), p. 230.

the border, if any of 'the surname, kin, or friends of the said party slain as shall for such slaughter allege deadly feud against the slayer and ride or make purpose to take the life of the said slayer or of any of his kin or friends', the wardens were to impose (if they could) sentence of death unless they could convince the parties openly to renounce and give good assurance for the final ending of the feud.[22] Here in the border region, some feuds took on the aspect of Italian vendettas, with particularly horrific killings meant to send messages as much as to remove enemies. Borderer Edward Armstrong was wanted for twelve murders and his kinsman John Armstrong 'for divers' others, but especially for 'ripping a woman's belly, taking out her child alive, cutting the woman's throat, and leaving her and her child dead in the road way ... by the direction of the said Edward Armstrong, who was also present at the deed doing'.[23] This sort of private satisfaction-seeking had to be stopped for subjects to trust in law and for royal justice to triumph.

After the union of the crowns in 1603, when James VI of Scotland became king of England as well, new border commissions had a special charge to root out this 'barbarous custom' by resolving existing feuds and preventing new ones. If parties to feuds then ongoing could not easily be brought to agreement, the Englishmen were to be gaoled in Edinburgh and the Scots in Newcastle until they would reconcile and take out bonds to keep the peace. For any new feuds that threatened, justice by the usual laws of both nations for any of the constituent crimes would be the order of the day. The commissioners received repeated reminders that they must 'labour by all possible good means to extinguish and pluck the same up by the roots, being the seminaries of bloodshed and murder'.[24] In practical terms, James's accession to the English throne helped drive feuding out of its last English strongholds: as Brian Levack has noted, while the union of the crowns did not bring a union of English and Scots law, it did complete 'the legal unification of the southern kingdom'.[25] With the abrogation of the distinctive laws and customs of the marches, common law thereafter ran to the border. With the disappearance of the armed frontier between the two countries, both the social and the legal conditions that had allowed feuding to continue diminished.

James had good experience dealing with feuds before he went to England. Indeed, historians of his Scottish reign have argued that he 'presided over the most dramatic reduction in violence in Scottish history', partly through successful mediation and partly through a legislative programme that allowed lawyers and royal officials greater roles in formerly private conflicts.[26] In Scotland, kin of a

---

[22] CAS (Whitehaven), D/CU Misc. On the continuation of feuding on both sides of the Anglo-Scottish border, see Maureen Meikle, *A British Frontier? Lairds and Gentlemen in the Eastern Borders, 1540–1603* (East Linton, 2004), pp. 27ff.

[23] CAS (Whitehaven), D/PEN 216, f. 59.

[24] CAS (Whitehaven), D/PEN 216, ff. 4, 5, 159.

[25] Brian Levack, *The Formation of the British State: England, Scotland, and the Union, 1603–1707* (Oxford, 1987), p. 19. On border laws before the union, see C.J. Neville, *Violence, Custom and Law: The Anglo-Scottish Border Lands in the Later Middle Ages* (Edinburgh, 1998). See also Diana Newton, *The Making of the Jacobean Regime: James VI and I and the Government of England, 1603–1605* (Woodbridge, 2005).

[26] Brown, *Bloodfeud*, esp. pp. 215, 239. See also Wormald, 'Bloodfeud', and Anna Groundwater, *The Scottish Middle March, 1573–1623* (London, 2010), esp. ch. 5.

homicide victim could seek a trial followed by execution, or they could instead openly and licitly seek compensation, known there as assythment: once the killer produced 'letters of slain', with the kin's acknowledgement of satisfaction received and their own foreswearing of any further violence or prosecution, then the king would pardon the killer.[27] Or the kin might use both, beginning a prosecution in the courts to encourage a settlement but letting the prosecution drop and offering their release once they received reparations. And the kin groups involved could extend several degrees beyond the immediate principals. As Michael Wasser notes, compensation remained far more common in Scottish homicide cases than did trials resulting in death well into the early seventeenth century, with expectations for assythment deeply rooted in Scottish society.[28] Too often, though, affronts and assaults degenerated into deadly violence. Parliamentary acts increased the punishment for killings committed in kirks and kirkyards—apparently favoured places for waylaying foes, despite their supposedly special status—and augmented the powers of the provost and bailiffs of Edinburgh to deal with disorders in the streets. A measure for 'removing and extinguishing of deadly feuds' followed in 1598 that established a structure for royal intervention in settling such disputes.[29] Arbitrations supervised by the courts were gradually pushing aside purely private settlements. The 1598 measure received confirmation in 1600, alongside a new act against 'singular combats', or what were coming to be known as duels and supplementing or (arguably) taking the place of feuds.[30]

In his *Basilikon Doron* (1599), James bemoaned the propensity of Scottish noblemen so often to run off to 'feides...for any displeasure that they apprehend to be done unto them by their neighbour...to bang it out bravely, he and all his kin, against him and all his'. In this book of guidance intended for his son, James counselled: 'rest not until you root out these barbarous feides, that their effects may be as well smoared down as their barbarous name is known to any other nation'.[31] Remarkably, for someone urged so vehemently from his infancy to seek vengeance first for his father's murder and then for his mother's execution, James evinced a clear sense of the dangers of such tit-for-tat reprisals. As Jenny Wormald noted, he was not above using the Scots traditions of assythment to seek satisfaction (i.e. money) from Queen Elizabeth after his mother's death, but his only interest in the destructive aspects of feuding focused on their suppression.[32] If any of the English had worried that their new king, born and bred in a nation known for its 'deadly feides', would bring this habit south with him, they need not have done so. At least as much as anyone in England and perhaps more, James saw feuds as antithetical to his laws and to the public justice of his new kingdom. What he found in his new southern

---

[27] See C.J. Neville, 'Royal Mercy in Medieval Scotland', *Florilegium* 29 (2012): pp. 1–31, and Grant, 'Murder Will Out: Kingship, Kinship and Killing in Medieval Scotland'.

[28] Michael Wasser, 'Violence and the Central Criminal Courts in Scotland, 1603–1638', University of Columbia doctoral dissertation, 1995, ch. 4 and p. 208. As Grant notes, a 1504 act sought to limit assythment and remissions for premeditated killings, but with what effect is unclear. See Grant, 'Murder Will Out', p. 23, citing *RPS*, 1504/3/108.

[29] *RPS*, 1592/4/30; 1593/4/54; 1598/6/2; 1600/11/44.   [30] *RPS*, 1600/11/33.

[31] *James VI and I: Political Writings*, edited by Johann P. Sommerville (Cambridge, 1994), p. 28.

[32] Wormald, 'Bloodfeud', p. 54.

kingdom was a society in which feud-like behaviour certainly still existed, but in which its frequency had been much reduced and in which the legitimacy of vengeance through deadly private reprisals had long since ceased to be recognized in all but its most northerly areas—a project he then helped to complete.

COMPENSATION

But what of the other side of feuding, satisfaction in currency other than blood? While the Scots still favoured assythment in cases of homicide into the early seventeenth century—as did the people of a good many other nations—the English, ostensibly, had no place for such payments.[33] In Scotland, as in many other jurisdictions abroad, both formal and informal justice allowed compensation, but not so in England. Private vengeance posed an obvious challenge to the Crown's claims to monopolize responses to homicide, but so too did privately secured payments that allowed a killer to evade royal justice. Homicide in early modern and much of medieval England's history technically afforded neither kith nor kin of the deceased any chance for compensation, in either civil or criminal law. Whereas the Scots, the Irish, and many others continued to use assythment, *éiric*, and other forms of 'blood money' to extract reparations for homicide, the English had formally abandoned such payments from the twelfth century, instead mandating that killers be subject to the corporeal sanctions of royal justice and forfeit their property to kings and lords. The great 'Angevin revolution in justice' associated most closely with

[33] In Portugal, in Castile, in various German towns, in Scandinavia, etc., compensation remained the norm, at least into the sixteenth century. Darlene Abreu-Ferreira finds the sources for her book on *Women, Crime and Forgiveness in Early Modern Portugal* (Farnham, 2015) in the remarkable notarized letters of pardon from homicide victims' kin, the *perdão de parte*, that killers needed to secure before they obtained pardons from the Crown. See also José Luis de las Heras Santos, *La Justicia Penal de los Austrias en la Corona de Castilla* (Salamanca, 1991), pp. 41–3; and Joachim Eibach, 'The Containment of Violence in Central European Cities, 1500–1800', in *Crime, Law and Popular Culture in Europe, 1500–1800*, edited by Richard McMahon (Cullompton, 2008), p. 57. In *Making Manslaughter: Process, Punishment and Restitution in Württemberg and Zurich, 1376–1700* (Leiden, 2017), Susanne Pohl-Zucker notes that in both areas she studied, reconciliations remained the norm, with elaborate rituals of penance and reconciliation accompanying payments in the *Totschlagssühne*, just increasingly brought under judicial supervision in the sixteenth century. The classic text by Bertha Surtees Phillpotts, *Kindred and Clan in the Middle Ages and After* (Cambridge, 1913) lists licit survivals of compensation payments in northern European regions well into the sixteenth century. Also instructive on comparative homicide law and the place of compensation are Christine Elkholst, *A Punishment for Each Criminal: Gender and Crime in Swedish Medieval Law* (Leiden, 2014), and Tyge Krogh, *A Lutheran Plague: Murdering to Die in the Eighteenth Century* (Leiden, 2011). Bruce Lenman and Geoffrey Parker, 'The State, the Community, and the Criminal Law in Early Modern Europe', in *Crime and the Law: The Social History of Crime in Western Europe Since 1500*, edited by V.A.C. Gatrell, Bruce Lenman, and Geoffrey Parker (London, 1980), pp. 11–48, do not distinguish between homicide and other crimes, but note the ubiquity of compensation, rooted in Germanic law as opposed to Roman, throughout much of Europe, describing its gradual displacement as 'one of the central (yet most neglected) developments of European history, constituting a revolutionary change in legal methods and in the techniques of social control' (p. 23). For Scotland, see especially Godfrey's essay, 'Rethinking the Justice of the Feud', which usefully emphasizes that when interpreting Scottish feuding, we must remember that there even formal justice continued to endorse compensation, without clear distinction between the criminal and civil functions of court remedies.

Henry II supposedly replaced wergeld payments to family with fines and forfeitures payable to the king and banishment or physical punishment of felons.[34] In Wales, too, the open, formal compensation for homicide known as *galanas*, payable from and to extended groups of kin, had been eradicated: within the Principality of Wales it had been banned from the 1280s, and it seems to have largely died out within the marcher lordships as well, even before the legislation of 1534–42 brought them into line with England and the rest of Wales.[35] Compensation of kin accompanied violent reprisal in the feuding that was being subordinated to royal laws.

Yet, in recent decades a number of medievalists have revealed that compensation survived informally in England, identifying cases into the fifteenth century. A bit of digging shows that compensation payments for homicide continued into the sixteenth century and beyond, too. As Edward Powell, Anthony Musson, and others have demonstrated for medieval England, extra-judicial appropriations of judicial mechanisms left space for compensation in some instances. Complemented by arbitration, appeal procedure allowed the immediate kin of some homicide victims to secure reparations, instead of the killer's execution.[36] The medievalists who have shown the persistence of extra-judicial reparations have been at pains to point out that reconciliation was not antithetical to law; arguing that the modern view that arbitration and litigation competed is anachronistic, they depict them instead as complementary responses. True. But the modern view gained substance in the sixteenth century. Sixteenth-century commentators, like some of their modern counterparts, also saw a conflict between the two as they drew clearer and more emphatic distinctions between 'public Justice', on the one hand, and both private revenge and private reconciliation on the other. So the survival of compensation—for even a crime as grave as homicide—into the early modern era needs some explanation.

[34] The phrase is Alan Harding's: *The Law Courts of Medieval England* (London, 1973), p. 49. Scholarship on this topic is voluminous, but for the broad context, see John Hudson, *The Formation of the English Common Law* (London, 1996). On the specific issue of the appeal of felony, see Kerr, 'Angevin Reform of the Appeal of Felony', pp. 351–91.

[35] R.R. Davies, 'The Survival of the Bloodfeud in Medieval Wales', *History* 54 (1969): pp. 338–57 explores the residual survival of such payments outside the principality after 1284, e.g. in Clun, and a few later payments of compensation as late as 1523, though with no mention of *galanas* as such. See also Llinos Beverley Smith, 'A Contribution to the History of *Galanas* in Late-Medieval Wales', *Studia Celtica* 43 (2009): pp. 87–94 for a case from 1430 in the marcher lordship of Dyffryn Clwd in which a *galanas* payment was effected alongside an appeal for homicide.

[36] Edward Powell, 'Arbitration and the Law in Late Medieval England', *Transactions of the Royal Historical Society* 33 (1983): pp. 49–67; Powell, 'Settlement of Disputes by Arbitration in Fifteenth-Century England', *Law and History Review* 2.1 (1984): pp. 21–43; Anthony Musson, *Public Order and Law Enforcement*, pp. 169–71, and 'Wergeld: Crime and the Compensation Culture in Medieval England', https://www.gresham.ac.uk/lectures-and-events/wergeld-crime-and-the-compensation-culture-in-medieval-england; and J.T. Rosenthal, 'Feuds and Private Peace-Making: A Fifteenth-Century Example', *Nottingham Medieval Studies* 14 (1970): pp. 84–90. On arbitration, see also Carole Rawcliffe, 'The Great Lord as Peacekeeper: Arbitration by English Noblemen and their Councils in the Later Middle Ages,' in *Law and Social Change in British History*, edited by J.A. Guy and H.G. Beale (London, 1984), pp. 34–54; Ian Rowney, 'Arbitration in Gentry Disputes of the Later Middle Ages', *History* 67 (1982): pp. 367–76; C.J. Neville, 'Arbitration and Anglo-Scottish Border Law in the Later Middle Ages', in *Liberties and Identities in the Medieval British Isles*, edited by Michael Prestwich (Woodbridge, 2008), pp. 37–55. Note, too, that while mediation and arbitration have distinct meanings in modern usage, they tended to be used more as synonyms in the period under study and in the works cited here.

Appeals decreased in number and came under tighter judicial control, but people could still use them to secure either revenge or recompense in some few cases. The victim of a serious offence—or in the case of a killing, the victim's widow or heir—launched the appeal, in which she or he managed the matter personally, and stood personally liable for costs should the suit fail. The defendant stood trial at the appellor's suit, not the king's. A male appellor put his life on the line to prosecute such a case, risking trial by battle to prove his claim. A woman was not thought able to pursue her cause with force of arms, and a man she accused was thus thought less able to defend himself, so she could in theory only launch appeals in a limited range of cases; as enshrined in Magna Carta, this included the death of her husband.[37] (When someone appealed a woman's death, it was typically a brother; no special provision allowed a man to appeal his wife's killer.) William Holdsworth and others have shown that the appeal was the keystone in bridging the old system of wergelds and feuds and the newer system of royal justice and Crown pleas.[38]

Over the thirteenth century and beyond, appeals tended to decline in number as more people preferred the safety of presentments and then indictments filtered through juries. Approvers' appeals had occasional surges in use, true, but these were a distinctive subset of the broader class, in which an offender confessed and agreed to appeal his confederates, often prosecuting by battle, upon a promise of his life if he succeeded in his appeals. Musson has found evidence that officials pressured offenders to turn approver at various times in the fourteenth century in the absence of more direct ways to start or prosecute cases against notorious criminals they wanted rid of, but to much complaint.[39] Otherwise, though, appeals tended to be used more sparingly. One set of early fifteenth-century gaol delivery records, for example, showed that only 13 per cent of all people arraigned for felonies were brought to court on appeals, though just under a quarter of those charged with homicides faced appeals. The rest were tried on indictments. The proportions found in East Anglian and Midland assize circuits in the early 1400s were even lower, with 3 to 9 per cent of prosecutions for all felonies initiated by appeals.[40] By pressing for

[37] See Klerman, 'Woman Prosecutors', who argues that in thirteenth-century England, judges sometimes ignored the restrictions on women's ability to sue unless the defendant objected. For various interpretations of the Magna Carta provision, see David Carpenter, *Magna Carta* (London, 2015), p. 107; see also p. 452.

[38] Holdsworth, *History of English Law*, vol. 2, pp. 198, 362.

[39] A.J. Musson, 'Turning King's Evidence: The Prosecution of Crime in Late Medieval England', *Oxford Journal of Legal Studies* 19 (1999): pp. 467–80, and *Public Order and Law Enforcement*, pp. 172–4, 242–8. As F.C. Hamil noted, this practice seems to have died out by the end of the fifteenth century. The last instance he found was in 1470. Thereafter, the term 'approver' was still sometimes used, but for a looser practice of turning 'king's evidence' and providing testimony to assist with a trial of one's criminal confederates, on indictment at the king's suit, and with an understanding though not a promise of a pardon. See F.C. Hamil, 'The King's Approvers: A Chapter in the History of English Common Law', *Speculum* 11 (1936): pp. 238–57.

[40] For thirteenth-century numbers, see Klerman, cited above. Karen Ellis examined the records surviving from Yorkshire gaol deliveries from 1399 to 1407, with 396 people arraigned. Looking specifically at homicide, fourteen of the fifty-eight people (24 per cent) charged with the crime came to court on appeals. See Karen E. Ellis, 'Gaol Delivery in Yorkshire, 1399–1407', MA dissertation, Carleton University, 1983, pp. 34, 92; Powell, *Kingship, Law, and Society*, p. 72. Writing about a set

a jury presentment or proffering a bill of indictment, an individual did not risk paying damages if the suit failed, and men did not risk needing to prosecute their claim with a trial by battle—though judicial discouragement of battle after 1300 lessened the risk, defendants might still insist upon it to encourage the appellor to withdraw. The rise of trespass actions, which allowed damages to the plaintiff, also diminished the attractiveness of the appeal procedure for a variety of non-felonious offences.[41] But appeals did not wholly disappear, for victims or their next of kin found them useful means to secure either revenge or reparations, depending on the case. As noted above, a royal pardon remitted only the king's suit against the offender, not the appellor's.[42] So victims or their immediate kin could push through with a suit to the deadly end, if they wished and were able, or strategically drop the suit once they received payment from the offender.

One might well assume, for a variety of reasons, that all this finally came to an end in the sixteenth century. Indeed, appeals did decline in number. The docket rolls for the civil pleas in the Court of King's Bench show that appeals continued throughout the sixteenth century, but in small and diminishing numbers. Christopher Whittick found that seventy-seven appeals of homicide advanced to the pleading stage between 1485 and 1495.[43] Looking at appeals for all sorts of felonies, John Baker suggested that their frequency more than halved between 1500 and the 1550s.[44] A further sampling of central court dockets for ten years drawn from the 1490s to 1570s finds eighty-three appeals of death, launched by sixty-eight people, thirty-nine of them women. The highest number in any of the years in this sample was twenty-four, in 1498/9, but from the reign of Henry VIII onward, two or three appeals of homicide per year proved more usual.[45] Appeals could also be held at the county assizes, but the trial records calendared by

of Yorkshire gaol delivery records from 1439 to 1460, however, Bellamy observes that 23 per cent of all those arraigned came up on appeals, noting that most of the appeals were for larceny, but offers no further details. Bellamy, *Criminal Trial*, p. 36.

[41] Holdsworth, *History of English Law*, vol. 2, p. 360; Klerman, 'Settlement and the Decline of Private Prosecution'. On the relationship between appeal and trespass, and efforts to quash feuding, see Hyams, *Rancor and Reconciliation*, pp. 176–7, 216ff. Some offences that could have been tried as felonies continued to be prosecuted as trespasses, but not, it seems, homicides: DeLloyd Guth, 'Enforcing Late-Medieval Law: Patterns in Litigation during Henry VII's Reign', in *Legal Records and the Historian*, edited by J.H. Baker (London, 1978), pp. 80–96.

[42] It is also worth noting a tellingly limited similarity to practice in Scotland and elsewhere in Europe. In Scotland, the king was not to pardon a killer until that killer could produce letters of slain from the kith and kin of the victim; similarly, in France, Portugal, etc., royal pardons for homicide were conditional on the satisfaction of the kin. In England, the king's power to pardon a killer was limited by considerations of kin and satisfaction, but not to the same degree: the king could pardon his own suit without regard or condition for the kin's satisfaction, though yes, the killer would have to stand trial upon the heir's appeal, if the heir was willing to take on the expense and labour of prosecuting such an appeal. On this point, see Grant, 'Murder Will Out: Kingship, Kinship and Killing in Medieval Scotland', p. 17, and Hurnard, *King's Pardon for Homicide*, pp. xi and 171ff.

[43] Christopher Whittick, 'The Role of the Criminal Appeal in the Fifteenth Century', in *Law and Social Change in British History*, edited by J.A. Guy and H.G. Beale (London, 1984), pp. 55–72.

[44] Baker, *Oxford History of the Laws of England*, p. 513.

[45] IND 1/1327 (13 Henry VII, 14 Henry VII); IND 1/1328 (20 Henry VII); IND 1/1329 (22 Henry VII); IND 1/1331 (12 Henry VIII); IND 1/1335 (30 Henry VIII, 21 Henry VIII); IND 1/1338 (1&2 Philip and Mary, 2&3 Philip and Mary); IND 1/1345 (20 Elizabeth I).

J.S. Cockburn for the reigns of Elizabeth and James for the five counties of the Home Circuit include only three appeals for homicide.[46]

The 1487 'Act against Murderers' contributed to this decline, both in expressing dissatisfaction with the way appeals allowed 'slayers and murderers' to escape the penalties of law and in making it more difficult to use the appeal as a bargaining tool. Whereas trials on indictment had previously been delayed for up to a year and a day to allow the victim's heir time to appeal, the 1487 statute stipulated that trial on indictment no longer had to wait, for 'the party is ofttimes slow, *and also agreed with*, and by the end of the year all is forgotten'.[47] Private appeal no longer took precedence over public prosecution on indictment. The victim's kin might still launch an appeal concurrently or even after the fact, as an acquittal on indictment did not bar a subsequent trial on appeal.[48] Nonetheless, the 1487 act presumably restricted both the time and the incentive for negotiating a settlement.

Given the significance of this act in establishing the primacy of trial on indictment, one wishes for more information about the impulses behind it than the meagre materials on legislation in this era provide. In his study of Henry VII's parliaments, Paul Cavill speculates that the measure was prompted by the problems that had emerged after the recent murder of William Welles, an alderman and former mayor of York, in the course of an attempt to arrest an offender. The burgesses of the city had petitioned the king for a commission to try the killer; they did not want to prejudice the interests of Welles's widow, but desired 'that the said heinous deed may be punished well in example of all other hereafter'.[49] Whatever the impetus, the provision was part of a significant set of changes in the prosecution of homicide that asserted the interests of the king's justice above other interests, and which must have complicated efforts to use appeals as leverage in securing compensation.

Another and perhaps more serious impediment to using the appeal to secure compensation emerged over the century, as manslaughter became more clearly separated from murder and as the charge became more common. Whether charged with murder or with manslaughter, a killer could be found guilty of the lesser charge and thus (if a man) be allowed to plead benefit of clergy to escape the noose. Over the sixteenth century, judges used this new feature to limit recourse to appeals: they decided that a conviction for manslaughter followed by a successful plea of clergy barred any subsequent appeal of murder. In 1579, Henry Borough tried to bring an appeal against Thomas Holcroft for the murder of his elder brother, but Holcroft had already pleaded guilty to an indictment for manslaughter and had then claimed his clergy; the judges debated whether to allow Borough's appeal to proceed based on flaws in the original indictment, having agreed that otherwise, the successful

---

[46] *CAR* Kent (Elizabeth), no. 243; *CAR* Surrey (Elizabeth) no. 571; *CAR* Sussex (James), no. 301.

[47] 3 Henry VII c. 2. Emphasis added. For discussion of the effects of the 1487 statute, see in particular Ernst, 'The Moribund Appeal', though he does somewhat overstate how 'crippling' the statute was in using the appeal to secure compensation.

[48] Much legal debate ensued on this point in later years, but both the statute and a subsequent proclamation clearly noted that an acquittal on the indictment did not preclude a subsequent appeal. See *TRP*, vol. 1, no. 30 (1493), *Enforcing Statutes against Murder (&c.)*.

[49] Paul Cavill, *The English Parliaments of Henry VII* (Oxford, 2009), p. 74; *York House Books, 1461–1490*, edited by L.C. Atreed, 2 vols (Stroud, 1991), vol. 2, pp. 561–2.

plea of clergy on the lesser charge of manslaughter was a bar to an appeal for murder.[50] In 1591, the judges offered an even clearer statement, though with an important caveat, in the case of Wrote *v* Wigges. A coroner's jury had deemed Thomas Wigges's killing of Robert Wrote an act of manslaughter. In court, Wigges confessed and prayed his clergy. Robert Wrote's widow Catherine then tried to launch an appeal for murder. As Sir Edward Coke noted in his report, the judges ultimately resolved that 'auterfoits [previously] convict of manslaughter, *and clergy thereupon allowed*, was a good bar in an appeal of murder'.[51] The only savings here put significant power in the hands of the judges: since a verdict of manslaughter alone did not suffice to bar an appeal, but needed to be followed by judgement and a successful plea of clergy, a judge could delay giving judgement after hearing the jury verdict, to allow an appeal to go forward. The judges acknowledged that it might seem odd or unfortunate that neither a pardon nor a full acquittal on a murder indictment prevented an appeal, but that conviction and judgement for manslaughter did; their reasoning implied that earlier precedents and statutes tied their hands on the matter of pardons and acquittals, but where they had the freedom to settle new issues, they chose to limit recourse to appeals.[52]

In one other way, too, the rise of manslaughter verdicts complicated people's ability to use the appeal to their own ends and allowed a bit more central intervention and control: a jury could find someone appealed of murder guilty only of manslaughter, and judges decided that the sovereign could pardon the convict for the manslaughter verdict, bringing the whole matter to an end. By law and long custom, the sovereign could not pardon an individual's own suit against a killer, but in the late sixteenth century, judges decided that if a jury found someone who had been appealed of murder guilty of a different crime—that is, manslaughter— the queen could pardon the offender from the burden of that offence. Thus, the judges decided in the case of Penryn *v* Corbet in 1595, 'that wherein he is found guilty is not for the party, but for the queen'.[53] The inability of the king or queen to release someone convicted on an appeal was, at times, a striking limitation of the sovereign power over life and death. In one notable case from 1512, for example, Henry VIII and his parliament had voided indictments brought by a supposedly corrupt jury against a royal sheriff who had killed in the course of an arrest, but had only been able to hinder and not halt the appeals brought against the sheriff by the families of the dead.[54] Elizabeth on one occasion ordered her justices to find a way to stay a widow's appeal against a number of men she had already pardoned for a killing—with what effect is unknown, but the fact that her pardon on its own could not guarantee these men their lives seems to have rankled.[55] So, a manslaughter verdict in a trial upon indictment could serve as a bar to an appeal for murder once benefit of clergy had been pleaded, and a trial on an appeal for murder could itself

---

[50] 74 *ER* 442.   [51] 76 *ER* 994. Emphasis added.
[52] 76 *ER* 994. See also 80 *ER* 134, Bradley *v* Banks, 9 Jac.
[53] 78 *ER* 702. For another such case, see 73 *ER* 578.
[54] 4 Henry VIII c. 20.   [55] *APC*, vol. 32, p. 490.

produce a manslaughter verdict, and with it the possibility of a royal pardon or the likelihood of a plea of clergy.

Both these changes—the 1487 statute's privileging of indictments over appeals and the judicial decisions allowed by the newly common manslaughter verdicts—must have diminished the ability to use appeals to negotiate settlements with offenders. And this fits with what we know of judicial distaste for appeals in particular and private vindictiveness and private settlements more generally. Judges did much to make appeals especially 'slippery actions', often holding prosecutors to high technical standards in pleading. Small flaws in proceeding could be used to block an appeal.[56] In one case from 1556, Richard Reade appealed a group of men for his brother's death, but one of them offered to defend himself by battle. Reade demurred and so lost his appeal. Judges ordered Reade to pay damages to the defendants and then had the defendants tried at the queen's suit—hardly a set of responses to make the appeal a useful device for prompting negotiations, nor entirely safe for securing retribution.[57] As Justice Dyer reportedly said, an appeal is 'but a suit of revenge, and therefore is not much favoured'—a sentiment echoed in Recorder Montague's dismissal of the appeal as an 'action of revenge'.[58] While better than purely private revenge, appeals sometimes suffered by association.

Even if private vengeance constituted the main contrast with 'public Justice', private settlements prompted concern, too. Whether arranged through appeals or even less formally, private settlements that let killers live attracted much criticism. In Wales and along its borders with England, although the formalities of *galanas* had disappeared, informal payments to lords to have them help an offender avoid criminal charges seem to have persisted under the guise of commorth or *cymhortha*. Details are few, but it appears that a lord might pay a victim's family if one of his men committed a killing, and then recover his expenditure through a levy imposed on the rest of his tenants. A Henrician statute of 1534 had decried such levies or exactions when used 'for redemption of any murder or any other felony', but in 1576, the Abergavenny lawyer David Lewis complained to one of Elizabeth's councillors that settlements effected in this manner continued and, in his estimation, contributed to disorder in the area. He wanted more punishments of the body rather than the purse.[59] Along the northern borders, too, compensation in lieu of punishment persisted. One Elizabethan letter writer complained that Northumberland's coroners and their juries eased compositions, forbearing from entering indictments or verdicts, 'to the end the hot blood of the parties grieved may have leisure to cool, and the murderer with [tract] of time and solicitation of friends may obtain the

---

[56] Pulton, *De Pace Regis et Regni*, ff. 157ff. For an example, see SP 46/75, f. 273, listing the reasons why the appeal against Edward Morgan was overthrown, including mistakenly identifying the time of the killing as '*circa hora*' and '*circa hora predicta*' rather than being more specific. See also Giles Jacob's discussion in *The Laws of Appeals and Murder* (London, 1719), esp. p. 100.

[57] Reade *v* Rochforth et al. (1556), 73 *ER* 263, 286.

[58] Cited in T.E., *Lawes Resolution of Women's Rights; Or, The Lawes Provision for Women* (London, 1632), p. 338. For Montague, see the notes from the lengthy discussion of appeals in the 1607 parliament in *The Parliamentary Diary of Robert Bowyer, 1606–1607*, edited by David Harris Willson (New York, 1971), p. 217.

[59] 26 Henry VIII, c. 6; SP 12/107, ff. 8–9.

easier composition'. To this practice, 'which is very openly and commonly done', the writer attributed the growing frequency of murders in the area.[60] Border commissioners later complained that allowing composition to settle a homicide meant that 'the murder of a man is as little or rather less feared than the stealing of a cow', and as a result, killings 'daily increased' in the region.[61]

While some might see compensation as a Christian act, contemporaries had other terms for the practice: composition, compounding, and concealing. It was most emphatically not civilized. On the borders, commissioners deemed composition a 'barbarous custom'.[62] So, too, when Englishmen looked to Irish practice. Both the characters in Sir Edmund Spenser's dialogue *View of the Present State of Ireland* agreed that the Irish custom of accepting reparation in lieu of a killer's execution was 'most wicked', repugnant to the laws of God and of man: 'by which vile law of theirs, many murders are mongst them made up and smothered'.[63] Sir John Davies cited the practice as a chief reason that those who follow Irish custom 'must of necessity be rebels to all good government, destroy the commonwealth wherein they live, and bring barbarism and desolation upon' the land, a custom far opposed not just to the law of England but also, he thought, to the laws 'of all other well-governed kingdoms and commonweals'.[64] Writing on England's own history, early modern scholars normally keen to document continuities with the ancient constitution of the pre-Norman past found nothing positive to say about wergeld, seeing it as a punishment that failed to punish, barbarous in allowing killers to escape with a payment rather than subjecting them to a proper penalty.[65]

Yet appeals in particular and compensation more generally continued, at least on occasion. Both the 1487 statute and the effects of manslaughter verdicts weakened the ability of individuals to use an appeal to compel an out of court settlement— unless judges cooperated, and they sometimes did. That is, survivors could still use the appeal to secure compensation, though they now found the connivance of judges increasingly necessary to do so. A sense that widows, at least, merited or required payment remained sufficiently strong to ensure such help from time to time.[66] Without doubt, homicide in sixteenth-century England became more fully criminalized, with the balance between private and public tipping more markedly towards the public. Public justice—public retribution rather than private reconciliation (or private revenge)—became more thoroughly accepted as the ideal, but widows' insistence on being compensated worked against this for a time.

---

[60] SP 12/284, f. 98.

[61] CAS (Whitehaven), D/CU Misc. See, too, BL, Cecil Papers 110/148, a complaint from May 1605.

[62] CAS (Whitehaven), D/PEN 216, f. 159.

[63] Edmund Spenser, *View of the Present State of Ireland*, edited by Andrew Hadfield and Willy Maley (Oxford, 1997), pp. 14–15.

[64] John Davies, *Discovery of the True Cause why Ireland was never entirely brought under obedience to the Crown of England* (London, 1747, printed from the edition of 1612), p. 167.

[65] Paul Christianson, 'Young John Selden and the Ancient Constitution, *c*.1610–18', *Proceedings of the American Philosophical Society* 128 (1984): pp. 271–315, at 277.

[66] For a related sense that widows of suicides and of executed felons merited some share of their husbands' forfeited property, see Kesselring, 'Coverture and Criminal Forfeiture', in *Female Transgression in Early Modern Britain*, edited by Richard Hillman and Pauline Ruberry-Blanc (Farnham, 2014), pp. 191–212.

A number of petitions from widows in the reign of Henry VIII certainly show a continued conviction that compensation was owed. Alice Warner asked the queen to intervene on her behalf. Warner noted that even as her husband lay dying after an attack by John Barnsby, the sacristan of Bury St. Edmunds, she went to the local steward to have Barnsby locked away, 'thinking to have some advantage of' him. The steward, however, allowed Barnsby to escape, and the killer fled to the sanctuary at Saint John in Colchester. Alice petitioned both to have the officer duly punished and to 'be recompensed for the death of her said husband'.[67]

At least nineteen widows sent to Henry VIII's lord chancellors bills of supplication, now filed among the records of Star Chamber, to seek justice of some sort after the killings of their husbands. That the justice they sought consisted first and foremost of compensation is a theme that runs throughout many of the suits. They approached the chancellor for a variety of reasons. Some noted explicitly the expense or exigencies of the appeal process. In 1520, Alice Dene sought the aid of Lord Chancellor Wolsey because her husband George had been killed in one county, but the murderer had fled to another and thus rendered a standard appeal impossible.[68] Isabel Goddeshalf maintained that she was too poor to proceed by common law appeal.[69] Margery Webbe noted that she had already sought justice for her husband's death by appealing the killers, but had seen the appeal quashed for a simple naming error.[70] As the killers of Alice Tilston's husband had fled to the Westminster sanctuary, she asked that the chancellor find some way to force them to make 'reasonable recompense and satisfaction unto your poor beadswoman for the loss of her husband'.[71] Others wrote that the killers had friends too powerful for justice to be obtained through usual means. Alice Davy complained of the local men who sought the acquittal of her husband's killer, 'to the utter undoing of her and her children'.[72] Isabel Kelke described in gory detail the murderous ambush of her husband as the pair travelled to a friend's wedding in Lincolnshire and noted that she had now launched an appeal against the killers, but doubted that she would see an indifferent trial, given the ties between them and local JPs.[73] Joan Bryce seemed in a better position than the others: she wrote that the gentleman who had killed her husband stymied local efforts to secure justice, but nonetheless 'has diverse times made labour to be agreed with her'. She asked the chancellor to order matters as he saw best for 'the profit of your poor obedient supplicant and her three small children... for she is a woman without any counsel'.[74]

Other women secured a settlement without going to the king or chancellor, instead relying upon local mediators and the sense that they merited some sort of compensation. Given the nature of such agreements, arranged privately outside the courts, evidence of them is scant or at least scattered and hard to find. The nineteenth-century archivist and antiquarian Joseph Hunter found a rather remarkable record of one such arbitration amongst family muniments and

---

[67] E 135/22/15. Warner's petition is undated and the queen unnamed.
[68] STAC 2/12, f. 186. [69] STAC 2/16, ff. 94–5.
[70] STAC 2/33, f. 45. [71] STAC 2/18, f. 287.
[72] STAC 2/12, f. 133. See also STAC 2/8, f. 115 and STAC 2/23, f. 66.
[73] STAC 2/23/66. [74] STAC 2/6, f. 262.

transcribed it in his history of south Yorkshire. This one arose from the long-running and eventually murderous dispute between the West and Darcy families in the 1550s. John and George Darcy, sons of Lord Darcy, had led a group of men who attacked the sons of Sir William West and their party in mid-April 1556, again in early May, and then a third time later that month. On this final occasion, reportedly at the head of some sixty men who were equipped with mail shirts and heavy weapons, the Darcys killed Lewis West. Mediation then ensued to ensure that the bloodshed go no further and to satisfy the widow sufficiently to have her forego her right of appeal. Margaret West agreed not to appeal the eldest Darcy son for murder, but reserved that option in respect to the younger Darcy and three of their confederates. The indenture bore the seals of the two local gentlemen who led the negotiations, William Fairfax of Gilling and Godfrey Bosvile. Hunter found it among the papers of the latter's family, and transcribes its contents as follows:

> Whereas great suit and variance hath been and be yet depending betwixt John Darcy, son and heir apparent of Sir George Darcy, knight, lord Darcy of Aston, and others, of the one part, and Margaret West, widow, late wife of Lewis West, late of Wales, esq., deceased, on the other, of and concerning the death of the said Lewis West: the said Fairfax and Bosvile, as friends to the parties, and at the earnest motion of sundry honourable and worshipful friends, have taken upon them to procure and make an accord and agreement as ensueth: Margaret West, in consideration of a friendship hereafter to be had between the said John Darcy, and other his friends and servants, towards the said Margaret, her children, and friends, and towards George West of Ashton and all other the kinsmen and friends of the said Lewis West, deceased, shall not sue or prosecute any appeal against the said John Darcy (reserving, however, to herself the right of prosecuting the appeal against George Darcy the younger, son of the Lord Darcy, George Parker, John Stringer, and Richard Grene, or so many of the said four persons as she shall think meet, but against no other), and shall give a sufficient release accordingly. On the part of Darcy it is agreed, that in consideration of the great cost and charges that the said Margaret hath sustained in suits and troubles, by occasion of the death of her husband, and by the loss and hindrance which she and her two daughters have sustained, he shall pay unto the hands of Bosvile, to be distributed at his discretion towards the charges of Margaret and the relief and preferment of the daughters, 500 marks, that is to say, 100 at the sealing and the rest in portions of 100 each, at days mentioned in obligations given. Also that John Darcy shall not show or procure any displeasure or inconvenience against Margaret West, Godfrey Bosvile, or George West, or any of the friends and kinsfolk of Lewis West, for any matter done before the date hereof; nor shall this indenture ever be alleged to the displeasure, hindrance, or slander of the said Margaret or any of her friends.[75]

Fortunately for the younger Darcy, his offence coincided with the brief revival of the Westminster sanctuary under Queen Mary. The London chronicler Henry Machyn noted George Darcy's presence in a procession led by the abbot of Westminster in December, where he was penitentially whipped for the killing. A little over a year

---

[75] Joseph Hunter, *South Yorkshire: The History and Topography of the Deanery of Doncaster*, 2 vols. (York, 1828–31), vol. 2, p. 173; Hunter is cited in Stone, *Crisis of the Aristocracy*, after a brief mention of the Darcy/West feud.

later he appeared in King's Bench, where Margaret's deputy launched an appeal against him, apparently offering to settle it by battle as in days gone by.[76] The battle seems not to have happened, but Margaret was still clearly seeking vengeance against some of her husband's killers, even while accepting compensation in lieu of prosecuting all of them.

We learn of a few more such settlements from litigation that resulted when they went awry. Elizabeth Symondes dropped an appeal against gentleman William Sculle for her husband's murder upon mediation and promise of compensation, though her son later had to sue the sureties to the original bond to secure the final payments.[77] Around 1530, Margaret Adams appealed two men as principals in her husband's slaying and several others as accessories. Arbitrators had her agree to let the suit fail in return for paying her legal costs as well as 20 marks. When the killers neglected to pay, she sued their sureties for debt in Chancery.[78] In the 1540s, Joan Curson dropped an appeal against her husband's killer after arbitration secured her a bond for payment of £100, but later sued the sureties when the final payments on the bond failed to arrive.[79] The killer of Elizabeth Stanger's husband obtained a royal pardon in 1556; to ensure his safety, he also had Lord Wharton negotiate a settlement with Elizabeth to have her drop her own appeal. Some time later, however, her son had to go to court to secure full payment of the bond from the killer's sureties.[80] These arbitrations left traces in the records only because they resulted in actions for debt. How many others may have happened, and for how long, we cannot know.[81]

We do know that a sense that widows merited compensation survived for a while yet, though. In Mary's reign, the justices endorsed a widow's right to appeal even as they determined that a widow who remarried could not then appeal the killing of her previous husband. They disagreed explicitly with the medieval legal text *Glanvill*, which had explained that women might appeal their husbands' murders because the two were 'one flesh', or '*una caro*'.[82] Instead, the chief justice now opined, 'the cause of an appeal is that she wants her husband; and the reason is, because the wife wanting a husband is not so well able to live'. A widow who appealed the death of one husband and then found another lost the grounds for her appeal, 'for the cause ceasing, the effect ceases'.[83] This decision and its rationale are interesting for a couple of reasons. It may have been a restriction of previous practice: in two thirteenth-century cases, widows had their appeals disqualified upon remarriage, but apparently because they had once more become *femes covert* and their new husbands failed to join the appeal, not because the remarriage itself proved a bar.[84]

---

[76] *Diary of Henry Machyn*, ed. Nichols, pp. 121, 165. My thanks to Shannon McSheffrey for this reference.

[77] C 1/363/66, date range 1504–15.   [78] C 1/685/36, 37.   [79] C 1/1114/60.

[80] C 1/1468/51. For the pardon, see *Calendar of the Patent Rolls...Philip and Mary* edited by M.S. Giuseppi, 4 vols. (London, 1937–39), vol. 3, p. 521.

[81] See William West, *The First Part of Simboleography* (London, 1615), pt. 1, section 169, sig. L3r and section 474, sig. Gg1v-Gg2r for templates of two releases of appeals in cases of homicide, one by a widow.

[82] *Glanvill*, ed. Hall, p. 174.   [83] 73 *ER* 853.

[84] *Select Pleas of the Crown*, edited by F.W. Maitland (London, Selden Society, vol. 153, 1888), no. 153 and pp. 98–9.

Otherwise it seems that the widows of murdered men who remarried could still launch an appeal. The judges in this Marian case cited a decision in a 1410 trial as establishing that a woman's appeal might be disabled by taking a second husband, though the record in that case is somewhat ambiguous. (Chief Justice Gascoigne observed of the matter that 'I have heard this often as a grand question, but never adjudged'.)[85] Whether or not the Marian decision represented a new limitation, however, the justices made clear their assumption that the appeal served to secure support for a woman deprived. Once she had a new husband to make her better 'able to live', though, the appeal had no ground. Whatever money might be extracted from the killer was viewed as support for a needy dependant, not a payment compensating for the loss or worth of the victim. Unlike such arrangements in other jurisdictions, no broad kin group was invoked in the collection or receipt of a payment; in England, it was sustenance for the immediate family alone.

The *Lawes Resolution of Women's Rights*, a remarkable legal treatise probably written late in Elizabeth's reign though not published until 1632, suggests both the continuing strength of the sense that widows merited payment and the discomfort with appeals. The author, signed only as T.E., called the appeal a 'vindicative' and 'revengeful action'. 'Feud was their mother', he noted. Appeal procedure began in attempts 'to appease such quarrels and capital enmities of families and kindreds as the northern men yet use and call feuds, which heretofore (but a long time since) were general, and overspread the realm'. He went into great detail on how appeals might be prosecuted and suggested their usefulness in prompting payment, but urged women not to pursue them to their deadly end. 'I advise a widow, that is full of spleen for the slaughter of her husband, . . . if composition be offered, not to refuse it . . . It is a more Christian thing to take five hundred pounds of a mankiller for a release, leaving him to agree with the king for his neck as good cheap as he can, than to seek blood and death (though of one which hath deserved it) in anger, malice and revengefulness.' Seek compensation, he urged, though the appeal itself remained 'but an image of deadly feud'.[86]

T.E.'s account, then, suggests a real distaste for the appeal, but also a continued belief that widows might rightly seek compensation. The trickle of such cases noted in the law reports and glimpsed elsewhere suggests that some widows pursued payment in this way for many years yet. The widow of the London fencer killed by Lord

---

[85] Seipp no. 1410.023 [11 Henry IV f. 48], from *Legal History: The Year Books*, compiled by David J. Seipp: http://www.bu.edu/phpbin/lawyearbooks/search.php. In later years, legal writers referenced this 1410 case as evidence for their verdict that 'the writ of appeal of a woman for the death of her husband is annex'd to her widowhood; so that if the wife of the deceased marry again, her appeal is gone': see Edward Coke, *Second Part*, p. 69, and Jacob, *Laws of Appeals*, p. 4. Whether it was understood as such before the Marian case is unclear. The report on one intervening case in 1481 refers to the 1410 report, but also in terms that suggest another interpretation: one justice noted that 'there has been a question where the widow sued the appeal for death of her husband . . . and the widow remarried another husband, now she has lost the advantage to sue execution, but as I understand to be law now, without doubt she can demand execution notwithstanding'. Seipp no. b1481.125 [21 Edw. IV, ff. 72b–73b].

[86] T.E., *Lawes Resolutions of Women's Rights*, pp. 373–5. For speculation on the author's identity, and the dating of the work's composition, see Wilfrid Prest, 'Law and Women's Rights in Early Modern England', *The Seventeenth Century* 6 (1991): pp. 173–5.

Sanquhar in 1612 reportedly pledged not to appeal in exchange for compensation, for example.[87] So, too, did the earl of Pembroke and Montgomery secure a release from threat of appeal from the widow of the man he killed in 1680—one assumes in exchange for financial support.[88]

Widows might seek compensation even without the dubious benefits of the appeal procedure, but had to find ways to do so that allowed for public prosecution. In 1653, two informants complained that Mark Badkin and his mother had taken money from Thomas Taylor in return for not testifying against him at the homicide trial for Badkin senior's death. According to the complaint, Taylor paid a bit of money upfront, more immediately after the assizes, and then made further payments on the May Day and Martinmas following. When hauled into court, the victim's son tried to argue that Taylor had paid his mother the money 'by way of gift, to relieve her because she was poor and had been sick long, but not in reference to his father's death'.[89] The widow of Edward Longueville's victim seems to have had a better idea of how this should be done. In 1676, in a petition for pardon from the penalties attendant on a manslaughter conviction, Longueville cited the 'reasonable provision' he had made for his victim's widow, alongside the standard invocations of the recommendations of people of good quality, his own youth, and the mix of provocation and sudden passion that led to the killing.[90] As a show of penitence or responsibility, the payment might help secure royal remission from the penalties of law, but should not be used to avoid them.

On the other hand, a few women—and men, too—continued to use the appeal to secure justice of a retributive rather than remunerative sort when dissatisfied with the outcome of a case by normal procedures. A participant in one Elizabethan killing claimed that the widow had pursued her appeal merely 'greedily seeking' blood and 'to revenge the same under colour and pretence of law'.[91] In the early seventeenth century, the killer of Reverend Storre obtained a royal pardon, but found that Storre's widow launched an appeal and adamantly refused his repeated offers to compound, despite her poverty and the needs of her five small children.[92]

How many women were able to use the appeal, or the threat of an appeal, to obtain either compensation or vengeance we cannot know. But use of the appeal did clearly decline, and with fewer appeals launched, one imagines that the threat of doing so lost its potency, too. The appeal survived, and continued to be used on occasion, but relied much more than before on the connivance of judges. When a jury convicted Mark Nurse's killer of manslaughter rather than murder in 1615, judges delayed giving sentence to allow Nurse's widow to appeal. Only when she

---

[87] Thomas Scot, *Philomythie* (London, 1616), sig. K4r.

[88] SP 29/415, f. 367. See also Holdsworth, *History of English Law*, vol. 2, p. 363 for a 1770 case in which the widow of one John Bigby compromised an appeal against his murderers in exchange for a payment of £350.

[89] ASSI 45/5/1, nos. 2 and 3. For a similar case, see also ASSI 45/1/5/75; citations from Vanessa McMahon, *Murder in Shakespeare's England* (London, 2004), p. 12.

[90] SP 44/28, f. 149. Thanks to Cynthia Herrup for this reference.

[91] STAC 5/W4/27, a case discussed in Hindle, ' "Bleedinge Afreshe"?', pp. 224–45.

[92] Francis Cartwright, *Three Bloody Murders* (London, 1613), sig. B2r. See also *The Life, Confession, and Heartie Repentance of Francis Cartwright* (London, 1621).

subsequently let the appeal drop—one assumes because she received payment—did the judges then allow him to plead his clergy and go free.[93] The widow of Henry Goring could bring an appeal against her husband's killer only because the judges delayed allowing him to plead his clergy.[94] So, too, with Widow Holborne's appeal against Sir Philip Lloyd, indicted for murder, convicted of manslaughter, but whose plea of clergy the judges delayed until Holborne appealed and (presumably) settled with Lloyd.[95] Similarly, the woman who secured the execution of her husband's killer at the Surrey assizes in 1680, despite his royal pardon, was helped by the judge's assistance in delaying the discharge. 'The crime and the fame of the person being notorious', the judge encouraged the widow to appeal. Passing sentence of death against the killer upon her suit, the judge reportedly told him 'he should certainly die and wished him to prepare for it, for that now his life was in the hands of that woman who had power to call for his execution when she pleased, which accordingly she did'.[96]

Two things (at least) stand out about this last case: one, the judge's intervention and two, its apparent novelty. The individual narrating this 1680 case in his newsletter clearly thought it noteworthy and unusual, 'having long wanted a precedent'.[97] A few cases can be found in the 1680s, but it does seem as if the increasing insistence upon public over private measures finally made the appeal all but an anachronism, with only rare uses thereafter largely reliant upon the good will of judges who used it to complement and correct public justice when they thought it had gone awry. In a sense, then, we see in the appeal's attenuated survival—not just in its decline— signs of the triumph of 'public justice' and the criminalization of homicide.

With all the easy logic afforded by hindsight, one cannot help but think that civil suits for damages for wrongful death would have done the job here, but in fact, the one reported case that might have opened that door instead served as the precedent cited to keep it shut for centuries to come. In 1607, one Higgins tried to sue Butcher, his wife's killer, for civil damages—perhaps opting for this route as husbands had never been able to appeal their wives' killers—but the judges said no. If the wife had survived her beating, she would have had a personal tort against Butcher, but that tort died with her. The law did allow a husband or master damages for injuries done to his wife or servant if those injuries resulted in a loss of services, but not for their deaths. With death, the judges decided, the injury became 'an offence to the Crown, being converted into felony, and that drowns the particular offence and private wrong offered to the master before'.[98] The wrong to the Crown trumped wrongs to the individual.

[93] *CAR* Sussex (James), no. 301.

[94] 87 *ER* 101. For the initial trial, see *Old Bailey Proceedings Online*, t16850716–10.

[95] 89 *ER* 870.

[96] *Calendar of State Papers... Charles II: Domestic Series, 1679–80*, edited by F.H. Blackburne Daniell (London, 1915), p. 623 (28 August 1680).

[97] Ibid.

[98] 80 *ER* 61. See Wex. S. Malone, 'The Genesis of Wrongful Death', *Stanford Law Review* 17.6 (1965): pp. 1043–76. Malone notes that in some of the colonies, this 'felony merger' doctrine was made to allow some exceptions, but that in England itself, the right to sue for wrongful death was not discussed in reported cases after Higgins for some two hundred years. Only in the nineteenth century

Two cases at the end of the period under study here demonstrate the still conflicted responses of judges to the appeal and all it represented, but also some of the intellectual distance that had been travelled. One closed the loophole that had enabled judges to delay accepting pleas of benefit of clergy to allow an appeal to proceed, thus further decreasing the likelihood of a successful appeal to secure either compensation or revenge. But the other offered a striking endorsement of the procedure.

The first, Armstrong *v* Lisle (1696), followed from Thomas Lisle's killing of one Richard Armstrong and his conviction for manslaughter rather than murder. Unhappy with this outcome, the victim's brother, John, sued an appeal before Lisle had read his book and had his claim to benefit of clergy accepted. All the judges agreed that a successful claim of clergy served as a bar to an appeal, but did they really have the right to delay allowance of clergy? They acknowledged the reported cases that had offered them this window, but described them as history rather than as binding precedents.[99] Offering a lengthy discussion of appeals, and emphasizing the importance of the 1487 statute, Chief Justice Holt observed that he had previously argued this issue both ways and cited recent examples of cases in which it had been affirmed that the courts might delay calling convicts to judgement to hinder them from pleading their clergy and thus to allow an appeal to proceed. Holt now maintained that he had always been unsatisfied with the idea that justices might arbitrarily decide whether and when to allow a plea of clergy. Beyond this specific point, he argued that proceedings in the interest of the 'public justice of the kingdom' should always take precedence over appeals, for 'the appellant seeks only revenge...without regard to the publick'. Justices should not hinder proceedings upon indictment, or hinder a convict from pleading his clergy, to ease an appeal. The 1487 statute was 'severe', he wrote, in subjecting someone who was acquitted to a second trial. At the time, such a severity might have been necessary to allow trial on indictment to take primacy over the appeal without denying this ancient privilege to the victim. But severe it was, and judges in this more enlightened age ought to avoid having an individual tried twice for the same offence. 'For the interest of the Crown, and the sake of publick justice, the Court ought to try the prisoner upon the indictment rather than upon the appeal'—and a man owed benefit of clergy upon that trial ought to be able to have it.[100]

---

did wrongful death statutes being to allow compensatory and/or punitive damages for homicide, or in response to negligent homicides, especially rail fatalities, i.e. the Fatal Accidents Act of 1846 (which was tied to the statute that finished off deodands). See Finkelstein, 'The Goring Ox', pp. 169–290. See, too, the complaint of the Interregnum law reformer William Sheppard, who noted that 'it is an hard law that not recompense is given to a man's wife or children for killing of him, whereas for the beating or wounding of him while he was alive, he should have had recompense for the wrong': *England's Balme* (London, 1657), p. 148.

99 In particular, Roy *v* Tothill, 82 *ER* 1129; see also 90 *ER* 615.

100 84 *ER* 1095–1108; see also 90 *ER* 300. Note, though, that despite Holt's assertions about the severity of using the appeal to re-try someone already acquitted of a murder, he presided over one such case in 1709, in which the accused, acquitted on indictment, was convicted and executed after the subsequent trial on appeal. 88 *ER* 999.

When discussing another contested case just four years later, however, Holt offered a rather more positive assessment of the appeal. The well-connected barrister, JP, and MP Spencer Cowper had been indicted and acquitted for the murder of Sarah Stout in a case that received much public attention. Sarah's mother then tried launching an appeal, but could not do so in her own name since she was not Sarah's heir; she had the writ done up in that heir's name, but the heir was underage and she was not his legal guardian. In the proceedings to determine whether the appeal could continue or be relaunched despite the irregularities, one justice reportedly argued 'that an appeal was a revengeful, odious prosecution, and therefore deserved no encouragement'. Chief Justice Holt, 'with great vehemence and zeal', wondered why so many deemed the appeal 'an odious prosecution'. He noted that it 'tends to the support of families and is of obvious necessity in some cases'. Even more boldly, he described it as 'a noble remedy, and a badge of the rights and liberties of an Englishman'. As such, he thought, 'judges ought to encourage appeals'.[101]

CONCLUSION

The appeal continued to find the occasional defender, sometimes grudging, sometimes effusive, but had been brought more firmly into line with royal justice. In his influential *Principles of Penal Law* (1771), for example, William Eden allowed that the appeal, while 'barbarous' and 'gothic', might nonetheless be at times 'an essential safeguard to the rights of the people'.[102] A culture of reconciliation and compensation persisted well beyond the twelfth-century reforms, but for homicide came largely to an end in the early modern period; it could not survive the increasingly strong belief that private settlements for deaths ran counter to 'the interest of the Crown and the sake of publick justice'.

A somewhat similar change took hold in Scotland, too, but one informative in its differences. As Wormald documented (paraphrasing Maitland), 'with marvellous suddenness' the Scots moved from expecting reparations to demanding death. They moved from an act in 1641 that reiterated earlier bans on royal remissions for homicide without assythment first being made to families, insisting upon the claims of kin to compensation, to one in 1649 that banned remissions altogether for any crime otherwise punishable with death. That very Calvinist parliament had decided to enforce the biblical injunctions that blood called for blood. Hearkening to passages such as Numbers 35:31, which inveighed that no recompense or satisfaction shall be taken for the life of a murderer, the measure noted that with remissions and respites, 'God's law is presumptuously dispensed with, the law and practice of the

---

[101] Rex *v* Toler (1700), 91 *ER* 1270 and Stout *v* Towler, 88 *ER* 1388. For this case, see Julia Rudolph, 'Gender and the Development of Forensic Science: A Case Study', *English Historical Review* 123 (2008): pp. 924–46, and Mark Knights, *The Devil in Disguise: Deception, Delusion, and Fanaticism in the Early English Enlightenment* (Oxford, 2011), pp. 10ff.

[102] William Eden, *Principles of Penal Law* (London, 1771), p. 184. For other, sometimes more effusive encomiums of the appeals, see Holdsworth, *History of English Law*, vol. 2, pp. 362–4, and the work he cites, John Lord Campbell, *Lives of the Lord Chancellors* (London, 1847), vol. 6, p. 114.

land made useless [and] ... a door opened to the committing of many heinous crimes without fear through hope of impunity'.[103] In this, the Scots echoed Swedes and other Protestants in endorsing the biblical directives that killers must be killed, at least in theory if not always in practice. In Scotland, as in Sweden and elsewhere, authorities sought a remarkably quick shift from a culture of composition to one in which death was the mandated punishment for all homicides.[104]

In England, as we will see, manslaughter verdicts themselves came in for some such criticism, in allowing killers to live. But their availability had already done much to ensure that killers would at least answer to the king's justice in one way or another—in part and perhaps unexpectedly by serving as a mechanism that judges used to limit recourse to the appeal. English law had long been fairly distinctive within Europe in not having an open, licit way of securing composition or compensation for homicides; the appeal had served as a safety valve, in part by allowing support for widows and children, but without endorsing any notion of a broader kin responsibility or loss. Over the sixteenth and seventeenth centuries, most other parts of Europe moved away from reparations, too. English law would once again become distinctive, though, in formalizing a punishment less than death for most instances of manslaughter as distinguished from murder, a change that oddly and indirectly helped further restrict the use of appeals as a public/private hybrid. Compensation and the appeal persisted longer than one might have expected, thanks in large part to the efforts and needs of widows, but under tighter judicial control and as an ever fainter 'image of deadly feud'.

---

[103] Wormald, 'Bloodfeud', pp. 93–5. See *RPS*, A1641/1/144, Act Prohibiting Remissions Granted without Letters of Assythment; 1649/1/117, Act gainst Remissions and Respites; 1649/1/118, Act anent the Several Degrees of Casual Homicide. Notably, the latter allowed that in non-capital homicides, the court might impose a fine 'to the use of the deceased's wife and bairns or nearest of kin'. Re: Numbers 35:31, the Geneva Bible referred to 'recompense' while the King James Version referred to 'satisfaction'.

[104] See Krogh, *Lutheran Plague*, pp. 106ff. While Krogh's book focuses on Danish developments, he presents a compelling argument for broad confessional differences in the laws and punishments relating to homicide, and also offers a useful entry point to works by Eva Österberg, Arne Jansson, Rudolf Thunader, and Jan Eric Almquist on the distinctive Swedish turn to Mosaic law in 1608 and its effects.

4

'That Saucy Paradox'
The Politics of Duelling in Early Modern England

The challenge private settlements posed to the triumph of public justice was one thing, but what of private vengeance? In the early seventeenth century, some fights between certain kinds of men took on the shape and label of 'the duel', and became the subject of much discussion. In one of the more famous accounts of such a combat, Sir Edward Sackville narrated his 1613 killing of Edward Bruce, the second lord of Kinloss and son of one of King James's most valued advisors. While in France, Bruce heard that Sackville had spoken ill of him and responded with a letter that challenged Sackville to fight. Bruce expressed his confidence that 'your honour gives you the same courage to do me right, that it did to do me wrong'. He urged Sackville to choose the weapons and to pick a place and time to meet. 'By doing this', he wrote, 'you will shorten revenge, and clear the idle opinion the world hath of both our worths.' Sackville readily accepted. The men decided not to meet in England, where the authorities might hinder their plans, but in a border village near Bergen-op-Zoom in the Netherlands, where the victor could easily fly for safety to another jurisdiction. Finally, in August 1613, the two met, accompanied by their seconds and their surgeons. Sackville later reported that they had 'fully resolved (God forgive us!) to despatch each other by what means we could'. Bruce ran him nearly through and with another stroke severed one of Sackville's fingers. Yet Sackville rallied, and in the end, he said, 'easily became master of him'. Bruce's surgeon ran to help, but found the nobleman 'weltering in his blood and past all expectation of life'.[1]

After killing Bruce, Sackville deemed it prudent to remain for a time on the continent: Bruce's friends and family reportedly threatened vengeance. The encounter between Sackville and Bruce could not have been more carefully premeditated; though holding the fight on foreign soil allowed Sackville to evade the dangers of England's common law, some people might well deem him a rank murderer nonetheless. Intended to 'shorten revenge' and assuage injured honour, the combat now exposed Sackville to reprisals and aspersions that he hoped his narrative of the killing might help to allay.

---

[1] Quotations are from the letters as reprinted by Richard Steele in *The Guardian*, nos. 129 (8 August 1713) and 133 (13 August 1713); the letters also appear, with minor variations, in *HMC Portland* (London, 1923), IX, 53–6. See also the account in Huntington Library, EL 244, which diverges in some respects from the narrative presented by Sackville.

Reportedly seeing the killing and its narration as affronts to his own honour, King James responded in part by issuing proclamations against this new phenomenon coming to be known as duelling. He denounced as a 'saucy paradox' gentlemen's mistaken belief that they could take vengeance into their own hands, 'the revenge of all private wrongs only belonging to Us (under GOD), into whose hand he hath put the sword for that purpose'.[2] But that was not the only paradox in play: James in short order forgave Sackville, as he would some other men who killed in fights deemed duels. Sackville, soon earl of Dorset, became a trusted privy councillor and ardent defender of royal prerogatives.[3] Like others, James repeatedly denounced duelling in the strongest terms in the abstract, but also repeatedly excused individual instances.

Another seeming paradox is the historiographical convention that the advent of duelling actually helped limit elite men's violence. Those who have studied the duel have often treated it as a civilizing agent that newly restrained and replaced the violence of the medieval feud. Lawrence Stone, for example, depicted 'the development in the minds of the landed classes of a new ethical code—the code of the duel' as 'a powerful cause of the decline of casual and unregulated violence involving the clash of groups of retainers, servants, and tenants'. Thanks to duelling, '[v]iolence in word or deed was thus regulated, codified, restricted, sterilized'.[4] In his analysis of the intellectual context of the duel, Markku Peltonen reiterated the notion that duelling helped limit and channel elite violence. He argued that the duel was not a remnant of a medieval honour culture, but that it arrived in England together with the Italian Renaissance notion of courtly conduct; rather than being a reaction against Renaissance civility, it served as one of its vehicles and thus helped minimize violence.[5]

Some scholars have, however, queried the supposed civilizing influence of duelling. Roger Manning portrayed the duel's antecedents and effects rather differently than Peltonen had. Manning agreed that Englishmen picked up the duel while

---

[2] James VI/I, *A Publication of his Maties Edict and Severe Censure against Private Combats and Combatants* (London, 1613 [1614]), p. 56; *SRP*, vol. 1, p. 296 (no. 132).

[3] His biographer deems him a 'constitutional royalist': David L. Smith, 'Sackville, Edward, fourth earl of Dorset (1590–1652)', *ODNB*.

[4] Stone, *Crisis of the Aristocracy*, pp. 242–50, quotes at pp. 243 and 244. Assertions of the duel's effects in limiting violence by replacing earlier, more violent retributive forms are strongest and perhaps most accurate in reference to Italian vendettas. See, in particular, Muir, *Mad Blood Stirring*. Much of the discussion of duelling as a civilizer remains rooted in the work of Elias, *The Civilizing Process*. For duelling, see also Donna Andrew, 'The Code of Honour and its Critics: The Opposition to Duelling in England, 1700–1850', *Social History* 5 (1980): pp. 409–34; V.C. Kiernan, *The Duel in European History* (Oxford, 1988); François Billacois, *The Duel: Its Rise and Fall in Early Modern France*, trans. Trista Selous (New Haven, CT, 1990); David Quint, 'Duelling and Civility in Sixteenth-Century Italy', *I Tatti Studies* 7 (1997): pp. 231–78; Markku Peltonen, *The Duel in Early Modern England: Civility, Politeness and Honour* (Cambridge, 2003); Roger B. Manning, *Swordsmen: The Martial Ethos in the Three Kingdoms* (Oxford, 2003); Jennifer Low, *Manhood and the Duel: Masculinity and the Duel: Masculinity in Early Modern Drama and Culture* (London, 2003); and Robert Shoemaker, *The London Mob: Violence and Disorder in Eighteenth-Century England* (Hambledon, 2004). Also useful in some respects, though its narrative of English developments confuses them with French measures, is James Kelly, *'That Damn'd Thing Called Honour': Duelling in Ireland, 1570–1860* (Cork, 1995).

[5] Peltonen, *The Duel*.

abroad but saw its fast diffusion in late sixteenth-century England as a product of a 'resuscitated honour culture', a remilitarization and 'rechivalrization' among men of the late Elizabethan aristocracy that produced more, not less, violence.[6] In his studies of violence in early modern France, moreover, Stuart Carroll has demonstrated beyond doubt that duelling did not always 'civilize', if by that we mean a lowering of levels of violence. He argued that duels did not replace feuds, but co-existed with them as elements of a wider, shifting 'system of vindicatory violence'.[7] Treating France as the exception to the rule, Carroll maintains that the introduction of the duel caused 'a huge escalation of elite violence, in which tens of thousands died in the century before 1660'.[8] English duels never numbered so high: while Stone made no claims that his count was complete, that his extensive search through newsletters and correspondence of the 1580s to late 1620s found mention of only some forty-seven duels and challenges involving aristocrats suggests a much lower incidence than in France.[9] Indeed, Linda Pollock briefly queries the duel's supposed civilizing effects in England precisely because so few seem to have happened there.[10]

True, duels had the potential to 'individualize' violence in ways that feuds—almost inherently collective endeavours—did not. In this way, we might see duels as limiting at least the numbers of participants in retributive encounters. Yet, one suspects that deadly feuds pitting one group against another rarely began over the sorts of slight that so often triggered duels. (The duke of Albemarle, we are told, challenged the earl of Tankerville to fight when the latter made fun of his gun.)[11] Both feuds and duels constituted vindicatory means of asserting honour and avenging injuries, but the sense of proportionality that historians of the feud have seen in their subject was often altogether absent from duels.[12] Feuds typically began with offences that might be deemed criminal, but duels started from lesser affronts. That the fights labelled as duels in early modern England so frequently lacked the formalities and conventions enjoined by theorists and seen more regularly in later duels also prompts a pause. We might, too, take more notice of the contemporaries who held duelling responsible for a truly alarming increase in untimely, bloody deaths. In his proclamations on the subject, King James asserted that duels aggravated the sorts of sentiment that lay behind feuds. 'Quarrels', he wrote, 'do not only become immortal but multiply.' He believed that with the

---

[6] Manning, *Swordsmen*, pp. 195, 243.

[7] Stuart Carroll, *Blood and Violence in Early Modern France* (Oxford, 2006), p. 9.

[8] Carroll, 'Introduction', *Cultures of Violence: Interpersonal Violence in Historical Perspective* (Basingstoke, 2007), p. 29.

[9] Stone, *Crisis of the Aristocracy*, pp. 245, 770.

[10] Linda Pollock, 'Honor, Gender, and Reconciliation in Elite Culture, 1570–1700', *Journal of British Studies* 46.1 (2007): pp. 3–29, at 7.

[11] He called it a 'coxcomb's fancy'. Richard L. Greaves, 'Grey, Ford, earl of Tankerville (*bap.* 1655, *d.* 1701)', *ODNB*.

[12] See Hyams, *Rancor and Reconciliation*, esp. pp. 8–9, and updated in Hyams, 'Was There Really Such a Thing as Feud in the High Middle Ages?', pp. 151–76. See also the introduction to *Feud in Medieval and Early Modern Europe*, ed. Netterstrøm and Poulsen.

advent of the duel, 'slaughters... have been strangely multiplied and increased in these later times'.[13] Others throughout the period voiced similar fears.

Ultimately, the question of whether the duel limited or encouraged deadly violence in early modern England seems impossible to answer with certainty. The question retains its significance, however, because studies of declining homicide levels over the early modern period regularly identify the sharpest declines in fatal conflicts between unrelated men and in killings by members of the elite.[14] The timing of the advent of duelling as a cultural phenomenon tempts one to look for links. Perhaps, though, it was not so much the duel itself that deterred violent encounters or offered a less deadly form of conflict, but the ways in which contemporaries defined this new phenomenon and responded to it that contributed to a gradual shift in elite men's violence. One must at least avoid the temptations to dismiss duelling as an 'excrescence... of an atavistic class', to romanticize it as something prettier than it was, or to reify it as a concrete, measurable thing, and instead try to determine what cultural work 'the duel' was made to do in its own time and place. Whatever else the advent of the duel may have done, people's use of the concept more firmly reoriented discussions of vengeance and violence towards the state. This chapter suggests that the conceptualization of certain kinds of conflict as duels created a special category for elite men's violence, one in some senses valorized, yet also marked as being 'private' and hence especially antagonistic to the king and to the 'public justice' he claimed to enforce.

Manning and Peltonen both mention the potentially political, subversive aspects of duelling: both the 'chivalric' and 'courtesy' strands of discourse about duelling could be seen to undermine royal authority.[15] Certainly, the men who penned King James's proclamations had no doubt that duelling denied the king's authority over wrongdoing, and that it undermined the 'public Justice of the State'.[16] In charges brought in the Court of Star Chamber, Attorney General Sir Francis Bacon described the new problem of duelling as a 'great and imminent peril to the state', a 'licentious abuse and presumption', and 'a matter full of derogation to your Majesty's imperial power'.[17] Duels took place at the shifting intersection of public and private. These contests challenged the state's claim to monopolize deadly force and to decide what constituted legitimate force more generally. Indeed, they forced clearer, stronger articulations of this claim. The growth of the early modern state helped limit interpersonal homicides by coercive, often brutal assertions of rights to determine the legitimate uses of such violence; it also relied on gentler means, particularly when dealing with its more powerful members, through elevating the status of the law and its agents. This chapter suggests that the creation of the duel as an abstraction to describe certain kinds of masculine violence, and the responses it engendered, assisted in this development.

---

[13] *SRP*, vol. 1, pp. 296, 303 (nos. 132 and 136).
[14] See, for example, Eisner, 'Long Term Historical Trends in Violent Crime', pp. 108ff.
[15] Peltonen, *The Duel*, p. 14; Manning, *Swordsmen*, ch. 7.
[16] *SRP*, vol. 1, p. 304 (no. 136).   [17] STAC 8/20/6 and 8/23/5.

INVENTING THE DUEL

How did contemporaries—and how ought we to—conceptualize the early modern duel? 'The duel' is not a stable entity with a continuous history: what went by that label in the early modern era differed from the duels of the eighteenth and nineteenth centuries, and from the single combats of earlier years. Indeed, the very novelty of the label attached to these fights alerts us to a shift: the word 'duel' entered the English language in the late 1500s and acquired common currency only in the early 1600s.[18] Some commentators, both early modern and modern, saw the duel of honour as an evolution of earlier judicial and chivalric combats, a cousin of the joust, rooted in and preserving elements of chivalry. Yet, others, in contrast, sharply and convincingly distinguished the duel of honour from these earlier forms, with some seeing the duel as a new import from the continent that embodied new notions of civil courtesy distinct from the honour codes of the feudal past.[19] The duel of honour, as conceptualized and as practised, did differ fundamentally from trial by combat and from chivalric competitions. But it also differed from the classic duel of honour as first conceptualized and practised on the continent. The key difference that many contemporaries chose to highlight? As they insisted, these other combats were public and explicitly licensed by a recognized authority. The English duel, in contrast, was private and unauthorized.

On the continent early duels of honour did have public license. French kings and Italian dukes set aside venues and days for such trials of truth and honour. In one of the better-known cases, for example, upon petitions from Guy Chabot de Jarnac, Henri II assigned a time and place for him to defend his honour against the seigneur de Châtaigneraie; in July 1547, Jarnac killed his opponent in front of the king, the court, and many others.[20] Such sanctioned, scripted combats—precisely the sorts of contests praised by Renaissance theorists of the duel—might in some ways be seen as an evolution of the chivalric or judicial combats of the past. But they had ended on the continent even before the duel appeared in England. The Council of Trent's decree against such fights, alongside growing royal and ducal discomfort with the practice, drove continental duellists into the fields and back

---

[18] The *Oxford English Dictionary* dates it to 1605. A search on *EEBO* produces a few earlier uses of the word: among these results, it first appears in L.H., *A Dictionarie French and English* (London, 1571) as a word needing translation. Sir Thomas Smith's *De Republica Anglorum*, published in 1583 but written in the 1560s, used the Latin *duellum* to refer to the French trials by combat and use of champions. Anthony Wingfield's *A True Coppie of a Discourse Written by a Gentleman, employed in the late voyage of Spaine and Portugall* (London, 1589) was the first, in an *EEBO* text, to use 'duel' in English, and in its current sense of a combat between two over a matter of truth or honour. (It should be noted, though, that text searches on *EEBO* are not comprehensive, and as such only suggestive, not indicative.)

[19] For a particularly strong statement of the novelty of the duel and its continental origins, see Peltonen, *The Duel*.

[20] Billacois, *The Duel... in Early Modern France*, pp. 49–56. Henri Morel, 'La Fin du Duel Judiciare en France et la Naissance du Point d'Honneur', *Revue Historique du Droit Français et Étranger* 42 (1964): pp. 575–639 argues that the Jarnac combat should in fact be seen as a judicial combat rather than a duel of honour, as the underlying dispute began over accusations of incest, a capital offence, thus serving to emphasize the difficulty in distinguishing these forms of conflict on the continent.

alleys.[21] As David Quint notes, proponents of the 'true' duel of honour disdained such developments: Annibale Romei deemed the secret and unsanctioned duel a 'diabolic invention', far inferior to the proper duel, which one fought before one's prince and others competent to judge one's merit.[22]

In England, such public, royally licensed combats had no recent precedents. Early modern writers had difficulty finding in English annals any chivalric contests intended as fights to the death. The most recent encounter they identified as such had happened in 1441, when Sir Richard Woodville fought a Spanish knight before the court, though the king stopped them after the third blow.[23] An attempt was made in 1632 to revive trial by combat before the Earl Marshal, but ended when the common law judges insisted that if either combatant killed the other he would be found guilty of murder.[24] Judicial combats had been used in the distinctive customs of the border against Scotland to settle cross-border allegations, and seem to have had a slightly longer life there than elsewhere, but on the border, too, such licensed fights seem to have ended by the second half of the fifteenth century.[25] Common law had allowed trial by battle both in Common Pleas in real causes and in King's Bench for criminal appeals. A judicial ordeal akin to the more infamous ordeals by fire and water, trial by battle had been thought to reveal the verdict of God in any particular case and could be fought by proxy with champions.[26] But this, too, had become increasingly rare over the fourteenth century and had all but disappeared in the fifteenth: the final criminal appeals to be settled by battle seem to have been those fought by approvers, with the last found in 1456.[27] The practice had not been formally abolished, though: Elizabeth's judges found with some consternation that they could not stop an appeal over a disputed parcel of land from proceeding to such a trial in 1571, and needed the queen herself to intervene with a last minute order to desist.[28] Judges similarly busied themselves in 1638 to find a loophole to prevent another property dispute from going to trial by battle.[29]

---

[21] See Quint, 'Duelling and Civility', pp. 247, 264, and Billacois, *The Duel... in Early Modern France*, pp. 83–111.

[22] Quint, 'Duelling and Civility', p. 264.

[23] See Anon., *Booke of Honor and Armes* (London, 1590), p. 88, and copied in William Segar, *Honor Military and Ciuil* (London, 1602), p. 137. See also Jean d'Espagne, *Anti-Duello: The Anatomie of Duells* (London, 1632), pp. 44, 63.

[24] *Cases in the High Court of Chivalry, 1634–1640*, edited by Richard Cust and Andrew Hopper (London, Harleian Society, n.s., vol. 18, 2006), pp. xviii–xix.

[25] Neville, *Violence, Custom and Law*, pp. 6, 40, 76–7, 134, 190. Meikle notes one later incident, in 1586, in which families on either side of the border arranged such a combat to settle a dispute, but they had no licence, and the authorities prohibited them from meeting: *A British Frontier*, p. 240. As she notes elsewhere, though, Scottish authorities did still offer some such licences within Scotland itself, citing an example from 1595.

[26] Robert Bartlett, *Trial by Fire and Water: The Medieval Judicial Ordeal* (Oxford, 1986), ch. 6.

[27] Hamil, 'Approvers', p. 256.

[28] Manning, *Swordsmen*, p. 220. A judicial combat did take place in Elizabethan Ireland, however: in September 1583, the Lords Justices in Dublin wrote to the Privy Council to note that they had allowed a combat enjoined between Conor M'Cormac O'Conor and Teige M'Gilpatrick O'Conor when they accused each other of treason. One died ('a very good riddance') but the other, while injured, survived ('the more was the pity'): SP 63/104, ff. 163–163d.

[29] The case was between Ralph Claxton and Richard Lilburne (father of the more famous John). Judges initially hoped that the hiring of paid champions might be used as reason to prohibit the

Even when single combats had the sanction of law, then, the authorities proved reluctant to allow them. Early modern English monarchs authorized nothing resembling the Jarnac combat. They had jousts, but nothing more. Such jousts could prove deadly, of course, but the combatants intended them as entertaining displays of martial prowess, not as ways to prove innocence or avenge a slight. The classic, continental form of the duel of honour, held publicly and licitly, which we might well see as an intermediate form growing from judicial trials of truth and chivalric displays of courage and ability, did not exist in England. In England, as so many contemporaries insisted, the duel was always somewhat covert, private rather than public, and unauthorized.

When early modern writers debated whether or not the duel of honour grew out of these other, earlier forms of combat, they often did so in efforts either to legitimize or delegitimize the duel. Admittedly, not all advocates of the duel saw such links or thought them useful to authorize their endeavours. An Italian fencing master who settled in London, Vincentio Saviolo, sought to counter objections that to be lawful a duel had to be licensed, as had been the combats of days gone by: he did so simply by asserting that those were entirely different sorts of combats that operated under different rules. He then adroitly bypassed the issue of princely permission altogether. The anonymous author of the 1590 *Booke of Honor and Armes*, in contrast, tried to graft the new combats on to the ancient and undoubtedly lawful trial by combat. 'Albeit I am not ignorant that public combats are in this age either rarely or never granted', he wrote, 'yet for that...no providence can prevent the questions and quarrels that daily happen among gentlemen and others professing arms, it shall not be amiss, but rather behooveful that all men should be fully informed what injury is, and how to repulse it, when to fight, and when to rest satisfied.' He insisted that 'trial by arms is not only natural, but also necessary and allowable'. Indeed, he treated these combats not only as lawful, though admittedly not legal, but as outgrowths of the old trial by battle that remained in some ways similar and alternative to court trials: as in days gone by, combat constituted a 'kind of judgement', with proofs and defenders and challengers as in any court. He compared the 'padrines', or seconds, to lawyers, performing the same offices as advocates in a court room. He referenced Castiglione and the newer modes of continental courtesy, but focused throughout on the combats, jousts, and triumphs of the English past to situate contemporary duels.[30]

A meeting of the Society of Antiquaries in 1601 drew forth a range of responses, but most carefully distinguished between 'lawful combat'—that is, the now largely defunct trial by battle—and the contemporaneous 'unlawful combats', treating the

---

combat, but ultimately had to settle for citing an error in the record, which one reporter thought 'wilfully done': DUL, MSP 52, ff. 43r–46v, 123r–124v. Only in 1819 did parliament formally abolish trial by battle, along with the abolition of appeals of felony, after one defendant in an appeal insisted on his right to defend himself in this manner: 59 Geo. III c. 46. See Hall, ed., *Trial of Abraham Thornton.*

[30] Anon., *Booke of Honor and Armes*, quote at sig. A2v. This work is sometimes thought to be by William Segar. At least, Segar's *Honor Military and Ciuill* offered a similar reading of the duel's history (e.g. pp. 115, 131ff).

latter as innovations with no real roots in native traditions.[31] In his own censure of duelling while prosecuting a case in Star Chamber, Sir Francis Bacon denied the links altogether. He and the judges who accepted his argument insisted that these 'private duels or combats were of another nature from the combats which have been allowed by the law as well of this land as of other nations for the trial of rights or appeals. For that those combats receive direction and authority from the law, whereas contrariwise these spring only from the unbridled humours of private men.'[32]

In his critique of duelling and the 'outrageous vanity of duellists', Sir Walter Raleigh did depict the duel as an offspring of judicial combats, but one of such a bastardly nature as not to live up to the parentage. In his description of the medieval judicial combat, a man accused of treason, murder, or some other offence that deserved death had to accuse his accuser of lying in order to deny the deed. After he had thus given his accuser 'the lie', the authorities then moved to a trial—sometimes by combat—to determine who spoke the truth. But, Raleigh wrote, the new fondness for duelling was for something rather different. He believed that it arose when King Francis I of France accused Emperor Charles V of lying after some breach of faith, and challenged him to personal combat. 'From this beginning', Raleigh opined, 'is derived a challenge of combat, grounded upon none of those occasions that were known to the ancients. For the honour of nations, the trial of right, the wager upon champions, or the objection and refutation of capital offences are none of them, nor all of them together, the argument of half so many duels as are founded upon mere private anger.' The causes that now drove men to fight festered from private, petty grudges and hurts. He insisted that 'the acting of a private combat, for a private respect, and more commonly a frivolous one, is not an action of virtue'. Unlike the public combats of yore, these private combats not only served private interests rather than public, but also tended to the diminishment of the public good.[33]

Thus, the fights called duels in early modern England differed, and were generally seen to differ, both from the earlier trials by combat that had a native ancestry and from the classic, early duels of honour that had a history on the continent. Commentators as diverse as Romei, Raleigh, and Bacon wrote of various elements that distinguished the duel as then practised from these other forms—the purpose, the nature of the underlying dispute, and so forth—but all noted as a key distinction the publicity and authorization of the one, and the private and unauthorized nature of the other. They repeatedly invoked the binary of public and private, locating the duel as 'private' both in the sense of being hidden from public scrutiny, and even more in being concerned with individual and particular interests rather than those of the 'public' more generally.

Commentators also broadly agreed in seeing the duel as intrinsically aristocratic. In one sense, we might say it was nothing of the kind. One can readily find

---

[31] T. Hearne, ed., *A Collection of Curious Discourses*, 2 vols. (London, 1771), vol. 2, pp. 172–215.

[32] Bacon, *The Charge of Sir Francis Bacon... touching duelis*, quote at p. 55. See also Bacon's memo, 'A proposition for the repressing of singular combats and duels', in James Spedding, ed., *The Letters and the Life of Francis Bacon*, 7 vols. (London, 1861–72), vol. 4, p. 397.

[33] Walter Raleigh, *The History of the World* (London, 1628), book 5, cap. 3, sect. XVII.

examples of men below the ranks of the gentry engaging in what they, and we, might call duels. In 1608, for example, Ralph Walker, a tailor in Bishop Auckland, died from a rapier thrust received in a prearranged fight.[34] Alexandra Shepard begins her account of masculinity and violence with a challenge to a duel between a tanner and a waterman, drawn from the Cambridge University court papers.[35] Other records do not tell whether the combatants issued challenges, but nonetheless describe deadly fights between men of moderate means using weapons that proved not to be the preserve of gentlemen alone. In 1630, for example, John Eve, described as a yeoman, killed John Remington with a rapier after the two argued about a game gone wrong.[36] Butcher Robert Strutt, accompanied by a tailor and a labourer, killed an unknown man with his rapier.[37] In 1637, labourer John Jasper gave Edward Wilkes a mortal wound in 'the left pap' with a rapier thrust.[38] The basic pattern of violent behaviour underlying the duel appeared among men of all sorts.

Yet, as conceptualized and either celebrated or condemned, the duel was almost by definition something fought by men of honour. Duelling was done by the armigerous, by those for whom the bearing of arms was itself a claim to status and privilege.[39] The *Booke of Honor and Armes* asserted that as 'the trial of arms appertaineth only to gentlemen, … it were not fit that any persons of meaner condition should thereunto be admitted'.[40] William Segar and Vincentio Saviolo repeated this limitation, noting as well that duels could not be fought by traitors, deserters, or any 'other man exercising an occupation or trade, unfit and unworthy a gentleman or soldier'. According to these writers, the only people born outside the ranks of the aristocracy who could participate were men who had taken on the profession of arms.[41] Bacon acknowledged that other men engaged in similar activities, but focused on the 'men of birth and quality', whom he hoped would abandon the practice once 'vilified and come so low as to barbers surgeon and butchers and such base mechanical persons'. Star Chamber judges described duelling as 'an offence which reigneth chiefly among persons of honour and quality'. The king's councillors concentrated their efforts on dissuading 'noble persons, or persons of quality' from challenging each other to such bloody private contests.[42]

---

[34] DUL, CCB B/218/4/12.

[35] Alexandra Shepard, *Meanings of Manhood in Early Modern England* (Oxford, 2003), p. 127. See, too, Garthine Walker's discussion of Cheshire court records, which notes that men of all status descriptions engaged in fights very much like duels: *Crime, Gender and Social Order*, pp. 37–8.

[36] Essex Record Office, T/A 418/105/13. Walker notes that references to weapons in indictments cannot always be taken at face value, as reference to 'swords' might only be a residue of the need, before 1545, to specify the use of weapons to support allegations of force and violence. (Walker, *Crime, Gender and Social Order*, p. 28.) The rarer and more specific mentions of 'rapiers', though, can presumably be more safely taken as accurate descriptions of the weapons used.

[37] Essex Record Office, T/A 418/116/31.   [38] Essex Record Office, T/A 418/154/24.

[39] See, for example, the discussion in Horder, 'The Duel and the English Law of Homicide', pp. 419–30, which maintains that a fight could diverge from the 'code duello' in any number of ways and remain a duel, but that the duel was 'in essence' an affair between gentlemen alone.

[40] Anon., *Booke of Honor and Armes*, p. 30.

[41] Segar, *Honor Military and Ciuill*, pp. 118–19; Saviolo, *Sauiolo his practise*, sigs. Cc3r–Cc3v.

[42] Bacon, *Charge*, pp. 6, 39.

As Victor Kiernan has noted of duelling, it constituted a class 'privilege', a way to distinguish the aristocracy from the rest.[43] In its early modern incarnation, it also served as a vehicle for marking and contesting distinctions of status within that elite. The English aristocracy, unusually for Europe, sharply split between a relatively small, titled peerage and then the lesser nobility, or knights and gentry, beneath them. All were aristocrats, though only the titled nobility enjoyed the generous legal immunities and privileges of the peerage.[44] According to theorists, all aristocratic men could fight duels, but they could not necessarily fight whomsoever they chose. Scholars who claim that the duel uniformly or equitably allowed any man of honour to demand satisfaction from any other are perhaps thinking of some later period. Among its early modern advocates, who could challenge whom remained one of the more deeply contested and divisive aspects of duelling, both as conceptualized and as practised.

Annibale Romei defined the duel as a 'battle betwixt two of equal interest'.[45] Segar and Saviolo devoted chapters of their works to 'whether a man of meaner title may challenge a greater, as when an earl challengeth a duke, whether lawfully he may so do'. As Segar noted, 'on this matter divers men have thought diversly'. He cited one authority who believed that a man with three generations of proven gentility behind him might well challenge a duke upon injury done. He thought that a duke could not deny the challenge of an earl, but deemed it 'not fit, that private gentlemen or barons should challenge a great marquis'.[46] Simon Robson's *Court of Civil Courtesy* offered a painfully precise disquisition into how to respond in any given situation, depending on whether one interacted with an inferior, an equal, or a superior, and whether one did so in the presence of one's inferiors, equals, or betters. How one jested, took compliments, gave thanks, responded to affronts, or reacted to challenges to fight all depended on status. An inferior could not really do one an injury. If he tried, one need not bother with the intricacies of a challenge and duel, but simply rap him on the face with a dagger or even just send a man by later to do the deed.[47] Having one's challenge deemed worthy of acceptance itself constituted a claim to status successfully staked.

Such distinctions appeared in practice as well as in the theoretical literature on duelling. When George Ivy asked Henry Richmond to carry a challenge to his local nemesis, Henry Moody, Richmond responded that Moody was 'a gentleman of a better rank than yourself, and that therefore he would not fight with you'.[48]

[43] Kiernan, *The Duel*, pp. 53, 327.

[44] This passage skates over a large literature on what an aristocracy consists of, and follows the arguments put forward in M.L. Bush, *The English Aristocracy: A Comparative Synthesis* (Manchester, 1984). For the privileges of peers, see pp. 20ff. For a contemporary treatment of the subject, see Harrison's *Description of England*, ed. Edelen, p. 94, which includes in the category of 'gentlemen' everyone from titled lords ('gentlemen of the greater sort'), to knights, esquires, and 'they that are simply called gentlemen'.

[45] Annibale Romei, *Courtiers Academie* (London, 1597), p. 131.

[46] Segar, *Honor Military and Ciuill*, pp. 118, 121ff. See, too, Saviolo, *Saviolo his practise*, sigs. Gg1vff.

[47] Simon Robson, *The Courte of Ciuill Courtesie* (London, 1577), esp. pp. 22–6; see also Thomas Churchyard, *Churchyards Challenge* (London, 1593), pp. 61–3.

[48] STAC 8/210/5.

When Sir Thomas Scott challenged Lord Willoughby to a duel, the latter spurned it with disdain, refusing to lower himself to fight such a 'paltry fellow'.[49] Sir Edward Norris sought to challenge his senior officer to a duel, with Sir Philip Sidney as his second, but the earl of Leicester intervened on the grounds that a junior officer could not challenge a superior.[50] Sidney himself famously gave the lie to Edward de Vere, earl of Oxford after the latter kicked him off a tennis court and called him a puppy, but found himself called before the queen. Elizabeth reportedly explained to him 'the difference in degree between earls and gentlemen, the respect inferiors ought to their superiors, and the necessity in princes to maintain their own creations, as degree descending between the people's licentiousness, and the anointed sovereignty of crowns'. Sidney argued that her father had allowed gentlemen to complain about peers, and indeed had deemed it wise to use 'the stronger corporation in number, to keep down the greater in power, inferring else, that if they should unite, the over-grown might be tempted, by still coveting more, to fall (as the Angels did) by affecting equality with their maker'. Elizabeth saw the danger coming from another quarter, however, and insisted that Sidney back down: gentlemen's insults against peers 'taught the peasant to insult upon both'.[51] For his part, Oxford refused to fight Sidney and for a time planned just to send men round to kill him, before friends talked him out of it.[52] Thomas Vavasour also found that Oxford felt himself too high to fight with the likes of him (though not too high to have an affair with Thomas's sister Anne): Vavasour challenged that 'if there be yet left any spark of honour in thee, or jot of regard of thy decayed reputation, use not thy birth for an excuse'.[53]

When Lord Eure wrote to Robert Cecil in 1609 about local gentlemen who had insulted and pressed his son to duel, he complained of the insolence of 'inferior persons...seeking to enable their reputation by quarrelling with the best'.[54] In the published Star Chamber decree against duelling, the judges noted as one reason for concern the 'confusion of degrees which is grown of late (every man assuming unto himself the term and attribute of honour)'.[55] Some men clearly did challenge their superiors, and some others did act upon the insults or challenges of lesser gentlemen. But when John Selden asserted that 'a duke ought to fight with a gentleman', this should be read as an intervention in a debate, not as a description of settled practice.[56]

In identifying certain kinds of conflicts as duels, both advocates and enemies thus generally conceptualized them as new, private, unauthorized, and almost inherently aristocratic, though in ways complicated by the finely graded and

---

[49] Louis A. Knafla, 'Scott, Sir Thomas (1534–1594)', *ODNB*, and BL, Cotton Galba D.vii, f. 111r.

[50] D.J.B. Trim, 'Norris, Sir Edward (*c*.1550–1603), *ODNB*.

[51] Arthur Collins, ed., *Letters and Memorials of State*, 2 vols. (London, 1746), vol. 1, pp. 101–2.

[52] See Alan H. Nelson, *Monstrous Adversary: The Life of Edward de Vere, 17th earl of Oxford* (Liverpool, 2003), pp. 199–200.

[53] BL, Lansdowne 99, f. 252.   [54] BL, Add MS 12514, f. 152.

[55] Bacon, *Charge*, p. 56.

[56] John Selden, *Table Talk* (London, 1689), p. 43. Cf. Peltonen, *The Duel*, p. 69 and Manning, *Swordsmen*, p. 203. For Stone's discussion of the blurring of boundaries, see *Aristocracy*, pp. 244–5 but also 249.

increasingly contested status distinctions within the aristocracy.[57] While some of duelling's defenders adopted for themselves the language of legality, opponents had no doubt that duels violated law; indeed, they often used 'private' and 'unlawful' as interchangeable, synonymous adjectives for the particular kind of combat coming to be known as the duel. As the barrister, antiquarian, and future justice James Whitelocke explained, 'unlawful combats are those that are fought by private men upon private quarrels arising upon points of honour or disgrace, as they term them'.[58]

DUELLING AND THE LAW

But how exactly to bring 'the law' to bear on these private combats among elite men proved a source of some debate and disagreement. When King James's councillors first sought to craft a response to the duels multiplying around them, they investigated the edicts issued against the practice by other European rulers, and turned to the common law judges for advice. Chief Justice Sir Edward Coke opined in 1609 that already the 'law of England forbiddeth any man to use any private revenge: for nothing is more opposite to monarchy, than for any man to take the sword of revenge in his hand but by lawful warrant from his sovereign'. He then surveyed the existing legal remedies. Duellists who killed their opponents did something illegal, of course: they faced the possibility of trial for murder or for manslaughter. (Coke himself believed that all deaths resulting from duels constituted wilful murder, clearly acts of premeditation rather than hot-blooded killings upon immediate provocation.) In theory, a duellist who injured his opponent could be tried for battery, a misdemeanour in these years. Coke observed that if antagonists threatened to duel they could be bound to keep the peace; if they fought, they could be charged with breaking the peace and thus fined. He acknowledged that initiating or fighting a duel violated no specific statute or common law, but suggested that existing common law remedies should suffice if adequately used, at least for those duels that took place on English soil.[59] Yet, some other jurisdictions had measures that specifically forbade duelling—the Scots parliament, for example, passed a statute against single combats in 1600—and some people in England seemed to think that something more than existing law was necessary there, too.[60]

---

[57] For this contestation see, e.g., Stone, *Crisis of the Aristocracy*, pp. 30–4, 54–6; C.R. Mayes, 'The Sale of Peerages in Early Stuart England', *Journal of Modern History* 19 (1957): pp. 21–37; Brendan Kane, *The Politics and Culture of Honour in Britain and Ireland, 1541–1641* (Cambridge, 2010), pp. 194–220. Contemporary complaints can be found in the College of Arms, MS Vincent 30, f. 391ff.

[58] James Whitelocke, 'Antiquity, Use, and Ceremony of Lawful Combats in England', in *Collection of Curious Discourses*, ed. Hearne, vol. 2, p. 190.

[59] Edward Coke, 'A Discourse Touching the Unlawfulness of Private Combats', in *Collectanea Curiosa*, ed. Gutch, vol. 1, p. 10. See also Coke, *Third Part*, p. 157, 'Of Monomachia, Single-Combat, Duell, Affrays and Challenges, and of Private Anger'.

[60] *RPS* 1600/11/33/. Note, too, that Northampton investigated Spanish and French measures against duelling before drafting the 1614 proclamation; see, example.g., BL, Cotton Titus C.IV, f. 503.

Observers expected some such bill to appear before parliament in 1609, but nothing did.[61] Instead, the king supplemented existing remedies by relying upon his royal prerogative, as expressed in proclamation and as enforced in the prerogative court of Star Chamber. A number of high profile duels and fatalities—including that of Edward Bruce, with which we began—drove King James and his councillors to pick up from their investigations of 1609. They clearly thought existing common law remedies inadequate for what they saw as a new and distinctive challenge. First, in 1613, the king issued a proclamation that did not deal with duelling as such, but banned the publication of challenges and descriptions of such combats.[62] Someone drafted a bill to deal with the problem 'wherein private men take upon them to be the judges and avengers of their own quarrels... to the great contempt of common justice' by allowing King's Bench to take cognizance of murders by the king's subjects on foreign soil, but it went nowhere.[63] (The resolutely territorial nature of English homicide law remained a problem until the nineteenth century.)[64] Early in 1614, the king did issue a proclamation specifically against 'private challenges and combats', though a proclamation sufficiently odd to require some comment. One of the longest of James's decrees, it resembles a treatise rather than a clear order to do or to desist, full of rhetorical flourishes and classical references but short on specific sanctions.[65] Moreover, it referred the reader or hearer to a separate 'edict' of over one hundred pages in length to get the full benefit of the king's 'severe censure' of the practice.[66] And as a proclamation it both lacked the force of statute law and touched a sore spot about the king's supposed efforts to make new law without parliamentary approval, a spot recently made especially sensitive: Coke and the King's Bench had insisted in a 1611 case that 'the king cannot create any offence by his prohibition or proclamation which was not an offence before... [T]he king hath no prerogative, but that which the law of the land allows him.'[67] The two councillors most active in James's anti-duelling campaign both saw a need for a parliamentary statute. James accordingly put a bill before

---

[61] BL, Add MS 72339, f. 38d [*HMC Downshire*, II, 86].

[62] *SRP*, vol. 1, pp. 295–7 (no. 132). [63] Parliamentary Archives, HL/PO/JO/10/1/7.

[64] With only the exception of Admiralty jurisdiction for offences aboard English ships or in English waters, and a short-lived measure passed in 1649, homicide law was otherwise limited to English shores until the nineteenth-century offences against the person acts began to make additional exceptions that allowed the prosecution of English subjects abroad, in some circumstances. See Michael Hirst, *Jurisdiction and the Ambit of the Criminal Law* (Oxford, 2003), esp. ch. 2. For the 1649 measure, see 'An Act for the Punishing of Crimes Committed upon or beyond the Seas', *Acts and Ordinances of the Interregnum*, edited by C.H. Firth and R.S. Rait, 3 vols. (London, 1911), vol. 2, pp. 254–6.

[65] *SRP*, vol. 1, pp. 302–8 (no. 136).

[66] James VI/I. *A Publication of his Maties Edict... Combatants*.

[67] The precise constitutional and legislative relationship of proclamations and statutes remains in some doubt now, and was in some dispute then. See the introduction to the *TRP*, vol. 1, pp. xxv–xxx, the 'Case of Proclamations' (1611), 77 *ER* 1352, and James's own comments about this particular—and peculiar—combination of 'edict' and proclamation when before the next parliament, quoted and discussed in Alan Stewart, 'Purging Troubled Humours: Bacon, Northampton and the Anti-Duelling Campaign of 1613–1614', in *The Crisis of 1614 and the Addled Parliament: Literary and Historical Perspectives*, edited by Stephen Clucas and Rosalind Davies (Aldershot, 2003), pp. 81–91. See, too, J.H. Baker's discussion of the mounting concerns *c.*1610 in *The Reinvention of Magna Carta, 1216–1616* (Cambridge, 2017), pp. 390–6.

parliament in 1614, even while defending his decision first to use proclamations, but to no avail. This so-called 'Addled Parliament' had enough difficulties for its failure to enact anti-duelling legislation perhaps to have been inadvertent. But the fact remains that, despite repeated promptings and foreign precedents, no such legislation passed in any subsequent parliament either.[68]

For the time being, King James fell back on Star Chamber and, as Peltonen, Richard Cust, and Andrew Hopper have shown, discussed plans to revive the ancient Court of Chivalry.[69] Francis Bacon, who had no patience for the code of honour, touted Star Chamber as a stopgap while awaiting a statutory solution. He pointed to the prerogative court's claim to jurisdiction over conspiracies to commit common law offences. Issuing or accepting challenges could be construed as conspiracy to commit murder, and thus, he argued, should be tried in Star Chamber.[70] It was a 'public court of justice' and also a space associated with the term-end exhortations on law and good policy given by the Lord Chancellor or sovereign to the great and the good before they dispersed to the counties; as such, it seemed an ideal venue to advertise the king's intentions.[71] Moreover, royal proclamations were generally considered enforceable in that court. With these proclamations now issued, Star Chamber could more robustly deal with duelling. The earl of Northampton, in contrast, also opposed duelling but proved more respectful of the demands of honour. As such, he recommended a revival of the ancient Court of Chivalry. He wanted the court reconstituted to meet more regularly so that gentlemen who felt their honour impugned could challenge the offenders in court rather than in combat. Nor could gentlemen be expected to use just any court for this purpose; Northampton felt that noblemen should not have to put their quarrels before juries of twelve lesser men. His death in 1614 put such plans on hold, however.[72]

James thus relied primarily on Star Chamber to deal with the duellist's 'saucy paradox'. While a few duelling-related cases had already come before that court, Bacon launched the new offensive in 1614, once appointed attorney general, by picking up a case begun under his predecessor against gentleman William Prest and Richard Wright, esquire. Prest had angered one George Hutchest at a dinner

---

[68] A bill to abolish trial by battle, which may have referred to duelling, was introduced to the parliament of 1624 but disappeared. See Peltonen, *The Duel*, p. 91 and *Commons Journals*, vol. 1, p. 798.

[69] Peltonen, *The Duel*, pp. 108–45; *Cases in the High Court of Chivalry*, ed. Cust and Hopper, pp. xii–xvi; Cust, *Charles I and the Aristocracy* (Cambridge, 2013), pp. 96–104, 140–56.

[70] Bacon, *Charge*.

[71] Some confusion seems to exist on this point, perhaps given the court's later reputation for dark deeds. But while the council met privately in the inner Star Chamber, court business was generally conducted in the larger, open outer chamber. See Pollard, 'Star Chamber', pp. 519, 525, 534, and William Hudson's distinction between the 'public court of justice' and the 'private board' of the council: 'A Treatise on the Court of Star Chamber', p. 62. True, in 1634 councillors did try to restrain the 'multitude of... persons of mean rank and quality' who resorted to the court, but otherwise satisfied themselves with guidelines for better behaviour in the room when the court was sitting. PC 2/43, p. 455.

[72] See Peltonen, *The Duel*; *Cases in the High Court of Chivalry*, ed. Cust and Hopper; Cust, *Charles I and the Aristocracy*; also Linda Levy Peck, *Northampton, Patronage and Policy at the Court of James I* (London, 1982), p. 164. For Northampton's distaste for juries of poor men, see Stewart, 'Anti-dueling Campaign', p. 24.

party; Hutchest declared himself a 'better man' than Prest and cuffed him a few blows. Prest then went by the home of his friend Richard Wright and asked him to deliver to Hutchest a written challenge to fight. No duel took place—Prest and Hutchest seemed to use a disagreement over whether to fight with rapiers or with staffs to defer the encounter—and Prest instead had Hutchest charged with battery at the next quarter sessions. Both had to take out bonds to keep the peace. A related attempt to charge Wright for carrying the challenge fell apart when he claimed immunity from the local common law court's jurisdiction thanks to his position in the king's household. Attorney General Hobart then brought the matter into Star Chamber, whence Bacon later picked it up.[73] In his lengthy charge before the court, Bacon warned that when 'revenge is once extorted out of the magistrate's hand, contrary to God's ordinancy' and 'private men begin once to presume to give law to themselves, and to right their own wrongs, no man can foresee the dangers and inconveniences that may arise and multiply thereupon'. Such actions brought 'peril upon the state, and contempt upon the law'.[74] The court accordingly sentenced both Prest and Wright to the Fleet and to massive fines—£500 in Prest's case—and ordered that at the next county assizes they publicly acknowledge their contempts of God, the king, and their laws. The judges ordered that Bacon's charge and their own summation be printed, and that their decree be read aloud at the next assize sessions throughout the country.

Coke continued to insist that duelling ought to be dealt with at common law, using existing charges and procedures. Richard Taverner, a man with a chequered past but the patronage of the queen, was brought to King's Bench in April 1616 on charges of murder, after he had killed a man in a single combat following an exchange of challenges some years previously. Judges spoke of the preceding, continuing malice. Coke took a particularly strong line. He maintained that 'this is a plain case, and without any question, if one kill another in fight, upon the provocation of him which is killed, this is murder...And we do all of us agree in this, that it is clearly murder in him.' A man ought not to fight in such a manner for any 'private provocation'. The jury followed the direction of the court, duly finding Taverner guilty of murder despite his pleas of provocation and defence of honour. The judges noted that Taverner had, if anything, aggravated his offence by going to the fight immediately after hearing a sermon on the biblical passage against killing. In the discussion leading to the sentence of death by hanging, Coke observed that 'If the cause be never so important, yet it cannot allow one to draw blood of a subject; if this were lawful, who should then live?...If this be not murder, what then shall be murder?' Taverner argued that he had fought his duel and killed his foe before the king's proclamation against duelling, bewailing 'his miserable and unfortunate chance, to be the first precedent in this case'. The court emphatically insisted that he was by no means the first precedent, 'for this was the common law before the king's edict': as a proclamation, the king's missive could not create new law but simply declare what already existed.[75] In the end, Taverner was pardoned,

---

[73] STAC 8/19/12 and 8/19/13.   [74] Bacon, *Charge*, pp. 9, 11.
[75] Taverner's Case (1616), 81 *ER* 144.

but Coke thought the court's insistence upon common law in dealing with duelling, and on the limits of royal proclamations, a worthy precedent to record.[76]

This decision came down around the same time that Coke offended the king through similar pronouncements on the relationship between prerogative and law. By November, the king had formally dismissed Coke from the bench and named a new chief justice. A few days later, Bacon created another opportunity to deal with duelling in Star Chamber. Lord Darcy had brought a complaint to the Privy Council that Bacon, freshly appointed to that body, suggested be heard in Star Chamber, a suggestion with which the newly appointed chief justice concurred.

Now as a judge, Bacon once more denounced the dangers of private revenge. Lord Darcy complained that Gervase Markham, esq., had written (though not delivered) 'a challenge to a challenge', after suffering insults from one of Darcy's men.[77] It was an odd case, but Bacon argued that it should be heard in Star Chamber, in that 'it is a cause most fit for the censure of the court, both for the repressing of duels, and the encouragement of complaints in courts of justice'. In the court itself, Bacon praised Darcy for dealing with his injury by law rather than on his own, and then launched into an attack on duelling. Deaths from duelling, he acknowledged, were sometimes seen not as murder but as manslaughter, but he posited this as a difference between Cain and Lamech, one 'insidious' and one 'insolent', but both equally grievous and to be punished as such. More generally, he noted that the king's law provided remedies for libel. He described those men with the presumption to right their own wrongs as akin to Anabaptists, writing laws for themselves in a manner that 'tends to the dissolution of magistracy'. Anyone who challenged a man challenged the law. Copies of this denunciation of duelling circulated publicly, too. According to one report of his speech, Bacon continued to insist that '[t]hese swelling tumours that arise in men's proud affections must be beaten flat with justice, or else all will end in ruin'.[78] The other judges then followed with their own criticisms of duelling as an affront or danger to the Crown—the two chief justices, Lord Chancellor Ellesmere, the Archbishop of Canterbury, the earl of Arundel, and the rest all took their turns. After the hearing, Bacon reported proudly that 'yesterday was a day of great good for his Majesty's service and the peace of this kingdom concerning duels, by occasion of Darcy's case'.[79]

King James used Star Chamber as a stage for another, much publicized warning against the practice early in 1617. In November of the previous year, officials had apprehended the young gentlemen Thomas Bellingham and Brice Christmas when word leaked of their intentions to fight. Even before receiving the Lord Chief

[76] On Taverner, see also *Letters of John Chamberlain*, ed. McClure, vol. 1, pp. 607, 610, 626; vol. 2, pp. 275, 288.

[77] Spedding, *Works*, vol. 6, pp. 105–15.

[78] Spedding, *Works*, vol. 6, p. 109. Two accounts of this speech survive. The other has a different version of this line: 'This doctrine of man-killing is grown to a tumour, and must be beaten flat by justice, lest that which is now man-killing should become judge-killing' (pp. 108–9; see BL, Harley MS 6807, f. 174.)

[79] Spedding, *Works*, vol. 6, p. 114.

Justice's warrant for the men, the port authorities in Dover had grown suspicious when Bellingham and a friend applied for passports for themselves and a surgeon; when asked if they intended to travel abroad to fight, the men denied it but then promptly ran off to try their way from Gravesend.[80] When both of the principals found themselves in Star Chamber, they may well have been surprised to find that the king himself appeared to deliver the judgement, a first for James.[81] The king had his new favourite, George Villiers, recently minted as earl of Buckingham, deliver his own maiden speech in the Chamber against the evils of duelling. James then spoke of himself as a shepherd who needed 'to keep and conserve his sheep from being spoiled', and as someone who sought to merit the sobriquet of *Rex pacificus*. To that end, he had come to pronounce sentence in a cause of duelling, a matter clean contrary to the laws of God and of nature, as well as his own.[82] He ordered that Bellingham and Christmas be imprisoned in the Tower so long as he deemed fit, that they each pay a fine of £1,000, and that they be denied access to the court, prohibited from wearing arms for seven years, and forced to make a public submission and apology.[83] Within a month, however, he discharged them from their imprisonment and fines, though not the rest, wishing 'to signalize his entry into his court of judicature by an act of mercy'.[84]

Star Chamber had numerous advantages for a campaign against duelling. A prerogative court not bound by common law restrictions, its judges could prove inventive in the punishments they allotted: while they could not sentence wrong-doers to death, they could otherwise craft sentences as they deemed best suited to the quality of the offence and offender. (In one case dealing with a challenge to duel, a couple of the judges wanted to make the defendant cut his 'long, ruffian-like hair', but were outvoted by their fellows.)[85] They could also deal more readily with the greatest in the land than could other courts: at common law, peers charged with felony or treason could insist upon a trial by their fellow lords, and need not swear on oath to anything they said in court on any charge. Not so in Star Chamber, where the privileges of peerage did not apply. The court claimed an extraordinarily broad competence, dealing with causes 'for which the law provideth no remedy in any sort of ordinary court, whereby the necessary use of this court to the state

---

[80] SP 14/89, f. 84.

[81] James had appeared in Star Chamber once before, in June 1616, to give a speech about the problems of competing jurisdictions and the derivation of all law from God, through him. See T.G. Barnes, 'A Cheshire Seductress, Precedent, and a "Sore Blow" to Star Chamber', in *On the Laws and Customs of England*, edited by Morris S. Arnold et al. (Chapel Hill, NC, 1981), p. 381, and James I, 'A Speech in the Starre-Chamber', in *The Political Works of James I*, edited by C.H. McIlwain (Cambridge, MA, 1918).

[82] SP 14/90, ff. 117r–d, 155.

[83] *Calendar of State Papers…Domestic Series, James I, 1611–1618*, edited by M.A.E. Green (London, 1858), p. 450.

[84] Ibid.

[85] See S.R. Gardiner, ed., *Reports of Cases in the Courts of Star Chamber and High Commission* (London, Camden Society, vol. 39, 1886), p. 115. In perhaps one of their more inventive punishments, they ordered that a convert to Judaism who made himself known with his diatribes against the 'eating of hogs' flesh' be fed a prison diet of pork. See Hudson, 'Treatise on the Court of the Star Chamber', p. 225.

appeareth'. William Hudson, its chronicler and ardent fan, referred to a disagreement that had arisen between Lord Chancellor Ellesmere and Lord Coke over the court's claim to deal with duelling. He himself admitted some reservations about its proceedings *ore tenus*—an 'extraordinary kind of proceeding, more short and more expeditious' that Bacon had recommended for duelling cases. In such cases, the accused received no formal charge or opportunity to consult with counsel, but was encouraged to provide a confession as the basis to proceed. Hudson tried to defend such proceedings as lawful and necessary, but wished that they might be used more sparingly, 'for that this course of proceeding is an exuberancy of prerogative'. This reservation aside, Hudson extolled Star Chamber as a venue to deal with duelling and with other offences, for it 'giveth life to the execution of law, or the performance of such things as are necessary in the commonwealth, yea, although no positive law or continued custom of common law giveth warrant to it'.[86]

Whatever reservations some others might have had about Star Chamber and its claims to deal with duelling, many turned to it. Thomas Barnes identified 204 files that related to duelling in his index of the records of Star Chamber from the reign of King James.[87] The king's attorneys general launched twenty-two of these cases, some upon the complaints of individuals, and private suitors the rest. A survey of seventy-two of these suits—those launched by the attorneys general, together with fifty of the others randomly selected—suggests how the particular abstraction of some kinds of conflict as 'duels', and hence especially dangerous to public justice and good order, came to be useful to individuals pursuing their own interests.[88] In surprisingly few of the cases does one find anything approaching the textbook definition of a duel. Here, where plaintiffs had an interest in making their charges conform to expectations as much as possible, one finds few reports of formal challenges to well-mannered single combats. Instead, plaintiffs referenced the king's proclamations then complained of words or deeds they portrayed as being intended to provoke them to issue challenges and hence dangerously criminal, however else they might otherwise seem. In those cases where violence had occurred, it often took the form of tussles between one man's servants and those of another in busy streets or at race meetings, or perhaps ride-by shootings from horseback after a protracted local spat.[89] In disputes that first manifested themselves in efforts to claim the best seating in church, or among JPs over the order in which they signed documents, for example, plaintiffs alleged that their opponents had thus tried provoking them to take vengeance by their own hands.[90]

Adding an accusation that one's foe had issued a challenge to fight, or tried to provoke a challenge, became a way to add weight to a standard list of complaints

---

[86] Hudson, 'Treatise on the Court of Star Chamber', pp. 87, 103, 107–8, 112, 127, 128, 139, 167, 207.

[87] *List and Index to the Proceedings in Star Chamber for the Reign of James I (1603–1625) in the Public Record Office*, edited by Thomas G. Barnes (Chicago, 1975), pp. 159–63.

[88] Steve Hindle has previously examined the range of ways in which plaintiffs sought to use Star Chamber prosecutions and procedures to their own ends; see *State and Social Change*, pp. 68, 78–87.

[89] See, e.g., STAC 8/24/4; 8/24/8; 8/24/11; 8/243/6.

[90] See, e.g., STAC 8/24/2; 8/184/19; 8/184/23; 8/239/17.

framed as conspiracy, riot, and rout. In his charge against Timothy Salter, for example, Garrett Fawcon repeated to his own purposes the notion that those who duel 'usurp the sword of justice to themselves and tempt God by taking vengeance unto their own hands'. How had Salter supposedly violated the king's injunction against duelling? It seems that Fawcon rented rooms from Salter's mother; when the two men disagreed about some aspect of the lodging, they fell to blows. Later, 'thirsting his blood and devising with himself how to provoke and incite the said Garrett Fawcon', Salter called him a 'base Walloon', a 'filthy lecher', and a 'most base coward'.[91] Similarly, Richard Bolle complained that his new son-in-law, Thomas Gilby, had turned his own wife against him, assaulted and insulted him, and called him a liar, 'whereby he might draw your said subject into your Majesty's displeasure and danger of the breaking of your Majesty's proclamation and edict, the which he is and shall be always careful to observe and keep'.[92] People made use of the king's proclamations against duelling in an effort to elevate charges that often amounted to little more than slander or libel to offences of the highest order.

And the king's councillors sitting as judges in Star Chamber continued to ratchet up the rhetoric about the particular dangers of duelling. When they did have fully fledged duelling cases brought before them, they tried to outdo each other in denouncing the practice. The court's files from the reign of King Charles do not survive, but reporters left summaries of noteworthy hearings. In one, launched *ore tenus* by Attorney General Heath in 1634, Peter Apsley faced accusations of 'high insolency' for challenging the earl of Northumberland to a duel. That Apsley challenged a man so much his superior, and indeed one then on a mission for the king, aggravated his offence. The attorney general regretted that they could not sentence him to death. One judge suggested that they ought to 'tie him up as they do mad men, grown into a frenzy'. Another declared that the Tower was too good for him, and that they ought to send him to Newgate, or to the Fleet at best. The earl of Dorset (the Edward Sackville with whose fatal duel this chapter began) initially suggested that Apsley also be perpetually barred from office of any sort, though after a moment's self-reflection, perhaps, later thought this a bit too much. Archbishop Laud observed that the people of other nations denied Christian burial to those who died in duels, as people who denied the law of God, and wished that they might do the same in England. Apsley would at minimum be imprisoned, pay a massive fine, and make his public submission to the king upon his knees, as well as an apology to Northumberland before the Lord Marshall. Secretary Windebank still thought this too little, for 'he that takes a sword in his hand to revenge himself doth as much as in him lieth depose the king, at whose dispose the sword of justice is'.[93]

At about the same time as Apsley faced them in Star Chamber, the king's councillors revived Northampton's plans for a reconstituted Court of Chivalry. After earlier, ad hoc meetings, this civil law court sat on a regular basis from 1634. Here,

---

[91] STAC 8/142/20.   [92] STAC 8/74/21.
[93] BL, Add MS 11764, ff. 4d–6d; SP 16/259, no. 71. He was eventually banished from the realm: PC 2/44, p. 90.

now, in addition to a court that could try the highest in the land was one available to the aristocracy alone. That it proved so busy so quickly suggests that a good many gentlemen found it useful: as Cust and Hopper note, some three-quarters of the 783 suits that survive for the six years from 1634 to 1640 dealt with 'words provocative of a duel'.[94] Here, as in Star Chamber, relatively few of the cases dealt with actual combats or formal challenges. Rather, gentlemen used the court to navigate their insecurities over status, elevating insults to words likely to incite private violence of the sort deemed so serious an affront to the king's justice. William Amcotts, for example, a JP and son of a Knight of the Bath, complained that Leon Shuttleworth had claimed to be 'a better man and a better gentleman than Mr Amcotts', thus surely trying to incite a fight. The court ordered Shuttleworth to pay damages and to submit publicly that Amcotts was, in fact, 'a better man than myself'.[95] Gentleman Thomas Rouse accused John Kippis of telling him that 'if he were a gentleman he was but a beggarly one', with a whore for a wife, and thus trying to provoke him to a duel.[96] Jenkin Vaughan charged that Ewan Lloyd had given him the lie and 'bid a turd in his teeth', thereby trying to start a fight.[97] Other affronted men brought charges that their foes had called them such things as 'a rogue rascal, no gentleman, and the son of a brewer'; 'a base fellow and the son of a cobbler and no gentleman'; 'a base, shitten, stinking gentleman'; 'a base scab...a base scurvy fellow... [and] an arrant liar'; or 'a bald-pated knave and a cheating rogue'.[98] All these insults became actionable in the Court of Chivalry since they could be construed as attempts to incite others to act in derogation of the king's sole prerogative to avenge wrongs.

By bringing their complaints to Star Chamber and the Court of Chivalry, men did not just use law in lieu of violence, but also endorsed the notion that retribution belonged only to the king's justice and, by extension, to the 'public Justice of the state'. Both courts, however, disappeared in the parliamentary attack on the royal prerogative in 1640–41. Royal efforts to deal with duelling had not just become caught up in, but had also contributed to, conflicts over law, prerogative, and jurisdiction. While James and Charles and their officials had expressed concerns about individuals who took the law into their own hands, some members of parliament in turn thought royal efforts to resolve the problem had become tied up in new and bigger threats to the law. Deemed a dangerous and arbitrary innovation that used something other than the 'laws of the kingdom', the reconstituted Court of Chivalry met for the last time in December of 1640.[99] The statute abolishing Star Chamber declared that its judges had not kept themselves to the remit of what MPs took to be the court's founding declaration, but rather, 'have undertaken to

---

[94] Richard Cust and Andrew Hopper, 'Duelling and the Court of Chivalry in Early Stuart England', in *Cultures of Violence: Interpersonal Violence in Historical Perspective*, edited by Stuart Carroll (Basingstoke, 2007), pp. 156–74. See also Cust, *Charles I*, pp. 140–56.

[95] *Cases in the High Court of Chivalry*, ed. Cust and Hopper, 3. Amcotts *v* Shuttleworth.

[96] Ibid., 566. Rouse *v* Kippis.   [97] Ibid., 658. Vaughan *v* Lloyd.

[98] Ibid., 21. Badd *v* Rigges; 35. Bawde *v* Dawson; 220. Foster *v* Booth, 656. Utber *v* Baldery.

[99] Ibid., pp. xxiv–xxvi. See also M. Jansson, ed., *Proceedings in the Opening Session of the Long Parliament: House of Commons*, 2 vols. (Rochester, NY, 2000), vol. 1, p. 254.

punish where no law doth warrant and to make decrees for things having no such authority, and to inflict heavier punishments than by any law is warranted'. Cases could and should be taken to common law courts rather than to Star Chamber, which MPs argued had become a 'means to introduce an Arbitrary Power'.[100]

How then would authorities deal with duels? When the civil war began, in 1642, the armies of both king and parliament adopted military codes that forbade private combats, but efforts to enact a law against duels in the population more generally continued to be made—and continued to fail.[101] In the 1650s, the parliamentary law reform commission recommended an anti-duelling bill. It mandated the loss of the right hand for sending or accepting a challenge, as well as banishment for those who fought; it ordered that any duellists who killed their opponents suffer as murderers without exception. As with many of the law reformers' efforts, though, this bill failed to become law.[102] Like James before him, Cromwell relied upon a proclamation to try to limit the practice, though one much more succinct and direct than that of 1614. This proclamation threatened six months' imprisonment to men who issued or accepted challenges, exile for participants in duels that resulted in no fatalities, and rigorous application of the penalties for murder for those duellists who did kill their opponents.[103] Its force came to an end with the Restoration. Parliament considered an anti-duelling bill in 1668, probably prompted by the duke of Buckingham's killing of the earl of Shrewsbury in that year, but with no result.[104] After the especially notorious duel of 1712 in which both the duke of Hamilton and Lord Mohun died, parliament again considered a measure to deal with duels, but once again it disappeared.[105]

As such, the early modern English duel was inherently unauthorized, but as a duel, violated no specific parliamentary statute. After the demise of Star Chamber and the Court of Chivalry, common law courts alone dealt with the offences comprising the duel under their traditional labels of breaking the peace, assault, battery, and homicide. The failure of so many legislative attempts to make duelling into an offence in its own right requires some comment. The loss of individual bills might well be attributed to the pressures of a particular moment, but their cumulative disappearance seems to speak to the same paradox that saw King James

---

[100] 16 Chas. I c. 10, referring to the legislation of 3 Henry VII c. 1, s. 1. For the mounting problems faced by civil lawyers and civilian jurisdictions, see Brian Levack, *The Civil Lawyers in England, 1603–1641* (Oxford, 1973). For the broader conflict over jurisdiction, see Louis A. Knafla, *Law and Politics in Jacobean England* (Cambridge, 1977), esp. pp. 123ff. H.E.I Phillips argues that Star Chamber was a casualty of the attack on episcopacy, but notes that abuse of procedure by *ore tenus* and other similar problems fed into the assault: 'The Last Years of the Court of Star Chamber, 1630–41', *Transactions of the Royal Historical Society*, 4th ser., 21 (1930): pp. 103–31.

[101] See, for example, *Laws and Ordinances of Warre established... by his excellency the Earl of Essex* (London, 1643), which banned the drawing of swords in private quarrels, and the more elaborated ban on duels in *Military Orders and Articles Established by His Majesty* (Oxford, 1643), esp. sigs. B1r–v.

[102] *Several Draughts of Acts Heretofore Prepared by Persons Appointed to Consider of the Inconvenience, Delay, Charge and Irregularity in the Proceedings of the Law* (London, 1653), pp. 16–17.

[103] *Acts and Ordinances of the Interregnum*, vol. 2, pp. 937–9; see also Manning, *Swordsmen*, p. 226.

[104] Parliamentary Archives, HL/PO/JO/10/1/331/168.

[105] See Victor Stater, *Duke Hamilton Is Dead! A Story of Aristocratic Life and Death in Stuart Britain* (London, 2000); Andrew, 'Opposition to Duelling', p. 410.

repeatedly denounce the practice in the strongest terms even while pardoning individual duellists. Pre-civil war bills ran up against concerns about prerogative encroachments on common law; post-Restoration bills became mired in disputes over differential legal privileges for lords and lesser aristocrats. They had difficulty distinguishing the essence of what made some fights duels. More generally, the men who sat in parliament may have agreed that in the abstract or the aggregate, duelling posed a dire threat, but more concretely, it was an activity engaged in by men of their own sort and perhaps sometimes excusable as a foible of the man of honour or military breeding. But at minimum, we might see these repeated efforts to enact specifically tailored legislation, as well as the repeated failure, or refusal, to pass such legislation, as yet more evidence of the conflicted conceptualization of and response to duelling.

DUELLISTS IN COURT

That same ambivalence shows itself in the prosecutions of duellists who became killers. The same individuals who denounced duelling one moment could in the next excuse it. Those men who killed their opponents in contests deemed duels rarely suffered the full force of the law as murderers. Obtaining a sense of the number of duels, let alone their outcome or punishment, is made difficult by the nature of surviving records, as much as by the nature of the offence and the offenders themselves. Since duelling did not become a common law or statutory charge, indictments never name it. One might, however, arbitrarily select indictments for homicide that sound as if 'duel-like' encounters lay behind them to serve as a rough working sample: from the larger set of some 3,600 accusations of homicide made between c.1480 and 1680, roughly seventy seem to meet the criteria. Of this number, outcomes are unknown for seventeen of the accused, seven were found not guilty, nineteen obtained verdicts of self-defence, twenty-six were found guilty only of manslaughter and thus most likely freed from fear of death (and a few of these men obtained pardons, too, to ensure that no punishment applied). Only one in this set was found guilty of murder. A search of the *Oxford Dictionary of National Biography* produces another rough working sample, revealing some ninety-seven fights in the years between 1570 and 1700 construed as duels. In these ninety-seven encounters, forty men died. What is particularly striking about these forty deaths from duels is that only one of the killers suffered death in turn.[106]

The one killer to die for his deed, moreover, did so in the unusual circumstances of a wartime trial under military law: Lt. Col. James Rochfort, who killed a Major Turner in a duel in 1652, was shot upon the sentence of a court martial some days later.[107] True, some other duellists may only have saved themselves from a similar

---

[106] One might also point to SP 46/174, f. 120, a list of precedents for condemnations for murder after duelling fatalities, drawn up in or around 1611 by someone hoping—in vain, as it transpired—to secure such a condemnation in the killing of John Egerton. The list identified only three instances, only one of which clearly resulted in an execution for murder.

[107] See the entry for his son: C.I. McGrath, 'Rochfort, Robert (1652–1727)', in *ODNB*.

fate by flight: Sir Thomas Lucas, for example, fled to the continent when the Privy Council issued a warrant for his arrest after he killed the brother of Lord Cobham.[108] Thomas Porter had already escaped with a mere branding after killing one man in a duel in the 1640s; when he later killed his friend Sir Henry Bellasis, he perhaps correctly thought himself safer abroad for a time.[109] Among those who did face trial, jurors found some guilty not of murder, but of the lesser crime of manslaughter— and thus if they could successfully plead benefit of clergy they faced only the forfeiture of their property and, depending on their status, branding. And some received pardons from the sovereign—even after the Restoration-era proclamations that promised not just to deny pardons to such individuals but that also forbade intercessions for such pardons.[110]

Part of the explanation for the conflicted responses not just to duellists in general but even to those who killed must obviously lie in the sorts of attitudes about homicide and legitimate or at least excusable masculine violence that T.A. Green, Cynthia Herrup, Garthine Walker, and others have charted: those that moderated harsh laws in particular cases, that saw 'hot blood' as a medical explanation not a metaphor, and that respected a 'fair fight'.[111] A good many fights recognized as duels failed to fit the convention of a pause between offence, challenge, and combat, but rather took place in the heat of the moment. As such, any killing that resulted met quite neatly the legal definition, as much as the broader popular sense, of manslaughter. Fatal duels that did see a significant gap between offence, challenge, and the actual contest might, in theory, have been considered cold-blooded, premeditated murder, but jurors seemed content to deem these acts of mere manslaughter as well.

But surely a large part of the explanation for the mixed responses and relative lenience also lies in the status of the killers and duellists more generally. The notion that law was even supposed to apply equally to all developed only slowly over this period; even when it did emerge, practice very often fell short of precept. It was presumably no accident that the men chosen for the high-profile Star Chamber attacks on duelling were lesser gentlemen. When prosecuting Prest and Wright, Bacon expressed his resolve to 'proceed without respect of persons in this business', but observed that 'it passeth not amiss sometimes in government that the greater sort be admonished by an example made in the meaner, and the dog to be beaten before the lion'.[112] In the Lord Darcy case, in which the peer stood as plaintiff not defendant, Bacon professed his hope he would not 'know a coronet from a hatband' in a matter that pertained to the safety of the king and his laws. 'God forbid', he continued, that 'the privileges of the peers should privilege them to wrong

---

[108] See the entry for his son: Barbara Donagan, 'Lucas, Sir Thomas (1597/8–1648/9)', in *ODNB*, and *APC*, vol. 28, p. 198.

[109] J.P. Vander Motten, 'Porter, Thomas (1636–1680)', *ODNB*.

[110] Charles II, *By the King: A proclamation against fighting of duels* (London, 1660); Charles II, *A proclamation against duels* (London, 1680).

[111] See, for example, T.A. Green, 'English Law of Homicide'; Herrup, *Common Peace*; Walker, *Crime, Gender and Social Order*.

[112] Bacon, *Charge*, p. 6.

any man', let alone the gentry who are 'second nobles', but 'yet there ought a distinction to be kept'.[113] Peers retained their legal privileges throughout these years, save for the republican era, immune from the ordinary courts of law for serious offences and facing trial only from fellow peers. Lesser aristocrats did not share this formal privilege, but nonetheless often enjoyed informal preferment, bestowed both by those above and those beneath them and by the men of their own sort who dominated the law's enforcement. Even had early modern monarchs wanted to proceed with capital severity against such men, they would have found it difficult to do so. Only when they themselves found law preferable to violence in meeting their needs would they turn more often to one from the other.

Some might see honour codes as obstructing such a shift, but recent work suggests that such codes could instead serve to mediate and allow it. A notion tenaciously persists in some quarters that the code of honour somehow impelled men to fight, and that a challenge compelled a man to accept or to face inevitable ignominy.[114] Yet, as noted above, even those men who did embrace duelling as an allowable defence of honour found in its code enough complexities and nuances to permit or even require that many a challenge be denied. Moreover, work by Richard Cust, Linda Pollock, Brendan Kane, Courtney Thomas, and others should by now have dismissed this notion by showing the multiplicity or multivocality of honour codes in the early modern period.[115] Much work on honour has appeared in response to Mervyn James's thesis that early modern political culture produced a shift in emphasis from an older honour culture based on lineage and manifested in chivalric codes to one inflected by Protestantism, humanism, and the nature of anw emerging modern state, a shift from a lineage to a civil society.[116] Some scholars working in this area have noted that because of the fissures and fractures in notions of honour, not all men would have felt compelled to fight when challenged. Alexandra Shepard's work has indicated the 'varieties of manhood' that existed, some of which would have utterly repudiated or even lightly dismissed a duel as a necessity.[117] True, the Renaissance stage hosted such encomiums of the duel as George Chapman's plays on the life of Bussy D'Ambois; conversely, one need only think of Shakespeare's *As You Like It* to know that the duelling code prompted mockery from its earliest appearance in England, surely a sign that its demands were less than hegemonic. Finally, as James Sharpe and others have noted, many men saw no shame in taking their disputes to court, at least supplementing

---

[113] Spedding, *Works*, vol. 6, p. 112.

[114] See, e.g., Low, *Manhood and the Duel*, p. vii.

[115] See, in particular, Richard Cust, 'Honour and Politics in Early Stuart England: The Case of Beaumont v. Hastings', *P&P* 149 (1995): pp. 57–94; Pollock, 'Honor, Gender and Reconciliation'; Kane, *Politics and Culture of Honour*; Courtney Thomas, *If I Lose Mine Honor, I Lose Myself: Honours among the Early Modern English Elite* (Toronto, 2017).

[116] Mervyn James, 'English Politics and the Concept of Honour', in his *Society, Politics and Culture: Studies in Early Modern England* (Cambridge, 1986), pp. 308–415.

[117] Shepard, *Meanings of Manhood*. See, too, Susan Amussen, ' "The Part of a Christian Man": The Cultural Politics of Manhood in Early Modern England', in *Cultural Politics in Early Modern England*, edited by Susan Amussen and Mark Kishlansky (Manchester, 1995), pp. 213–33.

and sometimes altogether replacing resort to violence.[118] The particular ways in which duelling was defined and responded to may well have allowed more men to come to such a decision.

CONCLUSION

Duelling, of course, continued for many years yet. Indeed, contests accorded this label seem to have become even more common in the Restoration era than before, and slowed in frequency only in the nineteenth century. In these later years, however, duels seemed to have become more formalized and formulaic. Willingness to participate, rather than ability to vanquish one's opponent, became the criterion by which advocates accorded honour. First blood, rather than death, became the expected end. The advent of pistol duelling made such fights even less deadly: in his study of eighteenth-century duels, Robert Shoemaker found that roughly a fifth of those fought with swords resulted in a fatality, whereas less than seven per cent of those fought with pistols did the same.[119] In these later years, perhaps, duelling did what historians have so often claimed for it, codifying, sterilizing, and limiting deadly violence among elite men. But arguably some of its cultural work had already been done indirectly, with its conceptualization helping to reorient revenge as a public rather than private matter for even the greatest in the land.

Mark Cooney, an historically minded criminologist, has theorized that 'lethal conflict is a function of the unavailability of the law, and law is effectively unavailable to disputants when its agents are either too high or too low in social status'. Today, it tends to be primarily members of marginalized groups who find the law unavailable to them; in the past, Cooney argues, men whose status superseded that of the law also engaged more frequently in violent conflict because law proved effectively unavailable to them as well.[120] This provides us with a hint at how duelling may well have contributed to a decline in homicides by elite men: whatever else duelling may have done, whether or not it eventually 'codified, restricted, [and] sterilized' the vengeance of powerful men into less deadly forms, the abstraction of the duel drew forth clearer articulations of the supremacy of law and its claims to effect retribution. And it did so in ways that many gentlemen found useful, or at the very least, not unduly threatening—thanks, again, in no small part to the utility of the manslaughter verdict. When these men took their grievances to Star Chamber and the Court of Chivalry, they endorsed these claims and helped to elevate the status of law.

---

[118] J.A. Sharpe, *Defamation and Sexual Slander in Early Modern England: The Church Courts at York* (York, 1980).

[119] Shoemaker, *London Mob*, pp. 179, 182. For the later history of duelling, see, too, Stephen Banks, *A Polite Exchange of Bullets: The Duel and the English Gentleman, 1750–1850* (Woodbridge, 2010); Nicholas Rogers, *Mayhem: Post-War Crime and Violence in Britain, 1748–53* (New Haven, CT, 2013); and Donna Andrew, *Aristocratic Vice: The Attack on Duelling, Suicide, Adultery, and Gambling in Eighteenth-Century England* (New Haven, CT, 2013).

[120] Mark Cooney, 'The Decline of Elite Homicide', *Criminology* 35.3 (1997): pp. 381–407, quote at 397.

The ways in which the language of 'lawfulness' pervaded discussions of duelling are striking: in the face of theorists who claimed for the duel its own kind of lawfulness, King James depicted it as a violation of the laws of nature and of God, as well as a violation of his own laws, which he equated with the 'public Justice of the state'. In time, however, some came to see the measures adopted by James and his son as also antithetical to law as properly understood. The 'law' became a public good, ostensibly above the interests of particular individuals, be they insulted gentlemen or monarchs. When even kings stood subject to the 'public Justice of the state', then law could more readily replace some interpersonal violence with violence of a different sort.

5

'For Publick Satisfaction'
Punishment, Print, Plays, and Public Vengeance

Homicide has a history. As old as Abel, its incidence, prosecution, and cultural salience nonetheless changed over time. Previous chapters have traced the rise and refinement of the manslaughter verdict, the increased regulation and reorientation of the coroner and his jury, the decline of the appeal and private payments for homicide, and the conceptualization of the duel as a form of violent encounter inherently opposed to something coming to be defined as 'public justice'. In all these ways, homicide became increasingly 'public', an offence against something more than the king, against a collectivity broader than those comprised by the individual victims and their families. Something else new about homicide in early modern England was its increasingly 'public' nature in the simplest sense of that term, when killers and killings came before audiences through public punishments, plays, and above all, in print. The rise of the commercial playhouse and changes in punishment regimes combined with the development of print to publicize individual killings and discussions of murder more generally in ways that distinguished early modern homicide from what had come before. Murder became more 'public' in these years in the most basic meaning of that word. This chapter explores links between the two ways of making murder public: that is, it posits a connection between the increasing publicity of homicide on the one hand and, on the other, its reconceptualization as an offence against 'public justice'.

Public conversations about killings did not just communicate ideas and describe behaviours but also participated in the processes that changed those ideas and behaviours. One of the key messages of many of the cheap murder pamphlets that multiplied from the late 1500s on, as Malcolm Gaskill has shown, was that 'murder will out': they regularly related the providential discovery of killers to support a belief in the likelihood of punishment. Gaskill alludes to statistics on homicide only to contextualize the pamphlets—to note that interest in homicide varied inversely with its incidence—and focuses firmly on what the pamphlets reveal about the cultural influences on the proscription, detection, and prosecution of murder.[1] But might we not also at least speculate about how print and publicity might have shaped the commission of the crime itself? That they might have done something more than simply report and reflect? Some scholars have claimed for reading, literacy, and the novel roles in an eighteenth-century 'humanitarian revolution' that expanded

---

[1] Gaskill, *Crime and Mentalities*.

circles of empathy and helped people see something of themselves in others, thus reducing levels of violence.[2] Might print and publicity not have played an earlier part in changing patterns of homicide by encouraging more people to leave vengeance to the law? The connection between the two is plausible, but hard to prove. At the very least, though, we can see in the new types of publicity afforded by punishment, plays, and print another mechanism by which homicide became more fully 'public'.

This chapter first traces the incidence not of criminal homicide but of capital punishment, a visible and brutal manifestation of the Crown's claims to monopolize the legitimate taking of life, yes, but also of its claims to provide vengeance. The notion that vengeance could or must be left to law received repeated elaboration in a variety of publications that came off the presses new to these years. The chapter then outlines the rise of 'true crime' reporting in pamphlets, plays (both printed and performed), and eventually in publications more akin to newspapers. Pamphlets and plays that narrated grisly murders providentially discovered and publicly punished constituted the most obvious sources of information about murder, but were also supplemented by the advent of more formal legal printing, too: statutes, treatises, manuals, and more, all contributed to making murder public. Finally and briefly, the chapter touches on publications relating to very political 'murders'—some imagined, some tied up in mystery, and some so deeply political that we might be more familiar with them as acts of treason. Punishment and print, offered at least ostensibly 'for public satisfaction', are examined here as mechanisms by which homicide became more fully criminalized.

PUNISHING PUBLICLY

While almost everyone reading this book will have seen fictionalized performances of homicide beyond number, few will have witnessed a person killing or being killed by another. Outside wartime, this is now a rare sight in many parts of the world. In contrast, most people who lived in early modern England probably saw such an event, and most likely through attending public executions. Residents of rural areas would have seen fewer hangings than their urban kin, true, but even they might have seen a few such deaths when travelling to markets, to court, or for other reasons. [3] When they categorized and catalogued the different types of homicides, legal writers of the era often included 'homicide by justice' or 'homicide...in execution of justice'. They obviously did not deem killing done in execution of

---

[2] See, e.g., Pinker, *Better Angels of Our Nature*, pp. 210ff, citing amongst others Lynn Hunt, *Inventing Human Rights: A History* (New York, 2007) on empathy and the epistolary novel. Though not focused on the decline of violence, G.J. Barker-Benfield offers a compelling discussion of the links between the rise of the novel and many of the individual behaviours that comprised Elias's 'civilizing process': *The Culture of Sensibility: Sex and Society in Eighteenth-Century Britain* (Chicago, 1992).

[3] Many people would also have seen homicides in war time, too: Paul Hammer has estimated that roughly 10 per cent of the population of late Elizabethan England had participated in military ventures: *Elizabeth's Wars: War, Government and Society in Tudor England, 1544–1604* (Basingstoke, 2003), pp. 245–8.

justice culpable or criminal, but they acknowledged it as homicide nonetheless.[4] And the simple fact holds that more people in early modern England died at the hands of those acting on behalf of the law than against it; while a developing state helped reduce interpersonal homicide, it did so at some cost. By extension, too, most people who went to the gallows died for offences other than murder or manslaughter: people condemned for theft, robbery, and property offences of various sorts outnumbered those executed for slayings.[5] Criminal homicides and judicial homicides shared any number of links; one of the most basic to be borne in mind is that many people would have learned something of what they knew about murder from watching the executions of killers strung up on early modern gallows, among a wider range of people condemned for offences against the king's peace.

Hanging was by far the most common form of capital punishment, used not just for criminal homicide but for the bulk of felonies, and prized for its supposedly exemplary, deterrent effect. These hangings were not the relatively quick affairs of later years: the standard drop and long drop developed only in subsequent centuries, meaning that earlier hangings typically consisted of slow strangulations that could take half an hour or more to kill a person, unless someone tugged on the body as it hung. For high treason, men were dragged through the streets, briefly hanged, then disembowelled and divided into quarters, though authorities typically substituted a beheading with block and axe for titled offenders. Judges ordered heretics to be burnt at the stake. So, too, for women found guilty of petty treason, most commonly for maliciously killing their husbands. While the English prided themselves on not having some of the more imaginative and gruesome forms of execution used on the continent, they did make exceptions for what they saw as exceptional crimes. Briefly after 1531, those people who used poison to kill risked death by boiling, a punishment imposed on at least two individuals.[6] Some punishments evoked parallels with the crimes committed: Alice Wolfe and her husband John, for example, were tied to a stake at the Thames's low tide and left there to drown as the waters rose, having killed foreign merchants while ferrying them across the river.[7] The authorities killed yet other offenders by gibbeting or hanging them in chains, or after first severing some offending body part.

Death came for many offences, in many varieties, and in many places. In and around London itself, the Tower offered the main site of execution for elite or exceptional offenders, either on full public view just outside the walls or somewhat more privately inside. The Smithfield market area, Wapping Dock, and, above all, Tyburn field served as favoured sites, but almost any church yard or open space that accommodated a crowd hosted executions, too. Charing Cross, Cheapside,

---

[4] See, e.g., Michael Dalton, *The Countrey Justice* (London, 1618), p. 207; Pulton, *De Pace Regis et Regni*, p. 120.

[5] As a quick example here: in his study of Surrey assize records, in a sample of twelve years drawn from 1663 to 1694, Beattie found that an average of eight people were sentenced to death each year, with an average of just under five hanged, with seven out of the total of fifty-six (12.5 per cent) executed for homicide and the rest for coining or property offences of various sorts. See Beattie, *Crime*, p. 454.

[6] See Kesselring, 'A Draft of the 1531 "Acte for Poysoning" ', *English Historical Review* 116 (2001): pp. 894–9.

[7] By a special parliamentary attainder: 25 Henry VIII c. 34.

St. Paul's Churchyard, Westminster's Tothill, and Old Palace Yard all saw executions in these years. After a set of riots in 1517, the authorities killed people at each of London's city gates, setting up special gallows at such places as Aldgate, Bishopsgate, Gracechurch Street, and Leadenhall Street.[8] Many people witnessed the power of the law to take life.

We have some reason to think that punishment became increasingly public in the late middle ages and into the sixteenth century. Medieval executions of traitors had long offered spectacles of power and pain, both bluntly brutal and intensely symbolic in their evisceration and elimination of subjects who violated their bonds of loyalty to their king. As Katherine Royer explains, over the thirteenth century the trials of selected traitors more often ended with ceremonialized 'urban spectacles' intended to punish and to demonstrate the power of the king, and also to 'announce the crime', with graphic displays performed for a public audience.[9] But authorities seem not to have orchestrated other executions for similar effect. Killers had long faced capital sanctions for their crimes, but only over the thirteenth century did England's kings try to monopolize the execution of law breakers, insisting that it be done by their agents or by their permission. Kings sought to limit or license others' use of gallows, and also to restrict capital punishment to those gallows.[10] Yet even then, evidence suggests that, in Henry Summerson's words, 'medieval executions for felony were commonly hole-in-corner affairs, with few witnesses, and it was not unknown for a condemned man to be left to hang in solitude'.[11] Gallows commonly stood at the edges of communities, rather than at their heart, at junctions and crossroads to edify passers-by rather than at sites likely to host crowds for the event itself, he notes.

J.G. Bellamy, James Sharpe, and others have argued that the early to mid-sixteenth century English witnessed an elaboration of the practices surrounding the scaffold.[12] The speech-making by the condemned, the participation of clergy, and some of the more ceremonial elements that early modern sources attest seem not to have been

---

[8] See Kesselring, *Mercy and Authority*, pp. 157–9, and contemporary Edward Hall's account, in *Hall's Chronicle*, edited by H. Ellis (London, 1809), pp. 587–90. For the full range of corporal punishments, also visible and violent, see, too, J.A. Sharpe, *Judicial Punishment in England* (London, 1990).

[9] Katherine Royer, 'The Body in Parts: Reading the Execution Ritual in Late Medieval England', *Historical Reflections* 29 (2003): pp. 319–39. Royer's article also helpfully sets out the reasons for caution in applying Michel Foucault's influential model of punishment to the late medieval period: Foucault had focused on the transition away from, not the creation of, a spectacle of the scaffold centred on the body, and dwelt on the development of a later system of interiorized punishment premised on surveillance. His discussion of the spectacle of the scaffold was also centred on absolutist France with its inquisitorial justice, and is not readily transferrable to a judicial system without routine torture and with more open, participatory modes of accusation and trial. See also Lorna Hutson, *The Invention of Suspicion: Law and Mimesis in Shakespeare and Renaissance Drama* (Oxford, 2007).

[10] Kenneth Duggan, 'The Ritualistic Importance of Gallows in Thirteenth-Century England', in *Crossing Borders: Boundaries and Margins in Medieval and Early Modern Britain*, edited by Sara M. Butler and K.J. Kesselring (Leiden, 2017), pp. 195–215.

[11] Henry Summerson, 'Attitudes to Capital Punishment in England, 1200–1350', in *Thirteenth-Century England VIII: Proceedings of the Durham Conference, 1999*, edited by Michael Prestwich, Richard Britnell, and Robin Frame (Woodbridge, 2001), p. 130.

[12] For Bellamy, see esp. *Crime and Public Order*, p. 189, and *Criminal Trial in Later Medieval England*, p. 154. Sharpe has made his argument most cogently in *Judicial Punishment in England*, pp. 31–4.

features of medieval felons' executions. In the meticulous accounts kept for a set of late sixteenth-century executions at Wapping Dock, we read not only of the 2*s* per man given to the executioner for the killing, cutting down, and burying or the 6*d* per man for a collar and pinioning cords, but also of fees for carrying bills to and from the Tower, for the minister who accompanied the condemned, for the rental of seven horses for the marshal and his men, for significant quantities of bread and beer for the warders who conducted the party to the execution site, and so forth.[13] Did earlier executions have the same? Bellamy notes that sixteenth-century chroniclers made more frequent mention than had their predecessors of executions and execution-day crowds. In part, to be sure, the argument for a shift in practice in the Tudor period rests on a lack of evidence for earlier executions: the primarily monastic chroniclers of the middle ages crafted few and perfunctory accounts of public punishments whereas sixteenth-century secular writers paid them more heed, but this may have reflected the different interests of the two groups of chroniclers more than changes to the practice of execution. Even so, other indications do suggest shifts towards more intensely visual, public performances of punishment: based upon London's urban records, Stuart Minson observes that authorities in the city began the carting of bawds and common women, the public whipping of vagrants and beggars, and the ducking of obstreperous women all in the early sixteenth century, with penitential processions proceeding more often and more widely through the city.[14] Martin Ingram notes that by the middle decades of the sixteenth century, public, corporal punishments such as whipping came to play more regular roles in the repertory of punishment, in a variety of urban centres.[15] Tyburn had long hosted many of London's executions, but obtained its infamous 'triple tree', a permanent gallows that could hold some two dozen bodies, only in the 1570s. Thus, executions were not just public throughout the early modern period, but may well have become somewhat more intentionally, intensively so over these years, and witnessed by more people.

Similar arguments for a shift in the publicity of capital punishments have been made for other parts of Europe. Writing of French history, Paul Friedland traces a general trend from the twelfth through the sixteenth centuries towards increasing severity and 'spectacularity' of punishment, identifying a shift from ritual to spectacle, from participants to onlookers, taking shape in the 1500s in particular.[16] Other historians have written of 'late medieval' changes in the culture of public

---

[13] HCA 1/101/8–19.

[14] Stuart Minson, 'Public Punishment and Urban Space in Early Tudor London', *London Topographical Record* 30 (2010): pp. 1–16.

[15] Martin Ingram, *Carnal Knowledge: Regulating Sex in England, 1470–1600* (Cambridge, 2017), pp. 286, 278. See also Ingram, 'Shame and Pain: Themes and Variations in Tudor Punishments', in *Penal Practice and Culture, 1500–1900: Punishing the English*, edited by Simon Devereaux and Paul Griffiths (Basingstoke, 2004), pp. 36–62. Much of this whipping was done publicly, but as Paul Griffiths reminds us, with the development of Bridewell in the latter half of the sixteenth century, whippings took place both 'privately' within and publicly without: *Lost Londons*, pp. 274–90. For London punishments of a later era, see Andrea McKenzie, *Tyburn's Martyrs: Execution in England, 1675–1775* (London, 2007).

[16] Paul Friedland, *Seeing Justice Done: The Age of Spectacular Capital Punishment in France* (Oxford, 2012).

punishment, typically locating those changes to the 1400s, with an intensification in the century that followed. In France, as Esther Cohen has noted, the *amende honorable* and elaborate ceremonies of both ejection and reconciliation had featured from at least the 1300s, but seem to have developed further thereafter as religious elements were added.[17] Friedland suggests that the executions of Lutherans and increasing numbers of heretics in the early 1500s helped intensify and redirect a shift long underway in France. As Tyge Krogh has shown, confessional differences manifested themselves in varying approaches to punishment across Europe in the Reformation era, and then in turn in differing patterns of criminal behaviour: in Lutheran areas, scaffold performances of repentance and ministerial support were such that people thought of them as a sure-fire way to be confident of their eternal salvation, and in post-Reformation Denmark, at least, this belief prompted a rash of suicide-murders.[18] Studies of other parts of Europe, then, give us some reason to think that capital punishments may have become differently 'public' than they had been before, even if the nature of that spectacle and its effects varied from one place to another.

Evidence also suggests that people had more executions to watch by the late Elizabethan years than they had had a century or so before. Exactly how many people died as convicted traitors, murderers, felons, and heretics in these years we cannot know, but the number was unquestionably high—certainly higher than the number of people who died as victims of interpersonal homicides—and seems to have peaked between *c.*1580 and 1620. True, the population of England and Wales increased dramatically over the sixteenth century, and especially in the decades on either side of 1600; without firmer numbers than we have at present, we cannot be sure that executions increased at a commensurate or greater rate, but that is at least the impression. And whether or not the rate increased, the number likely did. One frequently sees cited online and in older historical accounts claims that Henry VIII's agents executed some 70,000 thieves and vagabonds. This number comes from nothing more than the hearsay report of a visitor to England, however, which was then included (in slightly altered form) in an Elizabethan chronicle and thence passed on to posterity.[19] Turning to the archives gives us grounds for better

---

[17] For Cohen, see, e.g., *The Crossroads of Justice: Law and Culture in Late Medieval France* (Leiden, 1993), pp. 181–201. For the development of Bolognese confraternities to comfort the condemned and their various rituals and texts, over the 1400s and especially over the 1500s, see Nicholas Terpstra, ed., *The Art of Executing Well: Rituals of Execution in Renaissance Italy* (Kirksville, MO, 2008). Mitchell Merback writes of a late medieval shift to a distinctive mode of 'judicial spectatorship', using as evidence visual images dating mostly from the 1500s that show crowds at execution scenes: *The Thief, the Cross, and the Wheel: Pain and the Spectacle of Punishment in Medieval and Renaissance Europe* (London, 1999). Others have offered similar speculations about a sixteenth-century shift in execution rituals on the continent: see, e.g., R. van Dülmen, *Theatre of Horror: Crime and Punishment in Early Modern Germany*, trans. E. Neu (Cambridge, 1990), p. 59, and Pieter Spierenburg, *Spectacle of Suffering* Cambridge, 1984), pp. 43–4.

[18] Krogh, *A Lutheran Plague*.

[19] Sometimes cited as 72,000. William Harrison's 'Description of England', included in Raphael Holinshed's *Chronicles of England, Scotland and Ireland* (London, 1587), vol. 1, p. 314 seems to be the most commonly cited source for this number, but as Harrison notes, he acquired it only 'by report' passed on by one Gerolamo Cardano, a visiting Italian scholar, who in turn heard the number from the 'Bishop of Lexovia' (possibly Lisieux, in France). See Thorsten Sellin's tracing of the story in 'Two

estimates, but estimates nonetheless. Working from pockets of surviving court records, Philip Jenkins suggested that anywhere from 600 to 1,200 people a year suffered judicial executions in early modern England.[20] The archives that allow us even these imprecise numbers come mostly from the reigns of Elizabeth and her successors, though; relatively few court records survive from earlier years that provide the all-important indications of whether sentences were ultimately carried out.

Trying to find other sources of evidence to flesh this out, we might turn to the chronicle of Henry VIII's reign left by the royal herald Charles Wriothesley. Though he noted only the executions of high profile or unusual offenders and focused on the immediate environs of the court, he mentioned specifically the deaths of 234 individuals (together with 'diverse others', unspecified) between 1509 and 1547, with some 118 hanged and quartered, forty-three simply hanged, forty-three burnt, twenty-nine beheaded, and one boiled.[21] The letters that Christopher Jenney sent to Thomas Cromwell give some sense of executions for regular crimes, in another urban centre. Jenney was a travelling judge, sent out on the twice-yearly assize circuits that emptied gaols throughout the country. In one report on a court day in York in March 1535, he noted that he had tried seventy-six prisoners, with eighteen convicted, though one and possibly two of the condemned escaped execution thanks to their clerical status and a pardon.[22] His report of the August 1535 court date mentioned forty-two prisoners, of whom six went to their deaths. (In that letter, he noted too his stop at Hull, where he tried a 20-year-old 'boy' for 'meddling carnally with a cow': both the young man and the cow were killed, the latter burned in the place where the deed had been done.)[23] In a third letter, reporting a court session in April 1538, he noted that he had tried at York eighty prisoners, with eighteen executed, but had not bothered to travel to Durham as he had word that the city had no prisoners in its gaol at the moment.[24] We might choose to be impressed by either or both facts that only about twenty per cent of those people charged with capital offences suffered death, or that the small city of York witnessed a minimum of forty executions resulting from these three court days alone.

The diary kept by the provisioner Henry Machyn from 1550 to 1563 gives a sense of the number of executions a Londoner of the mid-Tudor years might have seen. Machyn noted the executions of a minimum of 347 people in and around London in those thirteen years. This is not a full tally: we have no reason at all to think that Machyn noted every execution—indeed, for some years he notes none at all—and the diary itself is now damaged and incomplete. Machyn seemed most interested in funerals, but also wrote about sermons, odd weather, 'monstrous'

Myths in the History of Capital Punishment', *Journal of Criminal Law and Criminology* 50 (1959–60): pp. 114–17.

[20] Philip Jenkins, 'From Gallows to Prison? The Execution Rate in Early Modern England', *Criminal Justice History* 7 (1986): pp. 51–71, at 52. Cockburn offered an estimate of 600–700 executions per year for roughly the same period: 'Punishment and Brutalization in the English Enlightenment', *Law and History Review* 12.1 (1994): pp. 155–79, at 158.

[21] *A Chronicle of England... by Charles Wriothesley*, edited by William Douglas Hamilton, 2 vols. (London, Camden Society, n.s., vols. 11, 20, 1875 and 1877), vol. 1, *passim*.

[22] SP 1/91, f. 144.   [23] SP 1/95, f. 33.   [24] SP 1/242, f. 10.

births, omens, and false prophets, as well as more unusual events such as the sighting of dolphins in the Thames and 'the greatest dinner that ever I saw'. Peppered through these notes, he included frequent mention of people pilloried or whipped through the streets for offences that ranged from adulterating food to bawdry to attempted murder. He also mentioned high-profile executions and busy Tyburn hanging days. Some of those 347 fatalities were for treason, including the forty-three men who died on St. Valentine's Day in 1554 for their parts in the revolts tied to Sir Thomas Wyatt, killed at sixteen locations spread around the city, much as had happened with the Evil May Day rioters of 1517.[25] Machyn's diary-keeping overlapped with Queen Mary's effort to stamp out Protestantism and as such, another forty-three of these victims burned for heresy. To pick one year to illustrate: for 1556, he recorded a total of fifty-eight executions in and around London, including nine for treason and twenty-one for heresy, as well as an additional twenty-eight for felonies that ranged from theft to piracy to murder. Of that final group, the pirates were hanged at the low water mark at Wapping, a common punishment for people whose crimes occurred at sea. Two of the other felons—whose trial for robbery saw one of the men stab a witness in court—had their hangings aggravated: one had a hand severed, the other had a hand burnt, and the man who had stabbed the witness was hanged naked. For this year, Machyn also noted that one of the men who suffered as a felon had himself previously served as the city's hangman, and had thus 'hanged many a man and quartered many, and [be]head[ed] many a noble man and other'. Machyn also made note of other criminals, usually heretics, who were condemned at Westminster but taken elsewhere to die, and recorded news of what must have been an exceptional court day in Oxford: on October 3, he noted, the justices at the Oxford sessions had condemned sixty people to death.[26] He deemed 6 April 1554 a noteworthy day: it saw eight felons hanged at Tyburn, even as five heretics burned at Smithfield and seven pirates drowned at Wapping.[27] Twenty-eight to thirty seems to be the rough average of felony executions noted in Machyn's diary per year, both in Mary's reign and in the earliest years of Elizabeth's.

This might seem extraordinarily high, but numbers of people subjected to capital punishment may well have climbed higher still at the end of the century. Annual numbers of executions in early to mid-sixteenth-century London were almost certainly more than those of the second half of the seventeenth century; but evidence suggests that the decades immediately on either side of 1600 saw the highest rates. We seem to see an increase near the turn to the seventeenth century before we begin to see a decline. We can look to the London bills of mortality for rough guides to the numbers of executions and deaths attributed to homicide for later decades. Kept intermittently from the late sixteenth century to track plague deaths, the bills became more regular and more detailed about the wide variety of causes of death as the seventeenth century progressed. Based on submissions from clerks in some 132 of the parishes in and near London, the bills from 1658 to 1700

[25] *Diary of Henry Machyn*, ed.Nichols, p. 55. [26] Ibid., pp. 109, 111, 115, 121–2.
[27] Ibid., p. 131.

mention 809 executions, or an average of 18.8 per year, alongside 634 homicides, an average of 14.7 per year. In most years—thirty-two out of forty-three—the number of people who died from executions exceeded the number identified as the victims of homicides.[28]

In the late Elizabethan and early Stuart years, though, execution rates seem to have been higher, certainly in London and also quite likely elsewhere in the country. As James Sharpe has shown, Cheshire saw its highest numbers of indictments for homicide in the 1620s, with roughly 110 charges laid in those years, and also witnessed its highest numbers and proportions of offenders executed in the same decade, with 166 people hanged for felonies of all sorts, 22 per cent of the total number accused.[29] Surviving court records show an average of about twenty-five executions per year in both Devon and Essex in the late 1500s.[30] Foreign visitors to London in 1599 and 1616 both estimated that some twenty-five people were executed on each of London's eight annual execution days.[31] James Cordy Jeaffreson found an unusually detailed gaol delivery register for Middlesex—not metropolitan London—that showed an annual average of 70.4 people hanged in each of the ten years after 1609, a 'penal death rate' that becomes all the more striking when we realize that an average of only 10.3 people were charged with murder and manslaughter in each of those same years. Most of the condemned suffered for crimes against property, not homicide. Jeaffreson provides reasons to think that the numbers of executions in the more heavily populated city must have been higher, but to avoid overstating his case, treats them as equal, suggesting an annual average of 147.2 executions a year in the greater London area.[32] (For context, London's population had soared from an estimated 70,000 people in 1550 to perhaps 200,000 by 1600, and was to double within the next fifty years.)[33] In early Stuart Middlesex, as elsewhere in these years, one stood a better chance of dying a violent death at the hands of the authorities than at those of common killers. Moreover, as Philip Jenkins has noted, evidence suggests that the English 'might have hanged more

---

[28] James Postlethwayt et al., *A Collection of the Yearly Bills of Mortality, from 1657 to 1758 Inclusive* (London, 1759). (On bills of mortality, see also Spence, *Accidents*, pp. 50–3.) As Postlethwayt notes, a number of omissions and sources of error complicate use of the bills: a few of the liberties were not included and a few parishes missing from the earliest years were added by the late 1600s; the clerks were sometimes negligent; and they tracked only burials in parish cemeteries and thus missed Catholics and dissenters who were buried elsewhere, as well as those who were buried in cemeteries belonging to the cathedrals and not the parishes. They have their deficiencies, then, as a source of reliable statistics. They do, however, have the added benefit of providing a bit of context for the numbers under discussion, reminding us that people were far more likely to die of diseases or injuries, whether wholly natural or inflected by social deprivation. In comparison to the 809 executions and 634 homicides noted in these returns, for example, some 11,641 women died in childbed, an average of 270.7 per year.

[29] J.A. Sharpe, *Crime in Early Modern England, 1550–1750* (London, 1995), pp. 87, 91, 92.

[30] Ibid., p. 92, and Cockburn, *History of English Assizes*, pp. 94–5; see also Steve Hindle's discussion of execution rates in *State and Social Change*, p. 119.

[31] *The Journals of Two Travellers in Elizabethan and Early Stuart England*, edited by Peter Razzell (London, 1995), pp. 36, 148; cited in McKenzie, *Tyburn's Martyrs*.

[32] *MCR* II, xvii–xxi. Nor does this amount include those who died from *peine forte et dure*, another 3.2 per year, on average, let alone those who died from imprisonment.

[33] Roger Finlay, *Population and Metropolis: The Demography of London, 1580–1650* (Cambridge, 2010), p. 51.

people between 1580 and 1630 than in *all* subsequent decades up to the virtual abolition of capital punishment in 1967'.[34]

Noting the scope and scale of judicial homicides can provide a salutary bit of context for talk of the criminal homicides they outnumbered. It reminds us that violence was not just an object of control, but also a means. Law was in some senses an alternative to violence, even while relying upon it. Beyond noting the ubiquity of state violence, it is important to observe as well that this violence was both mechanically instrumental and a form of political communication. Executions dispatched messages as well as offenders. They had a significance beyond mere numbers alone. Several studies have now examined executions for their ideological import, for the insights they provide into the construction of authority and obedience, and for the ways they allowed a state with limited policing capacity to display and augment its power.[35] Some have noted that the messages of the gallows and scaffold could be multivocal or contested; most obviously, the executions of Protestant 'heretics' or Catholic 'traitors' provoked conflicting reactions, but so too upon occasion could executions of the poor and pitiable who were condemned for regular felonies.[36] Executions did not always 'work' in their ostensible purpose of deterring criminals—an Elizabethan statute against pickpocketing noted with some consternation that these thieves worked execution crowds, for example, not mindful of the display 'ordained chiefly for terror and example of evil doers'. And a number of cross-national and historical studies have suggested that in so far as the severity of punishment and frequency of homicide are related, they rise and fall together.[37] At the very least, though, the publicly inflicted executions of killers, alongside those of offenders of all sorts, advertised the claims of the Crown to monopolize deadly vengeance.

Noting the scope and scale of judicial homicide also reminds us that people then viewed violence—that is, intentional physical harm—as morally neutral. They did not see force as intrinsically morally negative; judgement of the moral character of any given act of physical harm depended on the actors, context, and ends. Looking at the people who hanged on these early modern gallows and those who did not reminds us, too, that assault constituted at most a misdemeanour, and remained so for a long time yet. While those who stole goods of relatively small value might find themselves sentenced to die, those who caused a serious amount of physical harm, and even those who attempted murder, did not. What was being criminalized as felonious behaviour, offensive to king and to the public, was killing, not assault or physical harm. While the Crown might seek to arbitrate what constituted legitimate force, what it sought to monopolize was lawful slaughter. Only law could

---

[34] Jenkins, 'From Gallows to Prison?', quote at p. 52.

[35] See esp. James Sharpe, '"Last Dying Speeches": Religion, Ideology and Public Execution in Seventeenth-Century England', *P&P* 107 (1985): pp. 144–67.

[36] Peter Lake and Michael Questier, 'Agency, Appropriation, and Rhetoric under the Gallows: Puritans, Romanists, and the State in Early Modern England', *P&P* 153 (1996): pp. 64–107.

[37] 8 Elizabeth I c. 4. For the latter point, see, e.g., works summarized or cited in Wilson and Daly, *Homicide*, p. 290 and Michael L. Radelet and Traci L. Lacock, 'Do Executions Lower Homicide Rates?: The Views of Leading Criminologists', *Journal of Criminal Law and Criminology* 99 (2009): pp. 489–508.

legitimately take life. And asserting that claim—that killings by actors other than the Crown's agents were always and everywhere wrong, that lethal vengeance for slights had to be left to the law—took work.

PRINT AND PLAYS

While public executions did some of that work, print and other forms of publication also helped it along. The visibility and frequency of executions left no doubt of the Crown's claim that it had the authority to take lives legitimately; print and plays amplified, augmented, and elucidated that claim. If we want to enumerate what was new in these years that might have influenced the incidence and meaning of murder, we must surely include print in our list. Print did not just open up to us new sources of information about early modern crime and punishment, reporting to audiences then and now what was happening, but was itself a factor in the changes taking place.

William Caxton began working from the first English printing press in 1476, and over the coming decades printers produced ever more titles that embraced new subjects, adopted new forms, and reached new audiences. Printing transformed law reporting and legal culture, with statutes, abridgements, case reports, manuals, and treatises printed and distributed for ever wider readerships. Wider, faster dissemination of more and more texts allowed changes to legal scholarship of the sort Elizabeth Eisenstein proposed for scholarly culture more generally: extensive reading of relatively 'fixed' texts allowed authors to preserve and cumulatively build upon what had come before.[38] Chronicles of notable occurrences, long maintained in manuscript, moved into print and gradually 'dissolved' into a variety of distinct genres: shorter news pamphlets and broadsides first supplemented and then supplanted them, taking over some of their functions.[39] John Bellamy has traced the murder pamphlet's origins to the profusion of publications about the death of 'Protestant martyr' Richard Hunne at the hands of episcopal officers in 1514, but notes that it was only in the final three decades of the sixteenth century that such publications began to proliferate.[40] As the century progressed, chroniclers came to include in their works lengthier narrations of noteworthy murders. From the 1570s the genre of the murder pamphlet took shape, and from the first decade of the 1600s it took off. By the 1670s, dozens upon dozens appeared each year and

---

[38] On legal printing specifically, see Christopher W. Brooks, *Law, Politics and Society in Early Modern England* (Cambridge, 2008); David J. Harvey, *The Law Emprynted and Englysshed: The Printing Press as an Agent of Change in Law and Legal Culture, 1475–1642* (London, 2015); Richard J. Ross, 'The Commoning of the Common Law: The Renaissance Debate over Printing English Law, 1520–1640', *University of Pennsylvania Law Review* 146 (1998): pp. 323–461; and Sebastian Sobecki, *Unwritten Verities: The Making of England's Vernacular Legal Culture, 1463–1549* (Notre Dame, IN, 2015). For the classic work on the scholarly effects of print, see Elizabeth Eisenstein, *The Printing Press as an Agent of Change*, 2 vols. (Cambridge, 1979).

[39] Daniel R. Woolf, 'Genre into Artifact: The Decline of the English Chronicle in the Sixteenth Century', *Sixteenth Century Journal* 19 (1988): pp. 321–54.

[40] Bellamy, *Strange, Inhuman Deaths*, pp. 3–9 and ch. 2.

were accompanied by early newspapers and 'sessions papers' specially devoted to the range of criminal trials in London. Some publications focused on the crimes; others focused on the executions; many combined both. Works that sought to impose narratives on events and guide interpretations of their significance offered a mix of sensationalism, moralizing, and more, often conflating edification and entertainment.

In Leigh Yetter's words, printed accounts of executions became 'parts of the ritual of punishment itself'; in Todd Butler's, print became useful as a 'judicial technology'.[41] Randall Martin depicts the pamphlets as a form of 'preknowledge' that shaped readers' responses to subsequent events.[42] Indeed, Martin, Laura Gowing, Frances Dolan, Paul Griffiths, and others have noted that phrases from such texts later found their way into depositions, with words and ideas circulating from courtroom to quarto and back again. Some included ostensible transcriptions of courtroom testimony, lists of witnesses, and other such documentary evidence to assert the truth of their relation.[43] Malcolm Gaskill has examined the ways in which the pamphlets provided assurances that God's providence would unmask murderers if human efforts failed.[44] These 'true relations' insisted that murder could indeed speak 'with most miraculous organ': children born mute suddenly spoke to name the offender, bodies bled afresh in the presence of a suspect, drops of blood indelibly marked killers. Murder offended God so deeply that heaven itself would direct the hue and cry. As Gaskill notes, in these murder pamphlets, 'Thwarted escapes, monitory ghosts, revelatory dreams and bleeding corpses all explained the failure of secret murderers to keep their crimes secret.'[45] By the seventeenth century, many murder pamphlets followed the narrative of the killings and the providential discovery of their perpetrators with an account of the condemnation and execution of the killers, sometimes including effusively sorrowful gallows speeches or 'woeful lamentations'. Printed accounts of killings thus bolstered beliefs in the likelihood of punishment with reams of evidence. In the words of one author, 'that the bloody murderer never went to his grave in peace is experimentally known'.[46]

Some scholars have noted how these pamphlets singled out particular objects of fear. Murderous wives and mothers figured disproportionately in these texts in their first years. As Frances Dolan has observed, in their focus on domestic dangers, these pamphlets often located the threat to social order 'in the least powerful and privileged, in those most likely to be the victims rather than the perpetrators of violence'.[47] From about 1650, homicidal husbands begin to outnumber murderous wives in the surviving publications, but throughout the period, familial killings

---

[41] Leigh Yetter, *Public Execution in England, 1573–1868* (London, 2009), vii; Todd Butler, 'The Haunting of Isabell Binnington: Ghosts of Murder, Texts, and Law in Restoration England', *Journal of British Studies* 50 (2011): pp. 248–76, quote at 251.

[42] Randall Martin, *Women, Murder and Equity in Early Modern England* (London, 2008), p. 5.

[43] See esp. Frances Dolan, *True Relations*.   [44] Gaskill, *Crime and Mentalities*, pp. 203–80.

[45] Gaskill, *Crime and Mentalities*, p. 220.

[46] Anon., *Heavens Cry Against Murder* (London, 1657), p. 9.

[47] Frances Dolan, *Dangerous Familiars: Representations of Domestic Crime in England, 1550–1700* (Ithaca, NY, 1994), p. 15.

remained a common focus, out of all proportion to their actual incidence: in a sample of seventy-seven murder reports published before the 1670s, about half narrate household homicides. We read of the 'horrible, woeful, and most lamentable murder' by shearman John Kynnestar of his wife in 1573; the 'most wicked and secret murdering' of goldsmith John Brewen by his wife in 1592; the 'most cruel and bloody murder' of master Robert Heath by his own servant in 1609; the 'great and bloody murder' committed by Mary Champion upon her infant in 1647; and so on.

Some murder pamphlets pointed to the dangers of religious dissent and sought to use murderers to castigate the larger groups of which they were part. *The Parricide Papist, or Cut-Throate Catholicke* offers one example of the works that asked, essentially, 'how can the tree be good that beareth such Gomorrah fruit'?[48] One pamphlet recounts how the Catholic Inigo Jeanes clubbed his father to death before killing himself, while another narrates the killing by Enoch ap Evan, a fellow Catholic, of his mother and brothers. As Peter Lake has noted, puritans proved at least as popular as papists as targets for writers on a moralizing mission.[49] Words put into the mouths of watchmen commenting on murders by a fellow Londoner have one ask, 'Is this the fruits of saint-like Puritans? I never life such damp'd hypocrisy.' His fellow watchman derided the killer's sermon-gadding and belief that an oath 'would rend his jaws in twaine', yet his lack of scruple at murdering two people.[50] Anabaptists or members of radical religious sects in the civil war years also figured into pamphleteers' accounts of the horrible, unnatural murderers— often killing family members—who inevitably came to justice through God's own hue and cry.[51]

Murder pamphlets served to reiterate lessons on obedience and conformity of all sorts, but readers needed to fear not just the marginalized or the sectarian: murder might well be more common among the uncivilized or unsanctified, but was not the preserve of some criminal 'other'. Murder was a sin as much as a crime, and thus something to which all were prone. All people had within them the same blood as Cain. The same passions and humours that made murderers of some existed in all. A surprising number of these pamphlets warned their readers not about the dangers posed by others, but about the dangers within themselves. While the pamphlets often invoked the agency of the Devil in the acts of the killers, they did not show the killers to be demonized or dehumanized or fundamentally differ-ent from the reader: they remained all too familiar, as fellow sinners who had fallen

---

[48] George Closse, *The Parricide Papist, or, Cut-throate Catholicke* (London, 1606); quote from Richard More, *A True Relation of a Barbarous and Most Cruell Murther [com]mitted by one Enoch ap Euan* (London, 1633), sig. A4r.

[49] Peter Lake, 'Puritanism, Arminianism and a Shropshire Axe-Murder', *Midland History* 15 (1990): pp. 37–64.

[50] Robert Yarington, *Two Lamentable Tragedies* (London, 1601), sig. I1v.

[51] See, e.g., Anon., *Bloody Newes from Dover, being a True Relation of the Great and Bloudy Murder Committed by Mary Champion (an Anabaptist) who cut off her childs head* (London, 1647), and Anon., *Strange News from the North: Or, the Sectaries Sacrifice* (London, 1648).

prey to Satan's temptations. Anyone might become the Devil's instrument.[52] As Arthur Golding cautioned in one of the first murder pamphlets, his 1573 account of the death of George Saunders, the example of these killers' descent into sin thus brought to the 'open theatre' of judgement should 'drive us to the inward consideration of ourselves'. He continued, 'That we stand, it is the benefit of God's grace, and not the goodness of our nature nor the strength of our own will. That they are fallen, it was of frailty: where from we be no more privileged than they.'[53]

The invocations of providential discoveries offered not just reassurance that murders by others would be discovered, but also warnings that the readers themselves ought not to kill. Vengeance must be left to God, and would certainly be taken by God. If one suffered an injury, leave the punishment to God; if one caused injury, God would ensure retribution. Narrating the case of a woman who killed her spouse with her lover's assistance, one author asked that 'the Lord give all men grace by their example to shun the hateful sin of murder, for be it kept never so close and done never so secret, yet at length the Lord will bring it out'.[54] Another writer offered this moral to his tale: 'It therefore behooveth every one to have a special care what actions we commit, not seeking to murder those that have in some sort offended us, but to leave, as we ought, the revenge of all wrongs unto the Lord.'[55] John Reynolds's lengthy compendium of foreign murder tales, which had some sixteen reissues or editions between 1621 and 1680, was entitled *The Triumphs of God's Revenge against the Crying and Execrable Sinne of Murder, or his Miraculous Discoveries and Severe Punishments Thereof*; it was, according to its title page, 'very necessary to restrain and deter us from this bloody sin'.

Thomas Cooper's *Cry and Revenge of Blood* (1620) exemplifies this focus on the reader as the target of the moralizing message. A substantial work of some seventy-one pages, it related the greed-induced killing of three young adults at Halfworth, Suffolk, and the recent detection, trial, and punishment of the killers at the Bury assizes. As the title suggests, it insisted that through God's providence, murder would become known—though in this case, strikingly, God's providence operated in part through the skill of the surgeons who reconstructed the skeletons found at the bottom of a pond and the shrewdness of a judge who matched one skeleton to a mother's description of her missing son. Focused on this case and the assurance that God would take vengeance for blood, Cooper nonetheless began his tract with

---

[52] On the differences from witchcraft pamphlets in depicting Satan's agency in ways that reduced the 'empathic gap' between reader and criminal, see Nathan Johnstone, *The Devil and Demonism in Early Modern England* (Cambridge, 2006), esp. pp. 142–50. Karen Halttunen concentrates on modern constructions of murderers, but instructively traces a shift from early modern views focused on all-too-human sinners falling prey to evil, to assertions of moral distance from murderers depicted as monstrous, unhuman, unnatural, or (at best) diseased—though with interesting ambiguities produced by the lingering elements of older views: *Murder Most Foul: The Killer and the American Gothic Imagination* (Cambridge, MA, 1998).

[53] Arthur Golding, *A Briefe Discourse of the Late Murther of Master George Saunders* (London, 1573), sig. C4r.

[54] Thomas Kyd, *The Trueth of the Most Wicked and Secret Murthering of John Brewen* (London, 1592), p. 6.

[55] Anon., *Sundrye Strange and Inhumaine Murthers... wherein is described the odiousnesse of murther* (London, 1591), sig. A2r.

a twenty-five-page introduction that sought both to defend Protestantism and individual Protestants from their popish foes and also to dissuade his readers from killing. Cooper defended the people of the Gospel from popish aspersions based upon the profusion of killings—though certainly, he seemed to think that a truly reformed nation living more closely in accord with God's word would see fewer homicides, which he saw as characteristically Catholic failings. He also, bluntly and directly, urged individuals not to kill. Situating the causes of murder firmly in sin, he then devoted pages to the means by which to prevent killings. His advice did not focus on more effective policing, prosecution, and punishment, but on how people reading his work might better live at peace with God and their fellow man, and thus avoid becoming killers. A key 'preservative against this monstrous sin', logically enough, 'is wisdom to avoid the occasions thereof': pride, envy, lust, jealousy, ambition, covetousness, rage, bitter speaking, evil company, discontent, unlawful recreation, 'and the like'.[56] This was not a tract intended to reassure those who feared being killed, but to strengthen those who might fall prey to becoming killers.

True, some such pamphlets positioned their readers as potential victims rather than potential murderers. Some warned readers to take heed of these stories to ensure their own spiritual fitness should they die suddenly at others' hands; murder certainly showed that 'they that see the sun rise, are not sure to see it fall'.[57] Some urged people to be kinder to their servants or spouses lest they drive these people to violence. But the object of a good many warnings was to dissuade the readers themselves from the sin of murder. If the writer expected the reader to identify with anyone in his account—to think 'that could have been me'—it is typically with the killer, not the victim. One earnestly listed twenty-two 'pregnant inducements to deter men from murder or manslaughter'.[58] Others, too, offered 'remedies against murder' that looked inward rather than out. As Joy Wiltenburg has suggested, such texts not only sought to harness horror at private slayings to legitimize public executions, but also called upon personal introspection in the interests of public order.[59] Above all, they insisted, people ought not to seek their own vengeance or to loosen the reins on their own anger or other base impulses; they ought to leave vengeance to God, who would certainly punish those who acted on their own.

These pamphlets helped in a variety of ways to make murder more fully 'public'—both in the sense of 'not secret' and in the sense of being a shared, common concern. Some authors explicitly professed a desire to serve the public good as their reason for writing. One maintained that persons of authority who had a 'love of the weal

---

[56] Thomas Cooper, *The Cry and Revenge of Blood, Expressing the Nature and Haynousness of Wilfull Murther* (London, 1620), quotes at p. 23.

[57] Anon., *A True Report of the Horrible Murther, which was Committed in the House of Sir Jerome Bowes, Knight* (London, 1607), sig. B3r.

[58] More, *A True Relation of a Barbarous and Most Cruell Murther*, ff. 12d–17.

[59] Joy Wiltenburg, 'True Crime: The Origins of Modern Sensationalism' *American Historical Review* 109 (2004): pp. 1377–404. For a broader discussion of the dialectical and ideological relationship between internal and external restraints in this period, see Ethan Shagan, *The Rule of Moderation: Violence, Religion and the Politics of Restraint in Early Modern England* (Cambridge, 2011).

publique' had urged him to publish.[60] Another compared himself to a sentinel or night watchman, observing that 'the common good and preservation of my country's welfare, incites me unto this officious service'.[61] Authors justified their sometimes salacious accounts as deterrents to crime, much as the authorities justified the executions themselves as deterrents. Some wrote of their tracts as works intended 'for publique satisfaction', perhaps related to their assurance that justice, or vengeance, had been had.[62]

In these professions of public service, one is reminded of Thomas Heywood's *Apology for Actors*, which claimed for the stage, too, a profitable service to the 'weale publicke' in revealing individual murders and reiterating the wrongs that they did to the public more generally. When a tragedy is performed, Heywood maintained, 'we include the fatal and abortive ends of such as commit notorious murders, which is aggravated and acted with all the art that may be, to terrify men from the like abhorred practices'. And though the plays did not prevent all murders, he argued that they did nonetheless sometimes bring murderers to light: according to a story he told, one Norfolk woman had been conscience-struck and made her guilt known while watching a killing on stage.[63]

Indeed, plays supplemented print in presenting messages about murder to ever wider publics. The late sixteenth century saw the rise of popular, commercial theatre, with the opening of purpose-built playhouses from 1576, and with it, the profusion of plays marked by murderous violence and vengeance. Many of these plays themselves went to print, participating in the broader print conversations about murder, and some drew upon printed accounts of shocking, real-life murders.[64] *Arden of Faversham* (1591/2) is perhaps the best known of the plays that enacted a version of a true crime. In 1551, Alice Arden arranged the killing of her husband Thomas, a man of some status and means, so she might continue her adulterous affair. Her crime detected, she was burnt at the stake in Canterbury for petty treason, and her several accomplices were also burnt or hanged at Canterbury and in Smithfield. In the 1570s, Raphael Holinshed included an account of this murder in his *Chronicles* of British history. While he had included brief mention of other murders, for this one he went on at length, but apologized in striking terms for doing so: 'although otherwise it may seem to be but a private matter and therefore, as it were, impertinent to this history, I have thought good to set it forth somewhat at large'.[65] Other writers soon offered additional accounts of the killing, deeming it of interest or edification to an audience well beyond those who would have heard of the crime first hand or seen the executions: it appears in in John Stow's *Annals of* England (1592), in Thomas Beard's *Theatre of God's Judgements* (1597), and in a

---

[60] Anon., *A True Report of the Horrible Murther which was Committed in the House of Sir Jerome Bowes*, sig. A2r.

[61] Henry Goodcole, *Heavens speedie hue and cry sent after lust and murder* (London, 1635), sig. A1v.

[62] See, e.g. N. Partridge and J. Sharp, *Blood for Blood, or, Justice Executed for Innocent Blood-Shed* (London, 1670), title page.

[63] Thomas Heywood, *An Apology for Actors* (London, 1612), sig. G1v.

[64] See in particular Leanore Lieblein, 'The Context of Murder in English Domestic Plays, 1590–1610,' *Studies in English Literature, 1500–1900* 2 (1983): pp. 181–96.

[65] Holinshed, *Chronicles*, vol. 3, p. 1062.

ballad printed in 1633, for example.[66] Perhaps most striking, though, was its appearance in the play, on stage, and then again in print.

The play's dramatic re-enactment of a real murder soon inspired others of its kind. Four other true-crime plays survive that depict murders of the late sixteenth and early seventeenth centuries, and a few others seem to have been produced as well, though their texts are now lost.[67] *Two Lamentable Tragedies*, first performed in 1594 and printed in 1601, included a depiction of the recent murder of Robert Beech by his neighbour, the impecunious shopkeeper Thomas Merry, who killed him for his money. In it, personifications of Avarice and Homicide exult in their ability to induce the spilling of innocent blood, while Truth sadly wishes that 'the heart of man were not so open wide to entertain the harmful baits of self-devouring sin'.[68] A drunken gambler facing bankruptcy, Walter Calverley stabbed his wife and killed two of their three sons, a tragedy that prompted a number of publications and not one but two plays: both a pamphlet and ballad appeared shortly after the killings in 1605; George Wilkins dramatized it in his *Miseries of Enforced Married* (*c.*1605); and another playwright, likely Thomas Middleton, used it as the foundation for *A Yorkshire Tragedy* (*c.*1605). By the time the latter play came off the press in 1608, its title page advertised the story as 'not so new as lamentable and true'.[69]

Perhaps the most dissected of the real-life murders that ended up on stage was that of George Saunders in 1573. With echoes of the Arden killing, Saunders died at the hands of his wife's lover and his confederates. Adding further drama to the story were the uncertainties about his wife Anne's active involvement and the scandalous attempts of the enamoured prison pastor to clear her name. Holinshed also devoted some attention to this case, as did a number of other authors. Arthur Golding rushed into print *A Briefe Discourse of the Late Murther of Master George Saunders*, first published in 1573 and reprinted four years later. Another work entered in the Stationers' Register but now lost—*A Cruel Murder Donne in Kent*—likely dealt with this killing.[70] Anthony Munday's *A View of Sundry Examples Reporting Many Straunge Murthers* (1581), perhaps the earliest compendium of murder stories collected for moralizing ends, gave it pride of place. Then came the play, *A Warning for Fair Women*, in 1599, most likely written by Thomas Heywood. The play emphasizes the killers' immediate regret for their actions and the certainty that vengeance—divine vengeance—will follow. The personification of Justice

---

[66] See also *[The] Complaint and Lamentation of Mistresse Arden of [Fev]ersham in Kent... to the Tune of Fortune my Foe*, a ballad printed in 1633. Much has been written on the accounts of Arden's killing, but see especially Lena Cowen Orlin, *Private Matters and Public Culture in Post-Reformation England* (London, 1994), and Richard Helgerson, *Adulterous Alliances* (Chicago, 2003).

[67] *The Late Murder in White Chapel* (1624), by Thomas Dekker, John Ford, William Rowley, and John Webster is one example of a now lost play that likely dramatized a recent murder. For this and other possibilities, see Andrew Clark, 'An Annotated List of Lost Domestic Plays, 1578–1624', *Research Opportunities in Renaissance Drama* 18 (1975): pp. 29–44.

[68] Yarington, *Two Lamentable Tragedies*, Act V, Scene 5, ll. 35–6.

[69] Anon., *Two Most Unnaturall and Bloodie Murthers* (London, 1605); the play's title page also claimed 'W. Shakspeare' as the author: *A Yorkshire Tragedy* (London, 1608).

[70] So argues J.H. Marshburn, ' "A Cruell Murder Donne in Kent" and its Literary Manifestations', *Studies in Philology* 46 (1949): pp. 131–40.

assures everyone that measure will be given for measure, and 'lost blood for blood', but it will be effected through the actions of the queen's council and courts. A near miraculous revelation provides evidence of Browne's guilt, prompting characters to exchange tales of other, similarly providential revelations of murderers' secrets. In one, the characters share the same story Heywood did in his defence of actors, about the woman driven to confess her own act of murder when watching a killing performed on stage.[71] Speaking to the audience at the play's end, Tragedy allows that 'perhaps it may seem strange unto you all, that one hath not revenged another's death'. But this play, he notes, was based in truth, in a 'home-born tragedy'. They might see such retaliation in Histories or Comedies, but in this action, he said, the vengeance was divine.[72]

Modern literary scholars have situated these true-crime plays within a larger group of dramas they assign to a distinct generic category, that of the domestic tragedy. Unlike the classic tragedy focused on the deeds of the great and powerful, the plays gathered into this group centred on the household and family. These plays, fixed on real events, were performed alongside others that at least offered realistic scenes of domesticity as the site of tragic conflict. While these domestic tragedies did not deal directly with great affairs of state, literary critics have suggested that contemporary viewers might well have understood them as having public import, given the persistent analogizing of the 'little commonwealth' of the family and the polity writ large.[73]

With their focus on murder, these true-crime dramas also existed alongside a much bigger group of plays suffused with bloody violence and vengeance that presented entirely fictional murders to a viewing and reading public. Thomas Kyd's *The Spanish Tragedy* is sometimes seen as having inaugurated a whole new genre of intensely popular 'revenge tragedies'.[74] First performed around 1587 and printed in 1592, *The Spanish Tragedy* had at least twenty-nine performances within its first ten years as well as several reprintings. An enviable commercial success, it prompted other playwrights to emulate its tropes and themes. Dramatists rushed to stage tragedies that included one or more violent murders and then the protagonists' descent into an all-consuming pursuit of vengeance that led to their deaths in turn. In Kyd's prototype, Bel-Imperia, daughter of the duke of Castile, seeks revenge for the murder of her lover Don Andrea by Balthazar, who wanted her for himself. She turns to one Horatio instead, but he, too, is murdered. At this point Hieronimo, Horatio's father, takes up his own suit for vengeance, partly at Bel-Imperia's urging. When the well-connected killer blocks his attempts to seek vengeance from the king and law, Hieronimo mounts a play-within-the-play, using it as cover to slay the killers, before both he and Bel-Imperia kill themselves as well. The ghost of

---

[71] *A Warning for Fair Women*, Act IV, Scene 3, l. 34; Scene 4, ll. 37, 175ff.

[72] Ibid., Act V, Scene 4, ll. 184–5.

[73] Amongst many others writing on this genre, see Lena Cowen Orlin, *Private Matters*, and also Catherine Richardson, *Domestic Life and Domestic Tragedy in Early Modern England* (Manchester, 2006).

[74] Katharine Eisamann Maus, ed., *Four Revenge Tragedies* (Oxford, 1998), pp. 1–92. See also Molly Smith, 'The Theatre and the Scaffold: Death as Spectacle in *The Spanish Tragedy*', *Studies in English Literature* 32 (1992): pp. 217–32.

Bel-Imperia's murdered first lover, Andrea, serves as the chorus alongside the personification of Revenge: they conclude with a long recital of the many deaths seen in the course of the bloody sequence. The ghost and the play-within-a-play became common tropes alongside the multiple deaths and ill-fated ends of the revengers in a new batch of dramas produced thereafter; Shakespeare's *Hamlet* is the best-known example of this new genre.

While we might pick out a select group of early modern plays as fitting a particular set of generic conventions, some literary critics note that revenge was almost everywhere on the early modern stage—and that (private) vengeance was almost everywhere critiqued. Lily Campbell and, more recently, Bradley Irish note the Senecan and other precursors to the revenge tragedy, citing examples from at least the 1560s.[75] Vengeance extended outward from the narrowly defined revenge tragedy, too. To signal its ubiquity, Linda Woodbridge notes both that revenge appears as a theme in all but two of Shakespeare's plays, and that two of the era's three or four most frequently performed plays were unabashedly revenge dramas.[76] All this vengeance might at first seem to run counter to much of what has been discussed in these chapters thus far, but not so if we attend to Ronald Broude's influential reading of these plays. As he notes, an Elizabethan audience did not distinguish between (public) justice and (private) vengeance in quite the same way we tend to do: public justice was vengeance, too. Vengeance could be had through divine or public agency; revenge was not identical to 'extralegal retaliation', but could be had through the courts. The plays we call revenge tragedies very often show human retribution failing, whether sought through law or individually, and the latter failing quite spectacularly. Broude suggests that we can see the proliferation of these plays in the late sixteenth and early seventeenth centuries as a response to efforts by servants of the Tudors and Stuarts to reserve deadly vengeance to the sovereign alone.[77] Thomas Heywood may have been far too optimistic in his claims that witnessing tragedies on stage dissuaded people from killing or encouraged them to confess, but the plays—like the murder pamphlets more generally—may well have helped inculcate a sense of the dangers of personal vengeance and a preference for the king's justice, as supplemented by divine providence.

While the public, commercial stage went quiet in the revolutionary years of the mid-seventeenth century, to be reborn in altered guise at the Restoration, the printing of pamphlets that told of newsworthy murders and executions continued apace and spawned new genres. The newsbooks of the civil war and Interregnum became what we would recognize as newspapers; they began not just to report individual cases of homicide but also to advertise calls for information and rewards for assistance. *The London Gazette*, for example, included notices of rewards for information leading to the apprehension of named suspects, and requests for help

---

[75] Lily Campbell, 'Theories of Revenge in Renaissance England', *Modern Philology* 28.3 (1931): pp. 281–96, and Bradley Irish, 'Vengeance, Variously: Revenge before Kyd in Early Elizabethan Drama,' *Early Theatre* 12.2 (2009): pp. 117–34.

[76] Linda Woodbridge, *English Revenge Drama* (Cambridge, 2010), pp. 1–4.

[77] Ronald Broude, 'Revenge and Revenge Tragedy in Renaissance England', *Renaissance Quarterly* 28.1 (1975): pp. 38–58. See also James Sharpe's discussion of revenge drama in *Fiery & Furious People*, ch. 4.

in naming an unidentified victim of violence.[78] Perhaps most strikingly, from the early 1670s began to appear occasional compendia of highlights from the sessions at the Old Bailey, London's main criminal court. From 1678 these *Proceedings*, or sessions papers, became regular publications that described all the trials heard, and appeared almost immediately at the end of each court session, cheap and accessible to many and soon a commercial success.[79] A sister publication quickly appeared, too: the Ordinary of Newgate's *Accounts* narrated the behaviour and biographies of the condemned, accompanied by short accounts of their crimes and trials and ending with reports of their 'last dying speeches' at the gallows. As Andrea McKenzie notes in her study of these publications as both texts and artefacts, these serialized publications from the Newgate chaplain were indeed sensational, scripted, and tied to a religious agenda, but also very popular and influential. Published up to eight times a year for nearly a hundred years, they ensured readers a steady source of news and moralizing about crimes of all sorts and the sins that led one to the gallows.[80]

Print for a 'popular' audience—in the sense of being shared, open to both elite and plebeian, and in an age of increasing literacy—thus contributed to public discussions of homicide an awareness of individual cases, a focus on the providentially backed detection and punishment of killers, a highly personalized rhetoric of homicide based in the sinfulness of the individual, and repeated warnings that vengeance belonged to God. But, as noted previously, it was not just true crime and execution pamphlets that brought homicide before the public. Statutes began to be printed in the 1480s; the foundational measures on homicide and benefit of clergy of 1487 and 1489 were among the first to be printed, for example, with the text of acts thereafter more readily shared and studied. Medieval year books were printed and then abridged, then supplemented and superseded by printed law reports on noteworthy cases. The judge Anthony Fitzherbert was an early advocate of printed legal scholarship: he produced not just his 1514 'grande abridgement' of the year books to summarize English law and the *Nouvelle Natura Brevium* (1534), a treatise on the rules of common law, but also early guides for the work of justices of the peace, coroners, and other officers. About the same time that we start to see murder pamphlets appear in any number we also see printed legal treatises multiply, with William Staunford's *Exposition of the King's Prerogative* (1567) soon followed by works from William Fleetwood, Edmund Plowden, and others. Fleetwood, William Lambarde, and Richard Crompton began publishing more guidebooks for JPs, sheriffs, coroners, and other office holders in the later 1500s. The works we now use as sources helped shape and spread definitions of homicide as well as to standardize procedures for how to investigate and prosecute. These treatises and guides were meant for a narrower audience than the news pamphlets, but their

[78] See, e.g., *The London Gazette*, 27 October 1681 (p. 2); 17 April 1684 (p. 2); 5 April 1675 (p. 2); 20 October 1687 (p. 2.).
[79] They are all now digitized and available online. See Clive Emsley, Tim Hitchcock, and Robert Shoemaker, 'The Proceedings—Publishing History of the Proceedings', *Old Bailey Proceedings Online* https://www.oldbaileyonline.org, version 7.0.
[80] McKenzie, *Tyburn's Martyrs*.

writers also envisioned them as contributions not just to public conversations but also to a public good. In his abstracts and calendars of statutes then in effect, for example, Ferdinando Pulton insisted that making the laws better known in print worked to the 'profit and quiet of the commonwealth'. He expressed his hope that his work would be to the 'common benefit of all men'.[81]

Early modern audiences thus encountered homicide in a mounting number of genres and texts. Increasingly one sees a rhetoric of murder offending not just victim, but also God, king, and a 'public' more broadly defined. One sees this not just in texts explicitly focused on crime or on law, but in printed sermons and religious works as well. Indeed, even ostensibly stable, unchanging texts of religious truth were edited and annotated in ways that both drove and reflected this change. The Geneva Bible of 1560, for example, offered 'most profitable annotations' that moderated the responses appropriate to homicide. The marginal notes distinguished killings done 'wittingly and willingly' from those done 'suddenly', contrasting the more heinous killings with those done 'unadvisedly and not of hatred…without laying of wait'. While using murder as the generic label, the marginalia distinguished between those killings done 'of purpose or unadvisedly'. The notations firmly and repeatedly nuanced scriptural passages that enjoined vengeance, insisting that God intended that such vengeance be sought by or through the magistrates of the land. The 'avenger of blood' was the next of kin, true, but he was urged 'to pursue the cause' at law. Where the text decreed that the 'revenger of blood slay the murderer', the marginal note inserted 'by the sentence of the judge'.[82] To the stark injunction in Exodus that 'thou shalt pay life for life, eye for eye, tooth for tooth, hand for hand', the annotation added the emphatic assertion that 'the execution of this law only belonged to the Magistrate'.[83]

Sermons and texts based on the Ten Commandments mediated biblical injunctions against killing to early modern audiences, too, and came to do so in ways that also insisted on the role of the magistrate rather than the individual in exacting vengeance. Prior to the Reformation's opening of the scriptures in English to a lay audience, parishioners benefitted from paraphrases of the Decalogue, often in verse and metrical versions.[84] *The Arte or Crafte to Lyve Well* (1505) observed that the fifth commandment is '*Non occides*. That is to say, thou shall kill no person…be it to have their goods or by ire'. Killers might kill the body or the soul, or both together.[85] Richard Whitford's *A Werke for Householders*, a popular text with seven editions between 1530 and 1537, noted that 'We shall not slay or kill any person, neither in deed nor yet in willing or mind, nor yet may we hate any person in heart,

---

[81] Ferdinando Pulton, *A Collection of Sundrie Statutes, Frequent in Use* (London, 1618), preface (unpaginated).

[82] Numbers 35:16–29 and their notes.   [83] Exodus 21:23–24 and note to 24.

[84] See Ian Green, 'The Dissemination of the Decalogue in English and Lay Responses to its Promotion in Early Modern English Protestantism' and Jonathan Willis, 'Repurposing the Decalogue in Reformation England', in *The Decalogue and its Cultural Influence*, edited by Dominik Markl (Sheffield, 2013), pp. 171–89 and 190–204.

[85] Anon., *The Arte or Crafte to Lyve Well* (London, 1505), ff. xxvii, xxix(v).

for whosoever so doth, is an homicide and manslayer.'[86] With the Reformation came not just bibles in English but also greater focus on the Ten Commandments. With a renumbering and editing of the traditional text that highlighted the dangers of idolatry, Protestant versions of the Decalogue typically numbered the command against killing as the sixth. The translation that appeared in the Prayer Book editions of 1549 and 1552 observed simply 'Thou shalt do no murder'. New expositions on this core text of parish instruction appeared over the coming years. They sought to show that the injunction was more complicated, both broader in scope and yet also more limited, than it might seem. One might violate its spirit simply through hateful thoughts about one's neighbour or by omitting to feed the hungry; magistrates, however, had the right and duty to kill as needed to ensure that God's directives for vengeance be fulfilled.

   A Plain and Familiar Exposition of the Ten Commandments, with some twenty editions over the early seventeenth century, warned against taking it upon oneself to punish a killer, 'without any calling or authority', for 'hurting of our neighbour in revenge, God hath appointed to be punished by the Magistrate'. Might one not seek vengeance on one's own? Starkly, 'No: God gives no such allowance... Who made you a magistrate to take God's room? What commission have you to lay hands upon His image?'[87] In his *Learned and Pious Exposition of the Ten Commandments*, Lancelot Andrewes observed that with this simple commandment, God forbade not just murder itself but all its degrees and causes. He identified the chief motive for murder as anger, 'a boiling of the blood'; but God forbade only unrighteous anger, he noted. Indignation 'in God's cause, or for the public good, is a virtue'. Some people erred in thinking that '*non occides*' meant that one ought not to kill any creature of God, yet, he explained, kings and magistrates are in some cases not just exempted from this commandment, but even commanded to kill. Killing in a private cause was a 'crying sin' that called out to God for vengeance; it was a 'cursed sin', which brought God's wrath upon the killer. It was a sin against God and 'also against the commonwealth'. To those who argued that Christ had rescinded Old Testament injunctions to vengeance, he insisted that no, 'for it is not public but private vengeance that is prohibited. But for public vengeance, God tells us, it is his'. For this He established magistrates as his deputies.[88]

   Strikingly, though, some of these texts that urged a turning away from private to public vengeance expressed concerns about what had become the main mechanism for effecting this shift—that is, the development of the manslaughter verdict, and with it, what seemed to be the saving of many killers from the gallows. Blood *did* call for blood, after all. Quite aside from the difficulties in deciding what marked some killings as more serious than others, some people disliked drawing any such distinctions at all. The puritans who left England for Massachusetts initially denied

   [86] Richard Whitford, *A Werke for Householders* (London, 1530), sig. C1v.
   [87] John Dod and Robert Cleaver, *A Plain and Familiar Exposition of the Ten Commandments* (London, 1612), pp. 265–6.
   [88] Lancelot Andrewes, *The Pattern of Catechistical Doctrine at Large, or, A Learned and Pious Exposition of the Ten Commandments* (London, 1650), pp. 401–7.

such differences, making no division between murder and manslaughter in the law code they drafted.[89] Some civil war-era law reformers and lawyers criticized the distinction, too. Justice Richard Aske of the Upper Bench even asserted in 1655 that 'it was the Popish power' that introduced the differentiation between murder and manslaughter, insisting that 'by the law of God I find no difference...between hot blood and cold blood as we do now distinguish'.[90] These concerns made their way into print in a number of ways. Aske's concern echoed that of Thomas Cooper in his *Cry and Revenge of Blood*, who praised a judge who imposed sentence of death, for with such sentence was 'the law of God executed, that the murderer without any admittance of privilege or psalm of mercy must die the death, that so blood might be recompensed with blood, and the land may be cleansed from the guilt therefore'. He went on to express his thanks that no longer was justice frustrated by those 'popish receptacles of murderers'—places perhaps better known as sanctuaries. He continued, 'so happy are we that God hath taken from our necks that cruel and bloody yoke of Antichrist, who not only maintained his own tyranny by blood, but also protected others therein'.[91] Yet some writers acknowledged grimly that the toleration afforded some manslayers was not a popish holdover but a feature of their Protestant present. In a section of his reformist tome *England's Balme* (1657) on laws deemed defective because 'irreligious', William Sheppard complained that failing to punish manslayers with death, as one did murderers, was effectively to countenance slaughter, little different from the compositions allowed by appeals of murder, and thus a violation of God's command.[92] John March cited scripture to support the notion that anyone who killed knowingly and willingly must suffer death in turn, noting that the blood of the slain cannot be washed from the land without spilling the blood of those who shed it. Maintaining a distinction between murder and manslaughter was wrong: bluntly, 'He that killeth a man in hot blood, deserves to be hanged when it is cool.'[93]

In a work published in 1677, Zachary Babington drew on his years of experience as an assize clerk under many different judges to criticize manslaughter verdicts. His main point in writing was to urge all grand jurors in homicide cases to forego indicting people for manslaughter and instead to pen all homicide indictments for murder. Leave it to the trial jurors, he insisted, to determine the facts of the case, since they were the ones who would see all the evidence, and leave it to the judge to determine what kind of killing it had been at law. Throughout his tract, though, he also intimated his distaste for the verdict of manslaughter altogether. Like so many others, he cited the biblical injunction that God calls for the blood of those who kill. In grandiloquent terms that conflated divine and English justice, he insisted that this call for blood 'is within the Magna Carta of God himself, and by

---

[89] Steven Wilf, *Law's Imagined Republic: Popular Politics and Criminal Justice in Revolutionary America* (Cambridge, 2010), p. 27.

[90] 82 *ER* 867, cited in Horder, *Provocation*, p. 5.

[91] Cooper, *Cry and Revenge of Blood*, pp. 24, 53–4.   [92] Sheppard, *England's Balme*, p. 134.

[93] John March, *Amicus Reipublicae* (London, 1651), pp. 122–5, quote at 125. See also Anon., *The Law's Discovery: Or, a Brief Detection of Sundry Notorious Errors and Abuses* (London, 1653), p. 7. For context on the early Christian theology of bloodshed and blood guilt, see Whitman, *Reasonable Doubt*, p. 31ff.

an Act of Parliament made in Heaven, never to be repealed'. For many crimes, God allowed restitution and other satisfactions, but never in case of blood, 'for who can make satisfaction for the life of a man?' He opined that before the reforms of 1487 and the turn away from the appeal, murder was all too common since it was not commonly punished. In his own day, he worried that impunity and the license it afforded were reasserting themselves with jurors' too abundant use of the man-slaughter verdict: in this age, as in those when private appeals had pre-eminence over the king's suit, he believed there to be 'never more killing of men by duels, tavern and game-house quarrels, and yet never more impunity to such mankillers, such valiant murderers of their fellow Christians'.[94]

One anonymous writer concurred in his address to the members of the revolu-tionary Convention of 1688/9, expressing concern that the failure to punish killers appropriately brought punishment upon the people of England. 'Alas!', he wrote, 'the nation contracts the guilt of too much blood, almost at every assizes'—not because of all the executions, but because of 'it being ordinary for voluntary homi-cide, contrary to God's law, to go unpunished'. True, much of this impunity emerged from the failings of courts that proved too lenient with 'persons of quality or estates', but it came down to the 'ill distinction' drawn between murder and manslaughter. While he worried about the 'freedom of the kingdom from such blood-guiltiness', he worried more specifically that too frequent pardons and the impunity given to manslayers also brought guilt upon the throne.[95]

This writer, like others, alluded as well to the 'murder' of the earl of Essex in the Tower after his arrest for involvement in the Rye House Plot. This and other plots and conspiracies marked the age, infusing politics with talk of murder like never before.[96] The undoubted murder of magistrate Sir Edmund Berry Godfrey in October of 1678 had, infamously, fed into the machinations of Titus Oates and his revelations of a supposed 'Popish Plot' to kill King Charles II and replace him with his Catholic brother James. Found face down in a ditch, with a broken neck and impaled by a sword, Godfrey's mangled body was the focal point for intensive investigations and imaginings. Though three men hanged for it, authorities soon decided that the evidence upon which their convictions rested had been perjured. No shortage of publications about Godfrey's mysterious death poured off the presses to steep late Stuart politics in talk of assassination and dark, deadly deeds.[97] In this, late seventeenth-century political culture built on what had come before: as Alastair Bellany has shown in his study of the scandal surrounding the murder of Sir Thomas Overbury in 1613 by people connected to the king, and as Bellany and Thomas Cogswell have shown in their study of the rumours that King James VI/I had himself been fatally poisoned, murder attained a public salience in popular

---

[94] Zachary Babington, *Advice to Grand Jurors in Cases of Blood* (London, 1677), pp. 18, 92–3.

[95] Anon., *A Brief Collection of Some Memorandums, or, Things Humbly Offered to the Consideration of the Members of the Great Convention and of the Succeeding Parliament* (London, 1689), p. 14.

[96] See Zook, *Radical Whigs and Conspiratorial Politics.*

[97] See Claire Walker, ' "Remember Justice Godfrey": The Popish Plot and the Construction of Panic in Seventeenth-Century Media', in *Moral Panics, the Media and the Law in Early Modern England*, edited by D. Lemmings and C. Walker (Basingstoke, 2009), pp. 117–38, and Alan Marshall, *The Strange Death of Edmund Godfrey: Plots and Politics in Restoration London* (Stroud, 1999).

political culture over the Stuart years. Discussions of slayings both real and imagined, done by or to even the highest in the land, infused a nascent public sphere.[98] Murder had become political—tied up with *res publica*—in ways it simply had not been before.

Talk of the nature and necessity of revenge wove through many of these public conversations, and not least in those about the most extensively discussed murder trials of the period: those of Charles I and then of the men who had prosecuted him. Both the trial of the king in 1649 and those of the king's judges and prosecutors in 1660 were framed as treason trials, true, but in all of them, charges and imputations of murder figured prominently as well. The formal charge read against the king in the High Court of Justice accused him first and foremost of levying war to uphold his 'personal interest of will and power...against the public interest, common right, liberty, justice, and peace of the people of this nation, by and for whom he was intrusted'. By doing so, the charge added, Charles was guilty of all the subsidiary and constituent crimes, including murder. John Cook, the prosecutor, concluded that his people charged Charles Stuart as a 'tyrant, traitor, murderer, and a public and implacable enemy to the Commonwealth of England'.[99]

All this was publicly reported, as members of parliament had decided to try the king openly before witnesses and had also selected reporters to relay the happenings within Westminster to a broader audience. Since Charles refused to recognize the court or to enter a plea, though, Cook could not use much of the argument and evidence that he had prepared in court itself, so he had it printed instead. Here the talk of murder received even more elaboration, as did the question of whether a king could even be tried for such a crime. Beyond the bombast about Charles's 'massacres of myriads' or the jibes that Charles was no more affected by the deaths of thousands of men at the battle of Edgehill than by reading one of Ben Jonson's tragedies, Cook developed a case for Charles's blood guilt, and for seeing the law of the land as something separate from and superior to the will of the king. He brought up the suspicions that Charles's late favourite, the duke of Buckingham, had poisoned Charles's father, and that Charles had protected the duke from trial: 'He that hath no nature to do justice to his own father, could it ever be expected that he should do justice to others?' Cook suggested that if ever the king wanted a 'public spirited man' removed from his way, he could have the man killed and the killer found guilty only of manslaughter and thus freed, or, if the assassin was somehow found guilty of murder, then the king would pardon him, despite the

---

[98] Alastair Bellany, *The Politics of Court Scandal in Early Modern England* (Cambridge, 2002); Bellany and Thomas Cogswell, *The Murder of King James I* (New Haven, CT, 2015); and Thomas Cogswell, 'The Return of the "Deade Alive": The Earl of Bristol and Dr. Eglisham in the Parliament of 1626 and in Caroline Political Culture', *English Historical Review* 128 (2013): pp. 535–70. See also Kesselring, 'Assassination'.

[99] Kesselring, ed., *The Trial of Charles I* (Peterborough, 2016), p. 34. See, e.g., Gilbert Mabbott, *King Charls His Tryal* (London, 1649). For the print campaign, see especially Jason Peacey, introduction and 'Reporting a Revolution: A Failed Propaganda Campaign', in *The Regicides and the Execution of Charles I*, edited by Jason Peacey (Basingstoke, 1999). On the question of the king's 'blood guilt', see especially Patricia Crawford, 'Charles Stuart, That Man of Blood', *Journal of British Studies* 16.2 (1977): pp. 41–61.

Lord's injunction that murderers ought to die. Beyond the specific failings, though, loomed the broader charge of murder. How can it be murder, Cook imagined critics asking, for the king to raise forces against parliament? 'Where is the malice, that makes the killing of a man murder?' So he went on at length, building his case and insisting that Charles Stuart had to answer to the law, like anyone else. The malice, he said, could be implied by law. Like the blood of Abel, that of the innocent dead in all three kingdoms demanded justice against Charles, even if he was king.[100]

His judges, of course, found Charles guilty: he suffered a very public death as a 'public enemy to the commonwealth'. Hailed by some as an unprecedented example of justice of the highest sort, the act was denounced by others as murder of the basest kind. In 1660, with the monarchy restored and Charles's eldest son having claimed the throne, those men who had secured the late king's death then faced their own trials as murderers and traitors. A show of a trial was held for twenty-nine of the men. Talk of the son's duty to seek vengeance suffused the publications on the trial, together with occasional references to blood guilt, but now with careful attempts to limit that guilt to the few. The Lord Chief Baron told the grand jurors at the outset of the hearing that they were 'to enquire of blood, of royal blood, of sacred blood; blood, like that of the saints under the altars, crying, *Quosque, Domine*; *How long, Lord*, &c. This blood cries for vengeance, and it will not be appeased without a bloody sacrifice'.[101] John Cook and nine of the others were executed as 'murderers of his late sacred majesty', but signs of some disquiet from the crowds prompted the authorities to let the rest remain in prison. Blood calls for blood, but exceptions could be made, apparently, when politically prudent.

Defences of tyrannicide reached their apotheosis with the execution of King Charles, but had their printed apogee, perhaps, in the republican tract *Killing No Murder*. Charles was tried by law (of a sort); this tract encouraged the destruction of tyrants by anyone capable of doing the deed. A call for the assassination of the ever more kingly Lord Protector, Oliver Cromwell, it also defended in both biblical and classical terms the notion that anyone who put themselves above law ought to have no protection from the laws, which served as the very 'nerves and sinews of every state or commonwealth'. A tyrant, like a pirate, was an enemy of all human kind. For this reason, 'every man hath that vengeance given him, which in other cases is reserved to God and the Magistrate'. Blood did call for blood; if that blood was shed by a tyrant, scripture warranted the people to pick up Ehud's dagger. An individual *could* kill, not in pursuit of private vengeance but on behalf of the public good.[102] The tract was exceptional, obviously, as was the execution of a king. But it echoed talk of political killings in service of a public good that had been building

[100] John Cook, *King Charls his Case* (London, 1649), quotes at pp. 5, 12, 21.

[101] Heneage Finch, *An Exact and Most Impartial Account of the Indictment, Arraignment, Trial and Judgement (according to Law) of Nine and Twenty Regicides, the Murtherers of his Late Sacred Majesty* (London, 1660), p. 16.

[102] William Allen (pseud.), *Killing No Murder* (London, 1659), quotes at pp. 6, 7, 9. First published in 1657 in Amsterdam, and likely written by Edward Sexby and Silius Titus. On this pamphlet and its afterlife, see James Holstun, *Ehud's Dagger: Class Struggle in the English Revolution* (London, 2000), ch. 8, esp. pp. 358–61.

from the late sixteenth century. And Margaret Osmond, a London woman who was brought to court under Charles II for maintaining that the previous king had in fact been 'lawfully put to death', was by no means the only person to insist upon an interpretation of events at odds with an easy or complete restoration of monarchy as it had existed before the civil wars and Interregnum.[103] Killing violated a shared, public peace, one that might sometimes be construed as the property and prerogative of a community and not a king.

CONCLUSION

Over the sixteenth and seventeenth centuries, print, plays, and punishment contributed to public discussions of homicide of a sort that helped entrench notions that vengeance belonged to law. 'Murder' proved useful to think with, politically; and the political salience of murder-talk presumably helped make this personal sin and private tragedy a matter more readily conceptualized as an affront to the public as well. Over this period, thanks in no small part to the advent of print, 'public' increasingly became (as Geoff Baldwin puts it) both an adjective and a noun, a word used to describe and create not just common, collective interests, but also a community itself.[104] Print, plays, and punishments carried out in common view all called forth audiences, collectivities, or 'publics' in the Habermasian sense. The increasing use—and increasingly eclectic, promiscuous use—of the language of 'the public' over the early modern years also alerts us to shifts in the way people understood their world and their place within it. When we attend to its uses in discussions of homicide, we see signs of a sense that killing offended more than the victims, more than their families, and more than the king or queen who claimed them as subjects. We hear, too, assertions that a broader public was that which would demand and secure retribution. Satisfaction might still be had, but if it was to be lethal, it should be public rather than private. Interestingly, though, much of that vengeance or satisfaction was being had through the mechanism of the manslaughter verdict, one that typically did not secure blood for blood. Yet even so, such talk drew from and in turn helped justify high numbers of 'homicides by justice', higher even than the numbers of people who died at private hands.

[103] London Metropolitan Archives, MJ/SR/1214, no. 68. (See also *MCR* III, 304–5, where this is only one of many instances of words critical of the old king or the new reported around this time.)
[104] Baldwin, 'The "Public" as a Rhetorical Community', p. 212.

Conclusion

In April 1610, after long years of insults traded back and forth, John Egerton challenged Sir Edward Morgan to a duel. The two met in a Highgate field, with Morgan dressed for the occasion in a white satin suit and accompanied by his brother. Egerton died in the fight. No matter how much Edward Coke and other jurists argued that any death resulting from a prearranged duel constituted premeditated murder, much public sentiment backed the notion that deaths from a 'fair fight' represented no more than manslaughter. The coroner's jury doubted the fairness of this contest, though: provocations aplenty had arisen, but from both parties, and though Egerton initiated this particular encounter, his wounds were inflicted from behind, while his back was turned or while he lay prone on the ground. The coroner's inquest and grand jury both called Morgan's offence murder; the trial jury said manslaughter. The writer of one brief done up for the case explored the reasons why one ought to find not just Edward Morgan but also his brother and second, William, guilty of murder rather than manslaughter: he cited the now 'classic' cases of the sixteenth century, noting that judges had deemed Lord Dacre and his fellows murderers for their killing in the course of an unlawful act, and had found the servant in the Herbert case guilty of murder for having inadvertently killed a woman who had tried to stop a brawl. Malice might be express or implied by law, the author observed. As arguments and appeals threatened to drag the case out indefinitely, King James stepped in with a pardon for Morgan. The judges' brief to the king observed that Morgan's offence, 'by strictness of law as by the opinion of the judges of your highness's bench was thought to be murder, which otherwise the jury would have found to be but manslaughter, so by your judges' opinion, it was thought meet to refer Morgan to your majesty, the fountain as well of mercy as of justice'.[1]

King James had previously signalled his unwillingness to pardon murder. Manslaughter, yes, but murder, no, in accordance with scripture and in line with statute: an act of 1390, one of the first measures to offer any sort of formal distinction between murder and manslaughter, had sought to limit King Richard II's pardons for murderers, insisting that thereafter pardons 'in general words' for all felonies would not remit premeditated, forethought killings. If the king wanted to pardon a murderer, his pardon had to name the crime specifically. Thereafter, kings and queens issued plenty of pardons for murder, but did so with *non obstante* clauses

---

[1] Huntington Library, EL 199, 200, 205–7, 215–22, 244, but esp. 219, 220, and quote from 222, and also SP 46/174, f. 120, SP 46/75, ff. 92, 226, 228, 231, and 263. This case is also discussed in Thomas, *Honour*, pp. 62–4.

('notwithstanding' any statute to the contrary) and by naming the crime explicitly. James, in contrast, made something of a show of his refusal to pardon a crime so grave as murder. He did so, of course, but typically insisted that judges or petitioners find some reason to call the crime manslaughter instead.[2]

Morgan got his pardon and his freedom, but with some difficulty. Lord Chancellor Ellesmere, a kinsman of the victim (though not, it seems, a sympathetic one), turned his attentions to the history of pardons and their applicability to murder as opposed to simple homicide.[3] John Egerton's brother Rowland tried launching an appeal, arguing that proceedings thus far had been 'so dangerous to the state and commonwealth'. His appeal failed, however, because the judges objected to small errors in pleading even as the king had Morgan's court date moved forward. Thus, Edward Morgan killed a man, in a prearranged, premeditated fight, and suffered no fatal punishment in turn. A 'saucy paradox' indeed.

Yet, we see in Morgan's case, unusual as it was, some of the means by which homicide became more effectively criminalized, more fully a matter for the king's peace or public justice and less often treated as an offence that ought to provoke private vengeance or private composition. The rise of the manslaughter verdict, tied to benefit of clergy, allowed an increase in conviction rates. It gave judges, jurors, and others a way to debate and refine responses to homicide both in the abstract and in individual cases. It allowed the judicial redefinition of notions of malice, murder, and what counted as provocation. It helped limit recourse to the private appeal. It shifted discussions more often from whether a killing would be punished to how. The declining incidence of homicide was the product of many factors, of shifts in social realities and cultural codes, but the manslaughter verdict was one of the mechanisms by which people effected this change. Looking at this verdict and its uses clarifies both the social and legal histories of homicide.

Significantly, the manslaughter verdict also offered people a safety valve, of a sort, for dealing with elite killers. We see this with men such as Sir Edward Morgan, clearly, and homicide would not be more fully criminalized until men like him came more effectively within the law's reach. Men's violence is sometimes popularly assumed to be a primordial, unchanging thing, but studies have repeatedly shown that men of different social groups kill at differing rates across time; that men from the elite came in time to commit fewer killings and to turn vengeance over to the law is a crucial aspect of the early modern drop in homicide rates. The manslaughter verdict

---

[2] See, e.g., SP 14/164, nos. 62, 81.

[3] Huntington Library, EL 206, docket for the pardon; EL 207, memorandum of statutes relating to the granting of pardons. For the pardon, see C 66/1904, m. 12, dated 24 April 1611. Thomas Egerton, the Lord Chancellor, was John's kinsman, but the family had divided over a property dispute. Whether this falling out, or the manoeuvring of Morgan's own court connections amongst the Howards, helps account for Morgan's eventual pardon is unclear. See Louis Knafla, 'New Model Lawyer: The Career of Sir Thomas Egerton, 1541–1616', PhD dissertation, University of California, Los Angeles, 1965, pp. 220–5, but also Andrew Thrush, 'Egerton, Sir John (c.1551–1614), in *The History of Parliament: The House of Commons, 1604–1629*, edited by Andrew Thrush and John P. Ferris, 6 vols. (Cambridge, 2010): https://www.historyofparliamentonline.org/volume/1604-1629/member/egerton-sir-john-1551-1614.

helped with this, even with men from the very highest levels of the social hierarchy, titled members of the aristocracy.

In responding to peers who killed, the king or Crown might well find that either justice or mercy had potentially high costs. The very few peers to have been executed for their parts in killings have already been mentioned: Lord Dacre in 1541, Lord Stourton in 1557, and we might also add Lord Sanquhar, the Scottish lord hanged on a London gallows in 1612. But more lords than this bloodied their hands in this period, of course. Henry VII had Edmund de la Pole, earl of Suffolk indicted for murder in King's Bench in 1498 for his part in an affray that left three commoners dead. Given that Suffolk was the favoured Yorkist claimant to Henry VII's recently-won throne, and had only acquired the earldom after the death of his elder brother in battle against the king, one suspects that Henry VII all too happily took this chance to humiliate the man and to try to put him in his power. The earl was reportedly outraged by the unusual 'mark of disgrace' of being indicted as a common criminal; though the king offered him a pardon, with conditions, he fled to Flanders and began plotting in earnest.[4] Suffolk had an abundance of other reasons to turn to treason, but even so, his example suggests the political difficulties involved in charging a peer with such an offence. And, of course, in some cases the authorities might not want to prosecute at all. In 1567, the subsequently notorious Edward de Vere, 17th earl of Oxford and then seventeen years old, killed an undercook who chanced by when he was practising with foils. Oxford was not just the scion of an ancient house, but also the lucrative ward of Queen Elizabeth's chief minister, William Cecil, who had hopes of marrying the young earl to his daughter; the carefully packed coroner's inquest deemed the victim entirely responsible for his own death.[5] For their parts in the scandalous murder of Sir Thomas Overbury, Robert Carr, earl of Somerset and favourite of King James, and his wife Frances were found guilty in 1616 but subsequently pardoned. Notably, though, this lenience cost King James a good deal of political capital. As one contemporary reported, some people argued against mercy for Somerset, saying that 'justice must respect no person, and remembreth to the king of my Lord Sanquhar'.[6]

Arguments that justice ought to apply equally to all mounted around the Somerset case and others in the early seventeenth century. In the republican period, when the formal privileges of peerage disappeared, two lords were found guilty of manslaughter, in regular courts, and branded: Lords Chandos and Arundel of Wardour both had their flesh seared with hot irons upon their convictions.[7] Some faint sense, at least, that lords ought not to be able to kill with impunity and perhaps ought even to be treated equally with other killers survived into the Restoration period; notions of equality before the law would become key to the law's legitimizing claims

---

[4] See Steven Gunn, 'The Court of Henry VII', in *The Court as a Stage: England and the Low Countries in the Later Middle Ages*, edited by Steven Gunn and Anthuen Janse (Woodbridge, 2006), pp. 132–3, and Alison Hanham, 'Edmund de la Pole, Defector', *Renaissance Studies* 2.2 (1988), pp. 240–50.

[5] KB 9/619, pt. 1, m. 13. See Nelson, *Monstrous Adversary*, pp. 47–8.

[6] Bellany, *Politics of Court Scandal*, p. 234; Kesselring, 'Marks of Division', p. 274.

[7] C.H. Firth, *The House of Lords during the Civil War* (London, 1910), pp. 233–4.

in the years around the Revolution of 1688/9. The manslaughter verdict then gave the lords a way to pay some heed to this sentiment while still protecting their own kin and kind.

True, some noblemen who killed still went without any sanction, but a few faced trials and verdicts of manslaughter. In 1668, when the earl of Shrewsbury died of his wounds after he had challenged the duke of Buckingham to a duel, Charles II simply pardoned the survivor. In 1671, the king's illegitimate son, the duke of Monmouth, killed a man in a brawl outside a brothel along with Christopher Monck, duke of Albemarle; despite talk of a trial, Charles II decided just to pardon these killers, too. But a few such killers were at least publicly tried, even if by their peers and even if with little real chance that they would face punishment akin to that imposed upon men of lower status. Some of them had to await their trials in gaol, too, and complained about the cost and hardships of their confinement.[8] Lord Morley in 1666; both Lord Cornwallis and Philip, earl of Pembroke and Montgomery in 1678; Lord Mohun in 1692 and again in 1699, along with Edward, earl of Warwick and Holland on the second occasion: all faced trials from their peers upon charges of murder, whether in the House of Lords as such or in the court of the Lord High Steward with a jury of peers. In three of these trials, the lords ultimately acquitted the accused, but in three they found the men guilty of manslaughter.

At Lord Morley's trial for murder in 1666, after killing a man he felt had insulted him, the solicitor general, Sir Heneage Finch, argued that 'no provocation in the world can make that to be but manslaughter in the case of a peer that would be murder in the case of a gentleman... The same duty to the king, the same obedience to his laws, the same reverence to human nature, the same care to avoid effusion of Christian blood is expected from a lord, which is required from the meanest commoner of England.' The lords who tried Morley were not yet ready for this sort of even-handed accountability: while two deemed him guilty of murder, the rest thought a manslaughter verdict best. We might see any finding of guilt significant, but perhaps the better indicator of change came in the content of Finch's arguments before the court. Whereas earlier homilies warned of the perils that followed failure to recognize degree, Finch now spoke of the dangers of special favour. Finch was no republican; he had just recently tried the regicides. But now he warned the lords: if the people 'put their trust in the law, as the great avenger of blood in the world, and once find themselves deceived, who knows the consequence that may follow? What feuds in private families? What massacres it may produce at last?'[9]

While Finch and others might now speak of a rule of law that must apply equally to all, they retained a sense that a public trial—an open inquisition for blood—was itself a punishment of a sort for men of 'honour'. A few years after Morley's trial, Finch was elevated to the peerage and served as the Lord High Steward in the trial of Philip, earl of Pembroke and Montgomery. Then he opened his comments by observing that 'doubtless the shame of being made a spectacle to such an assembly as this' must to a gentleman 'be a penance worse than death itself, for he that

---

[8] Parliamentary Archives, HL/PO/JO/10/1/493/1181 (d, e); HL/PO/JO/10/1/515/1387 (a).
[9] Howell, *State Trials*, vol. 6, cc. 770–86, quotes at 783, 784.

outlives his own honour can have very little joy in whatsoever else he lives to possess'. In this case, the accused did not try to plead provocation at all, but to cast doubt on whether his beating of the victim had caused the man's death: witnesses spoke of the victim's previous problems with drunken fits. Thus, the decision of his peers to find him guilty of manslaughter speaks clearly to the utility of the verdict in such a case: six of the lords accepted the Crown's evidence and deemed the earl guilty of murder, eighteen were moved by Pembroke's arguments to vote for a verdict of not guilty, but forty opted for manslaughter.[10] At the trial of Lord Cornwallis on charges of murder later in 1678, Finch again spoke of the accused being 'exposed to the shame of a public arraignment and (which to a man of honour is much less) to the hazard of both his life and estate'. Cornwallis had been present at a beating death in a drunken late-night encounter; while six of the lords deemed him guilty of manslaughter, twenty-four of his peers decided that his presence at the scene did not amount to aiding and abetting and acquitted him of all charges.[11]

A few years later still, the fifteen-year-old Charles, Lord Mohun was also acquitted, upon charges that arose from similar circumstances. He had been drinking heavily with his friend Richard Hill, who waylaid and killed the man he thought responsible for an actress not succumbing to his advances. While the attorney general produced much evidence of Hill's prior malice towards the victim, the lords let themselves doubt whether Mohun had known of an intent to kill, and if he did, how such knowledge might matter in law. Mohun's young age likely played a part in the lords' decisions, too. Ultimately, fourteen lords deemed him guilty of murder, but a clear majority—sixty-nine—said not guilty.[12] At the end of the century Mohun was acquitted on murder charges yet again, this time upon accusations that he had aided and abetted Edward, earl of Warwick and Holland when he killed a man in a fight. On that occasion, while the lords acquitted Mohun they did find the earl guilty; but again, just of manslaughter, and this by a unanimous vote of all ninety-three lords present. The Lord Steward advised the earl that he could not have the benefit of freedom upon a manslaughter verdict twice—that a second such verdict might well see him hang—and expressed the hopes of the house that the earl would take 'more than ordinary care' of his behaviour in future. 'Take warning by what has now happened', he urged.[13] For his part, Mohun assured the lords that he would avoid any action that might bring him to trouble them yet again. In a way, he did: his next fatal encounter, a duel in 1712, ended in his own death.

Mohun might well make one doubt the efficacy of the warning afforded by such trials, but we should not be too hasty. That none of this batch of aristocratic killers faced more than a stint in gaol to await their days in court and then whatever indignity the hearing itself offered might seem a less than impressive assertion of the rule of law and supremacy of the king's peace, let alone any broader notion of

---

[10] Howell, *State Trials*, vol. 6, cc. 1310–1350, quote at 1318.
[11] Howell, *State Trials*, vol. 7, cc. 143–158, quote at 147.
[12] Howell, *State Trials*, vol. 12, cc. 950–1050.
[13] Howell, *State Trials*, vol. 13, cc. 939–1033 (earl of Warwick) and cc. 1034–1060 (Mohun), quotes at 1032. For Mohun, see also Stater, *Duke Hamilton*.

public justice. But the manslaughter verdict did allow a trial and something of a reprimand, for lords as for so many lesser men. These trials happened against the backdrop of intense debates over lordly privilege, royal prerogative, and the powers of the Commons in parliament. In such a context, the trials and the occasional public findings of guilt that the lesser verdict allowed might well be seen as signs of change. Finch's orations at three of these trials, first as solicitor general then as Lord High Steward, remind us of the political weight of such killings and the responses to them. He deemed the privilege of peers to be tried by their own kind an institution as old as monarchy itself, a privilege that could not be taken away without risking the dissolution of government. Yet, he argued forcefully, while lords might be permitted special trials, they needed to be held to the same laws as everyone else. He asserted that the incidence of killings in any given society varied depending on the type of government, and that the security of the government they then had relied upon the prosecution of slayers, no matter their status. After what he saw as the horrors of the republican years, he reminded his hearers that 'we, who have the happiness to live under a monarchy (the best of governments) and under a king (the best of monarchs) have all our lives secured to us, by his majesty's own royal and immediate protection'. If the lords wanted to keep their privileges, they had to submit to the king's peace, he argued. They had to sanction their fellows who broke its protection of all the king's subjects.[14] These aristocratic trials offered lessons, at least, on the changing understanding of law and justice in the late seventeenth century. Even those people who still called the peace the king's understood it to have broadened in scope. The manslaughter verdict alone did not make lords subject to law, but the ways in which people used it helped.

The significance of the verdict is suggested, too, by cases in which it did not effectively apply. While women could be found guilty of manslaughter, the verdict meant little as they could not claim benefit of clergy. In 1645, Susan Adams beat her servant Hester Pride to death. The trial jurors accepted Adams's story that she had only beaten Pride 'with a small stick, by way of correction... for some fault which she had committed'. They found her guilty of manslaughter rather than murder, thinking thereby to impose some punishment but one well short of death. They were alarmed, then, to find that they had mistaken the law, and petitioned parliament to secure her a pardon, explaining their mistake.[15] Another group that found itself without recourse to clergy consisted of men convicted of killings at sea or on the rivers and waterways claimed by Admiralty jurisdiction, where benefit of clergy did not apply. In the eighteenth century, until the Offences at Sea Act of 1799 rendered this workaround unnecessary by allowing clergy in the Admiralty Sessions, judges and juries simply acquitted men who committed killings that they deemed acts of manslaughter rather than murder, in recognition of the disparity with those who did their deeds ashore.[16] In the sixteenth and seventeenth centuries, though, men found guilty of manslaughter in Admiralty were not so fortunate.

[14] Howell, *State Trials*, vol. 6, c. 783 and vol. 7, cc. 147, 148.
[15] *Lords' Journal*, vol. 9, p. 4 (11 February 1646).
[16] Prichard and Yale, eds., *On Admiralty*, p. ccxvii.

In a 1588 case, Jacob Henrickson accidentally stabbed his father when the elder man tried to break up a drunken fight between him and another man on board *The Fortune*, afloat in the Thames. Jurors and judges showed some pity, agreeing that the killing occurred 'by misfortune without any pretended malice', and found an interesting solution: they convicted Henrickson of mayhem rather than homicide, assuring punishment but short of death.[17] In two early seventeenth-century cases, though, in which mariners killed their boatswains when defending themselves during beatings, the judges deemed the killings manslaughter and reprieved the killers in hopes that they might be able to obtain pardons, but none proved forthcoming. The petition of John Nicholls, one of the killers, sets out the problem: 'your petitioner received many blows before he did strike', and so the court found him guilty of manslaughter rather than murder, but 'forasmuch as that court admits no clergy', he needed a pardon to survive. He pledged his hearty sorrow and willingness to serve the king, but to no avail.[18] The manslaughter verdict, when attached to benefit of clergy, allowed killings into the courts while permitting the offenders to live. It provided an essential flexibility in how jurors and judges might respond to killings and in so doing helped to further the criminalization of homicide. But it did not apply to everyone.

Both of these exceptions remind us, too, of the broader limits on where and to whom the law applied at all. Statutes passed in this period made it easier to try homicides across England and Wales, lowering the barriers posed by internal borders between the two nations and between one county and the next.[19] But as with Admiralty Sessions's jurisdiction over crimes committed at sea, common law did not apply to homicides of any sort committed by English people abroad—despite the talk of passing such a law in the midst of the Jacobean campaign against duelling, noted in chapter four, and a brief attempt during the republican period. Figuring out quite how far common law applied in English colonies became an increasingly vexing issue over the eighteenth and nineteenth centuries. And the complexities of jurisdiction over place compounded issues of personhood at law for one growing group: the enslaved.

Writing in the early seventeenth century, Coke had asserted that homicide law applied to the killing of any 'reasonable creature', any man, woman, or child, 'subject born or alien, persons outlawed or otherwise attainted of treason, felony, or praemunire, Christian, Jew, Heathen, Turk or other infidel, *being under the king's peace*'.[20] But a person could be outside the king's peace, and the public peace, in more ways than one. It had long been the case in England that even outlaws—even those people ostensibly, formally outside the law's protections—could not be killed with

---

[17] HCA 1/3/132, 133 (case cited in Prichard and Yale, eds., *On Admiralty*, p. ccxix).

[18] HCA 1/101/73, HCA 1/7/128, 130 (cases cited in Prichard and Yale, eds., *On Admiralty*, p. ccxx).

[19] See Hirst, *Jurisdiction and the Ambit of the Criminal Law*, ch. 2; on trying homicides across county lines, see 33 Henry VIII c. 23 and 2 & 3 Edward VI c. 24; on Wales, see 26 Henry VIII c. 6, 27 Henry VIII c. 26, and 34 & 35 Henry VIII c. 26. See Kesselring, 'Marks of Division' for a discussion of crimes and criminals that crossed the Anglo-Scottish border.

[20] Coke, *Third Part*, p. 47. Emphasis added. He went on to clarify that this definition meant that the termination of a fetus might be a 'great misprision', but was not homicide.

impunity, at least not by anyone without royal warrant. At the beginning of the 1300s, one might have received a reward for killing an outlaw; at the end of the 1300s, one might at best hope for a pardon for doing so.[21] So, too, had English law come to see serfs as being protected even against their lords (at least in theory—in practice, a fair few masters who killed even free servants found themselves only convicted of manslaughter or even misadventure). Villeinage, or serfdom, still existed as a formal status in England into the late sixteenth century, so it was no antiquarian point when Coke noted 'that the life and members of them, as well as of freemen, were in the hands and protection of kings, and that he that killed his villein, should have the same judgement as if he had killed a freeman'.[22]

And yet, within a few decades, English colonists began to create their first slave codes, and set aside even this small protection. While they may have drawn in some respects on the precedents of villeinage in England's past to justify their current efforts, this assertion of royal or public oversight of a master's violence was left aside.[23] Beginning in 1660, these codes included laws for the 'better ordering and governing of Negro slaves' that, on the one hand, deemed a slave who killed morally culpable and punishable for the crime, but on the other, mandated little to no punishment at all for the destruction of an enslaved person. In the Caribbean codes of the late seventeenth century, if a master killed his own slave 'accidentally' in the course of correction, he had to account to no one; if he accidentally killed someone else's slave, he needed to compensate the owner. If he with 'bloody minded and cruel intention willfully' killed an enslaved person, then fines and financial penalties were owed—to the owner of the victim, and also to the king and 'public treasury'. When presented with a Jamaican act setting out such penalties in 1683, King Charles II's agents back in London briefly objected that some better provision than a fine was needed 'to deter men from such acts of cruelty': the Jamaicans accordingly stipulated a bit of imprisonment and a bigger fine.[24] Everyone avoided

[21] Holdsworth, *History of English Law*, vol. 3, p. 605; Bellamy, *Crime and Public Order*, p. 105; see relevant cases in the law books: Seipp no. 1328.017 [Y.B. 2 Edw. III. Hil. Pl. 17]; Seipp no. 1328.140ass; Seipp no. 1353.166ass.

[22] Edward Coke, *First Part of the Institutes of the Laws of England* (London, 1628), Lib. 2, ch. 11, sect. 172.

[23] James Stephen, *The Slavery of the British West India Colonies Delineated* (London, 1824), pp. 17–18, 21 explored the contradictions in claims that slave laws were based on common law villeinage, highlighting the differences around homicide. See also Edward Long, *History of Jamaica*, 3 vols. (London, 1774), vol. 2, pp. 493–8.

[24] See the Barbados act of 1661, CO 30/2, ff. 16–26 and the Jamaica act of 1664, CO 139/1, pp. 66–9. For the king's response as delivered by the Lords of Trade, see CO 138/4, pp. 128d–129. Note that the provisions of the Jamaica act copied closely those of the Barbadian act. For context and discussion, see Andrew Fede, *Homicide Justified: The Legality of Killing Slaves in the United States and the Atlantic World* (Athens, GA, 2017), and Elsa Goveia, *The West Indian Slave Laws of the Eighteenth Century* (Barbados, 1970), esp. pp. 24, 29. Goveia notes that a Jamaican act of 1696 made the second wilful killing of a slave an act punishable as murder, but that Tobago, in 1775, was the first of the British islands to make the first offence a capital crime at law. See also Edward B. Rugemer, 'The Development of Mastery and Race in the Comprehensive Slave Codes of the Greater Caribbean during the Seventeenth Century', *William and Mary Quarterly* 70.3 (2013): pp. 429–58; and David Barry Gaspar, ' "Rigid and Inclement": Origins of the Jamaica Slave Laws of the Seventeenth Century', in *The Many Legalities of Early America*, edited by Christopher Tomlins and Bruce H. Mann (Chapel Hill, NC, 2001), pp. 78–86.

references to murder or manslaughter. It is striking and salutary to remember that even as the English more successfully asserted for the state or 'public justice' a monopoly over lawful killing at home, the English abroad specifically excluded one big and growing group of people from the protections of law, relegating them to the private.

The criminalization of homicide has been depicted here as largely synonymous with 'making murder public'—that is, with the treatment of homicide as a wrong to be punished by 'public justice' and an offence against something coming to be seen as 'the public peace'. These terms can seem chameleon-like, taking on different hues in different contexts. At minimum, their use denoted a further tilting of the balance away from private responses, whether of vengeance or compensation, to public. In this, the king's peace and the public peace might be seen as coterminous. (And it is, of course, the queen's peace and the Crown that continue to be invoked in definitions of homicide and the law's operation today.) What was happening here was, in part, a stage in a process begun centuries before, in which kings and their agents sought to assert royal remedies over private settlements—and rather distinctively so when compared with other places in Europe. Developments in the years from roughly the 1480s to the 1680s helped effect this transition: acts passed by Henry VII's parliaments, the development of Star Chamber and the manslaughter verdict, the accession of the Scottish King James and his preoccupations (and the reactions thus provoked) all contributed. But, more generally, we also see a sense developing that a polity or collectivity beyond the monarch alone is being injured and is also capable of offering protection or retaliation. This shift can be tied, in part, to developments in high politics and political thought, shaped in turn by confessional conflict and shifting social cleavages. It also grew from the participation of a wide swathe of society in the law's operation, as first-finders, witnesses, inquest participants, trial jurors, matrons judging pregnancy, and so on. An even broader swathe of society participated, after a fashion, by serving as the readers of tracts or engaged members of audiences at plays, inquests, trials, and public executions. The 'public' was a metaphor, but also a metonymy that reflected a degree of participation in the law's operation—at a level that was also unusual in Europe at the time—and in parish governance more generally. The peace these people helped to enforce was not just the king's; it was theirs, too.

Now, of course 'they' and 'theirs' could be quite limited. Invocations of a 'public', or of a public, collective good to which all contributed and from which all benefitted, were often exclusionary and factitious. This talk of 'public justice' was both a product of participation and a rhetoric useful in the art of governance. Homicide and the public peace it violated could both be political in all sorts of ways. Most obviously, who killed whom, who became victims, who was prosecuted and for what crime (manslaughter or murder or even petty treason), and who ended up being hanged (or burned, or branded, or transported, or pardoned, or simply acquitted) were all facts inflected by relationships of dominance and subordination. More broadly, while the development of a 'public peace', promoted by widespread participation, helped to restrain interpersonal homicides, its early modern manifestation also produced and helped to legitimize extraordinary levels of judicial homicide.

By invoking the 'public' and the ways in which homicide came to be treated as an offence against the public peace, to be punished by public justice, are we simply adding yet another imprecise, overly capacious term to our lexicon, to vie with 'state' or 'Crown'? Perhaps; like these keywords, 'public' has many inflections. Some of its uses are mutually reinforcing, some faintly contradictory. But it is a term that came to be widely used in the era in which homicide rates declined and in which legal definitions of homicide that endured into the present took shape. The new language should alert us to underlying shifts in the way people understood wrongs and how to right them. It manifested and channelled a change in the way people imagined their society and their place within it. Medievalists have shown us that the emergence of a notion of 'the king's peace' mattered deeply in the histories of crime and law and governance; that 'the king's peace' was supplemented and to a degree subordinated in the early modern era is worth highlighting. As with 'the state'—another term newly deployed in these years—we need to be careful in treating the 'public' as both a tool and a subject of analysis, but it gives us an additional point of entry into the framing within which early modern homicide's history took shape.

By the late seventeenth century, then, murder more clearly violated a 'public peace'. John Beattie and others have traced the distinctive directions the criminal law, crime, and punishment took in the years after the Revolution of 1688/9.[25] Pardons became less often personal gifts of a king or queen and increasingly part of the new cabinet's 'management of death', for example. Statutes depicted the forfeitures of criminals' property not as the due of a betrayed king or as rewards for royal favorites, but as assets collected by the Crown to the 'use of the Publick'. Rates of both criminal and judicial homicide continued to decline, and the latter perhaps somewhat surprisingly so, given the profusion of statutes that made ever more felonies and mandated death for ever more crimes. The era of the 'Bloody Code' was about to begin, but with it, too, the developing use of punishments secondary to death, first transportation and then imprisonment. Homicide—both criminal and judicial—remained deeply political. Ultimately, though, that so much about murder proved mutable and unfixed shows that even a story as grim as this might contain within it some sparks of hope.

---

[25] See especially J.M. Beattie, 'The Cabinet and the Management of Death at Tyburn after the Revolution of 1688–89', in *The Revolution of 1688–89*, edited by Lois Schwoerer (Cambridge, 1992), pp. 218–33, and Beattie, *Crime, passim*. See, too, classics such as E.P. Thompson's *Whigs and Hunters* (London, 1975) and Doug Hay et al., *Albion's Fatal Tree*, and newer works, e.g., Tim Hitchcock and Robert Shoemaker, *London Lives: Poverty, Crime and the Making of a Modern City, 1690–1800* (Cambridge, 2015).

The Records and the Database

The database of homicide accusations is based largely on already calendared English records, but as these sources only become numerous from about 1558/9, supplements them with roughly one thousand manuscript coroners' inquisitions from the early 1500s, taken at five-year intervals, as found in the Court of King's Bench indictments files found in record class KB 9 (and occasionally KB 8) at The National Archives.

It was compiled from records calendared in the following:

R.F. Hunnisett, ed., *Calendar of Nottinghamshire Coroners' Inquests, 1485–1558* (Nottingham, 1969); *East Sussex Coroners' Records, 1688–1838* (Lewes, 2005); *Sussex Coroners' Inquests 1485–1558* (Lewes, 1985); *Sussex Coroners' Inquests, 1558–1603* (London, 1996); and *Sussex Coroners' Inquests, 1603–88* (London, 1998).

John Cordy Jeaffreson, ed., *Middlesex County Records*, vols. 1–3 (London, 1886–92).

J.S. Cockburn, ed., *Calendar of Assize Records: Home Circuit Indictments, Elizabeth I and James I.* 11 vols (London, 1975–82) and *Kent Indictments, 1625–1688*, 4 vols (London and Woodbridge, 1989–97).

Data compiled by James Sharpe and R. Dickinson for Cheshire, in Violence in Early Modern England: A Regional Survey, 1600–1800: Cheshire [computer file], Colchester, Essex: UK Data Archive [distributor], July 2002, SN: 4429, http://dx.doi.org/10.5255/UKDA-SN-4429-1.

Calendars of the Essex assize records in the Essex Record Office, T/A 418.

Anne Cummings's assistance in entering the data was invaluable. Both because of the nature of the surviving records and the choices made when entering data into the database, this dataset vastly underrepresents excusable homicides (misadventure and self-defence). Nor does it include suicides, although early modern contemporaries treated self-slaying as homicide, too. Otherwise, it should serve as a reasonably representative sample of the events identified by contemporaries as felonious homicides.

As abundant as early modern coroners' inquisitions into homicides are, they are not complete and cannot be used to calculate accurate homicide rates for much of the period and for most of the country. A statute of 1487 ordered coroners to submit reports of their inquests into felonious deaths to the justices of gaol delivery on their next visit; any suspects then in gaol were tried on the relevant records, and the justices of gaol delivery were to submit the rest to the central Court of King's Bench upon their return (3 Henry VII, *c.* 2). How fully both the coroners and the justices' clerks complied is not clear, but certainly, many of these records no longer exist. We do find in KB 9 batches of inquisitions that were called or sent up to King's Bench, but typically those for which some action was to be taken there, e.g., prosecution of the case *coram rege* or fining a coroner for neglect of some sort. And the problem of incompleteness is greater for homicide than for suicide: inquisitions resulting in trials before the travelling assize justices often stayed in their files without going on to King's Bench, and these assize files survive only from 1558 forward, only for a few counties, and not in complete runs. To illustrate: when Hunnisett calendared all the inquisitions surviving from Sussex, he found 243 for 1485–1557, but 582 for 1558–1603. This increase reflects in part a higher number being called or sent into King's Bench and saved in what is now KB 9, but also the survival of the Sussex assize files after 1558. In that 582 total, he found 388 in the KB files but the rest in assize files and borough archives. Thus, the records in KB 9 simply cannot provide homicide rates, with the difficulties compounded by uncertainty over population numbers. They can, however, provide minima and, unlike the pockets of assize records that survive from 1558, they contain material from all regions. They also provide useful indicators of patterns within the broader category of homicide. The hope was thus that a dataset compiled from these records would provide a picture of the rough contours of early modern homicide.

J.A. Sharpe and J.S. Cockburn have probably said about as much as can be said about homicide rates in early modern England given the issues with the surviving records. As noted in the text, both suggest that the period as a whole saw a decline in homicide rates, but note what seems to be an interruption of this downward trend, most marked from the 1580s to the 1620s. Sharpe's work on Cheshire records, for example, indicates a significant increase in indictments for all sorts of felonies, including homicide, from the 1580s, peaking in the 1620s, and declining thereafter.[1]

Matthew Lockwood has recently argued that the increase in homicide indictments from *c*.1580 to 1620 was a trick of record keeping, not a reflection of a real increase in homicide numbers or rates.[2] While he is undoubtedly correct to note the increased supervision and improved record-keeping of these years, the evidence and analysis offered in support of this argument are not sufficiently convincing. He draws his evidence from Hunnisett's calendars of Sussex coroners' inquisitions, observing that, yes, the absolute numbers of inquisitions from 1580 to 1620 are higher than for the forty-year periods preceding and following, but that there was no proportional increase in homicides in that batch of reports: 23.5 per cent of the inquisitions from 1530 to 1580 (96/407) were for homicide, and 24.7 per cent of the inquisitions from 1580 to 1620 were also for homicide (143/578). Thus, he argues, we do not have an increase in homicides but improvements in holding inquests and producing records. The decision to look at homicide inquisitions in the context of the other inquisitions—those on suicides, accidents, and natural deaths—makes sense, and at first glance, Lockwood seems to have a point in noting that the roughly consistent proportion of homicides indicates that the 'rise' in homicides is thus likely a symptom of improved practices amongst coroners. Closer examination points to some difficulties with this interpretation, though.

As Hunnisett's introductions to his volumes indicate, the inquisitions he has calendared cannot be treated as reflecting either 'absolute numbers of homicides' in Sussex or even the absolute numbers of inquests performed, and we cannot assume that coroners returned inquest reports into all categories of deaths in the same way throughout the period. For one, the statute of 1487 had *not* asked that *all* inquisitions be submitted (*pace* Lockwood, *Conquest*, p. 277) but only that those into felonious deaths be given to the assize justices. Given that coroners were only promised payment for inquests into felonious homicides, and later threatened with fines for failure to investigate deaths by misadventure, they had less incentive, too, to retain or return records into other deaths. When one examines the KB 9 files and sees the ways in which inquisitions from an individual coroner were grouped together, one gets the impression that the coroner was asked by a special writ to provide a particular one and then sent whatever else he had on hand. We do not know if coroners

---

[1] Sharpe, *Crime in Early Modern England*, 82, 83–4, 86; see also Cockburn, 'Patterns of Violence', pp. 70–106, esp. 78.
[2] Lockwood, *The Conquest of Death*, chapter 7.

were in the habit of submitting all inquisitions, or even all reports of all inquests into felonious deaths, to the assizes justices on any sort of consistent basis, or that the assize justices were in turn submitting them all to King's Bench; but if they were, the records were not being saved in what became record class KB 9. Second, as noted above, what Hunnisett had found and calendared came from different sources pre- and post-1559: his pre-1559 inquisitions came primarily from the King's Bench files, with a smaller number of reports found in town archives (Rye's in particular), but after 1559, the date from which the records of Sussex's assize courts begin to survive, he was also able to supplement finds from KB and town archives with many more inquisitions found in those assize files (ASSI). The mix of inquisitions found in KB files and what is in the ASSI files are not identical; inquisitions travelled different routes and for different purposes to end up in each.

For my own purposes, I retain some doubts whether the collection of inquisitions and indictments into felonious *homicides* pre- and post-1559 are wholly comparable, given that the first consists largely of cases of interest to the judges in King's Bench for one reason or another, and may reflect different types of killers or killings than in the latter. (The former may over-represent cases in which no killer was available for trial and upon which process of outlawry was to ensue, for example.) But certainly, the proportions in the broader sets of all surviving inquisitions in Hunnisett's calendars cannot be trusted to reflect actual proportions of inquests carried out. That the proportion of inquisitions in Hunnisett's set from 1485 to 1530 dealing with homicides was much higher—61.7 per cent (42/68)—than in later sets is shaped by their origin in KB files rather than in the more mixed set of ASSI files and cannot safely be treated as reflecting higher actual rates of homicide.

Quite aside from the comparability of pre- and post-1559 sets of inquisitions, the changing proportions of inquisitions in Hunnisett's collection after 1620 also suggest that what we are dealing with are changing habits amongst coroners in what they handed to visiting assize clerks or delivered to King's Bench, as well as problems with the completeness of the surviving assize files. Lockwood notes that from 1620 to 1660, the total number of inquisitions in Hunnisett's Sussex collection dropped to 236, with the number of homicides dropping to 109—that is, a drop of 24 per cent from the 143 between 1580 and 1620—but that the number of reports on suicides dropped by 81 per cent, accidental deaths by 66 per cent, and natural deaths by 69 per cent. This is admittedly a matter of interpretation rather than evidence, but I cannot see variations like that as reflecting actual inquests; instead, it seems probable that coroners were much less likely to send their files on suicidal, accidental, and natural deaths in to the assizes at this point in time than they had been before, or that the assize clerks were much less likely to hand them along for storage. As Hunnisett himself concluded, given the variability in record survival, both over time and from one type of death to another, 'there would be little to gain by comparing the total numbers of each category of verdict'.[3]

And while the decision to look at homicide inquisitions in the context of all other inquests into sudden death is laudable, the separation of the homicide inquests from indictments for all other felonies seems a mistake. As Sharpe and others have noted, trials for *all* sorts of felonies increased from 1580 to 1620. Lockwood's arguments for improved oversight of coroners' practices have no bearing on rising indictment levels for burglary, robbery, and other crimes. The context of rising criminal indictments more generally lends some support to the notion that the higher rates of homicide cases coming before the

---

[3] For the quote and for Hunnisett's discussion of variability in record survival, see Hunnisett, *Sussex 1603–88*, pp. xii–xiv and xxi.

courts were not 'simply a trick of the archives', at least not in the way that Lockwood suggests (p. 264).

As should be clear from the rest of the text, however, I agree with Lockwood about the significance of greater oversight from the Privy Council and through the Court of Star Chamber—whether in asserting greater state control of [lethal] violence, as is his focus, or in more fully criminalizing homicide and making it an offence against the king's peace and public justice, as is the focus here.

Bibliography

ARCHIVAL SOURCES

British Library, London: Add MS 11764, 12514, 31028, 72339; Cotton MS Galba D.vii, Titus B.I, Titus C.IV; Harley MS 1021, 2143, 5141, 6807, 7581; Lansdowne MS 3, 99, 639; Cecil Papers Proquest database [originals are held at the Hatfield House Archives].

Cheshire Archives and Local Studies: QCI/6/1–13; QCI/7/1–10; DDx.196.

College of Arms, London: MS Vincent 30.

Cumbria Archive Service, Whitehaven: D/CU Misc, D/PEN 216.

Derbyshire Record Office: D 258/36/1/20.

Durham Cathedral Library: RAI 126.

Durham University Library: MSP 49, 52; CCB B/218/4/12.

East Riding of Yorkshire Archive Service: DDCC/139/65.

Essex Record Office: D/B 3/3/210; T/A 418.

Herefordshire Archive and Records Centre: BG 11/8/4.

Huntington Library, California: EL 199; EL 200; EL 205–7, 215–22, 244.

Lambeth Palace Archives: MS 720, 3199, 3216.

London Metropolitan Archives: MJ/SR/1214; COL/CA/01/01/18.

The National Archives, Kew: ASSI 45; C 1; C 82; CO 30/2; CO 139/1; E 135; HCA 1; IND 1; KB 8; KB 9; PC 2; PSO 5; SP 1; SP 10; SP 12; SP 14; SP 16; SP 46; SP 63; STAC 1; STAC 2; STAC 5; STAC 7; STAC 8.

Nottinghamshire Record Office: DDE 67/1.

Parliamentary Archives: HL/PO/JO/10/1/7; HL/PO/JO/10/1/331/168.

Suffolk Record Office, Bury St. Edmonds: D 11/11/1.

PRINTED AND ONLINE PRIMARY SOURCES

Acts and Ordinances of the Interregnum, edited by C.H. Firth and R.S. Rait, 3 vols. (London, 1911).

Acts of the Privy Council 1542–1628, edited by John Roche Dasent, 43 vols. (London, 1890–1949).

Allen, William (pseud.). *Killing No Murder* (London, 1659).

Andrewes, Lancelot. *The Pattern of Catechistical Doctrine at Large, or, A Learned and Pious Exposition of the Ten Commandments* (London, 1650).

Anon. *The Arte or Crafte to Lyve Well* (London, 1505).

Anon. *The Enquirie and Verdite of the Quest Panneld of the Death of Richard Hune* (Antwerp, 1537?).

Anon. *A True and Summarie Reporte of the Declaration of some Part of the Earle of Northumberlands treasons delivered publicly in the Court at the Starrechamber... by her Maiesties special commandement... touching the maner of his most wicked & violent murder committed upon himself* (London, 1585).

Anon. *Booke of Honor and Armes* (London, 1590).

Anon. *Sundrye Strange and Inhumaine Murthers... wherein is described the odiousnesse of murther* (London, 1591).

Anon. *Two Most Unnaturall and Bloodie Murthers* (London, 1605).

Anon. *A True Report of the Horrible Murther which was Committed in the House of Sir Jerome Bowes, Knight* (London, 1607).

Anon. *Three Bloody Murders* (London, 1613).

Anon. *[The] Complaint and Lamentation of Mistresse Arden of [Fev]ersham in Kent...to the Tune of Fortune my Foe* (London, 1633).

Anon. *Bloody Newes from Dover, being a True Relation of the Great and Bloudy Murder Committed by Mary Champion (an Anabaptist) who cut off her childs head* (London, 1647).

Anon. *Strange News from the North: Or, the Sectaries Sacrifice* (London, 1648).

Anon. *The Laws Discovery: Or, a Brief Detection of Sundry Notorious Errors and Abuses* (London, 1653).

Anon. *A True and Lamentable Relation of the Most Desperate Death of James Parnel, Quaker, who wilfully starved himself in the prison of Colchester* (London, 1656).

Anon. *Heavens Cry Against Murder* (London, 1657).

Anon. *The Whole Business of Sindercome* (London, 1657).

Anon. *Account of How the Earl of Essex Killed Himself in the Tower of London, the 13th of July 1683, as it appears by the Coroners Inquest, and the several informations following* (London, 1683).

Anon. *A Brief Collection of Some Memorandums, or, Things Humbly Offered to the Consideration of the Members of the Great Convention and of the Succeeding Parliament* (London, 1689).

Babington, Zachary. *Advice to Grand Jurors in Cases of Blood* (London, 1677).

Bacon, Francis. *The Charge of Sir Francis Bacon...touching Duells* (London, 1614).

Bacon, Francis. *The Letters and the Life of Francis Bacon*, edited by James Spedding, 7 vols. (London, 1861–72).

Bacon, Nathaniel. *An Historical and Political Discourse of the Law and Government of England from the First Time to the End of the Reign of Elizabeth...Collected from Some Manuscript Notes of John Selden* (London, 1689).

Braddon, Laurence. *Murther Will Out* (London, 1692).

Brugis, Thomas. *Vade Mecum, or, a Companion for a Chyrurgion* (London, 1652).

Calendar of the Patent Rolls...Philip and Mary, edited by M.S. Giuseppi, 4 vols. (London, 1937–39).

Calendar of State Papers...Charles II: Domestic Series, 1679–80, edited by F.H. Blackburne Daniell (London, 1915).

Calendar of State Papers...Domestic Series, James I, 1611–1618, edited by M.A.E. Green (London, 1858).

Cartwright, Francis. *The Life, Confession, and Heartie Repentance of Francis Cartwright* (London, 1621).

Cases in the High Court of Chivalry, 1634–1640, edited by Richard Cust and Andrew Hopper. Harleian Society, n.s., vol. 18 (London, 2006).

Chamberlain, John. *The Letters of John Chamberlain*, edited by Norman McClure, 2 vols. (Philadelphia, 1939).

Charles I. *Military Orders and Articles Established by His Majesty* (Oxford, 1643).

Charles II. *By the King: A proclamation against fighting of duels* (London, 1660).

Charles II. *A proclamation against duels* (London, 1680).

Churchyard, Thomas. *Churchyards Challenge* (London, 1593).

Closse, George. *The Parricide Papist, or, Cut-throate Catholicke* (London, 1606).

Cockburn, J.S., ed. *Calendar of Assize Records: Home Circuit Indictments, Elizabeth I and James I*, 10 vols. (London, 1975–82).

Cockburn, J.S., ed. *Kent Indictments, 1625–1688*, 4 vols. (London and Woodbridge, 1989–97).

Coke, Edward. *First Part of the Institutes of the Laws of England* (London, 1628).

Coke, Edward. *Third Part of the Institutes of the Laws of England* (London, 1669).

Coke, Edward. *Fourth Part of the Institutes of the Laws of England* (London, 1797).

Coke, Edward. *Second Part of the Institutes of the Laws of England* (London, 1797).

Collectanea Curiosa, edited by J. Gutch, 2 vols. (Oxford, 1781).

Cook, John. *King Charls his Case* (London, 1649).

Cooper, Thomas. *The Cry and Revenge of Blood, Expressing the Nature and Haynousnesse of Wilfull Murther* (London, 1620).

Crompton, Richard. *Loffice et auctoritie de iustices de peace* (London, 1587).

Crompton, Richard. *Star Chamber Cases* (London, 1630).

d'Espagne, Jean. *Anti-Duello: The Anatomie of Duells* (London, 1632).

Dalton, Michael. *The Countrey Justice* (London, 1618).

Danvers, Henry. *Murder will out, or a clear and full discovery that the Earl of Essex did not murder himself, but was murdered by others* (London, 1689).

Davis, John. *Discovery of the True Cause why Ireland was never entirely brought under obedience to the Crown of England* (London, 1747).

The Diary of Henry Machyn, Citizen and Merchant-Taylor of London, from AD 1550 to AD 1563, edited by John Gough Nichols. Camden Society, vol. 42 (London, 1848).

Dod, John and Robert Cleaver. *A Plain and Familiar Exposition of the Ten Commandments* (London, 1612).

Eden, William. *Principles of Penal Law* (London, 1771).

Emsley, Clive, Tim Hitchcock, and Robert Shoemaker, *Old Bailey Proceedings*: https://www.oldbaileyonline.org, version 7.0.

Essex, Robert Devereux, earl of. *Laws and Ordinances of Warre established… by his excellency the Earl of Essex* (London, 1643).

Ferguson, Robert. *Enquiry into and detection of the barbarous murther of the late earl of Essex* (London [?], 1684).

Filmer, Robert. *Patriarcha, or, The Natural Power of Kings* (London, 1680).

Finch, Heneage. *An Exact and Most Impartial Account of the Indictment, Arraignment, Trial and Judgement (according to Law) of Nine and Twenty Regicides, the Murtherers of his Late Sacred Majesty* (London, 1660).

Fitzherbert, Anthony. *La Graunde Abridgement* (London, 1516).

Flenley, Ralph, ed. *A Calendar of the Register of the Queen's Majesty's Council in the Dominion and Principality of Wales and the Marches of the Same (1535) 1569–1591*. Cymmrodorion Record Series, no. 8 (London, 1916).

Foxe, John. *Acts and Monuments* (London, 1570).

Gardiner, S.R., ed. *Reports of Cases in the Courts of Star Chamber and High Commission*. Camden Society, vol. 39 (London, 1886).

Golding, Arthur. *A Briefe Discourse of the Late Murther of Master George Saunders* (London, 1573).

Goodcole, Henry. *Heavens speedie hue and cry sent after lust and murder* (London, 1635).

Greenwood, William. *Bouleuterion, or, A Practical Demonstration of County-Judicatures wherein is amply explained the Judiciall and Ministeriall Authority of Sheriffs and Coroners* (London, 1664).

Hale, Matthew. *Historia Placitorum Coronae*, edited by Sollom Emlyn (Philadelphia, 1847).

Hall, Edward. *Hall's Chronicle*, edited by H. Ellis (London, 1809).

Harrison, William. *The Description of England*, edited by Georges Edelen (Ithaca, NY, 1968).

Hawarde, John. *Les Reportes del Cases in Camera Stellata*, edited by W.P. Baildon (London, 1894).

Hearne, T. ed., *A Collection of Curious Discourses*, 2 vols. (London, 1771).

Heywood, Thomas. *An Apology for Actors* (London, 1612).

Holinshed, Raphael. *Chronicles of England, Scotland, and Ireland* (London, 1586).

Howell, T.B., ed. *A Complete Collection of State Trials and Proceedings for High Treason and Other Crimes and Misdemeanours*, 21 vols. (London, 1816–28), vols. 1–7, 12, 13.

Hudson, William. 'A Treatise on the Court of Star Chamber'. In *Collectanea Juridica*, edited by F. Hargrave, 2 vols. (London, 1742), vol. 2, pp. 1–240.

Hunnisett, R.F., ed. *Calendar of Nottinghamshire Coroners' Inquests, 1485–1558* (Nottingham, 1969).

Hunnisett, R.F., ed. *Sussex Coroners' Inquests, 1485–1558*. Sussex Record Society, vol. 74 (Lewes, 1985).

Hunnisett, R.F., ed. *Sussex Coroners' Inquests, 1558–1603* (London, 1996).

Hunnisett, R.F., ed. *Sussex Coroners' Inquests, 1603–1688* (London, 1998).

Hunnisett, R.F., ed. *East Sussex Coroners' Records, 1688–1838*. Sussex Record Society, vol. 89 (Lewes, 2005).

Hurst, Thomas. *The Descent of Authority* (London, 1636).

Jacob, Giles. *The Laws of Appeals and Murder* (London, 1709).

James VI/I. *A Publication of his Maties Edict and Severe Censure Against Private Combats and Combatants* (London, 1613 [1614]).

James VI/I. *The Political Works of James I*, edited by C.H. McIlwain (Cambridge, MA, 1918).

James VI and I :Political Writings, edited by Johann P. Sommerville (Cambridge, 1994).

Jansson, M., ed. *Proceedings in the Opening Session of the Long Parliament: House of Commons*, 2 vols. (Rochester, NY, 2000).

Jeaffreson, James Cordy, ed. *Middlesex County Records*, vols. 1–3 (London, 1886–92).

Jennings, Abraham. *Digitus Dei, or, An Horrid Murther Strangely Detected* (London, 1664).

The Journals of Two Travellers in Elizabethan and Early Stuart England, edited by Peter Razzell (London, 1995).

Kesselring, K.J., ed. *The Trial of Charles I* (Peterborough, 2016).

Kyd, Thomas. *The Trueth of the Most Wicked and Secret Murthering of John Brewen* (London, 1592).

Lambarde, William. *Eirenarcha* (London, 1581).

Legal History: The Year Books, compiled by David J. Seipp: http://www.bu.edu/phpbin/law-yearbooks/search.php

Letters and Memorials of State, edited by Arthur Collins, 2 vols. (London, 1746).

Leslie, John. *A Treatise of Treasons* (Louvain, 1572).

Locke, John. *Two Treatises of Government*, edited by Peter Laslett (Cambridge, 1988).

Long, Edward. *History of Jamaica*, 3 vols. (London, 1774).

Mabbott, Gilbert. *King Charls His Tryal* (London, 1649).

March, John. *Amicus Reipublicae* (London, 1651).

Milton, John. *Paradise Lost*, edited by Barbara Lewalski (Malden, MA, 2007).

More, Richard. *A True Relation of a Barbarous and Most Cruell Murther [com]mitted by one Enoch ap Euan* (London, 1633).

More, Thomas. 'A Dialogue Concerning Heresies'. In *The Complete Works of St Thomas More*, edited by T.M.C. Lawler, 15 vols. (New Haven, CT, 1981), vol. 6.

The Narrative of the Persecutions of Agnes Beaumont, edited by Vera J. Camden (East Lansing, MI, 1992).

The Parish Register of Horsham in the County of Sussex, 1541–1635, edited by R. Garraway Rice. Sussex Record Society, vol. 21 (London, 1915).

The Parliamentary Diary of Robert Bowyer, 1606–1607, edited by David Harris Willson (New York, 1971).

The Parliament Rolls of Medieval England, edited by C. Given-Wilson et al. Internet version. Scholarly Digital Editions (Leicester, 2005).

Partridge, N. and J. Sharp, *Blood for Blood, or, Justice Executed for Innocent Blood-Shed* (London, 1670).

Plowden, Edmund. *Les Commentaries, ou Reportes de Edmund Plowden* (London, 1588).

Ponet, John. *A Shorte Treatise of Politike Power* (Strasbourg, 1556).

Postlethwayt, James et al. *A Collection of the Yearly Bills of Mortality, from 1657 to 1758 Inclusive* (London, 1759).

Prichard, M.J. and D.E.C. Yale, eds. *Hale and Fleetwood on Admiralty Jurisdiction*. Selden Society, vol. 108 (London, 1993).

Pulton, Ferdinando. *De Pace Regis et Regni* (London, 1610).

Pulton, Ferdinando. *A Collection of Sundrie Statutes, Frequent in Use* (London, 1618).

Raleigh, Walter. *The History of the World* (London, 1628).

The Records of the Parliaments of Scotland to 1707, edited by K.M. Brown et al. (St. Andrews, 2007–17).

Robson, Simon. *The Courte of Ciuill Courtesie* (London, 1577).

Romei, Annibale. *Courtiers Academie* (London, 1597).

Scot, Thomas. *Philomythie* (London, 1616).

Segar, William. *Honor Military and Ciuil* (London, 1602).

Selden, John. *Table Talk* (London, 1689).

Select Pleas of the Crown, edited by F.W. Maitland. Selden Society, vol. 153 (London, 1888).

Several Draughts of Acts Heretofore Prepared by Persons Appointed to Consider of the Inconvenience, Delay, Charge and Irregularity in the Proceedings of the Law (London, 1653).

Sheppard, William. *England's Balme* (London, 1657).

Smith, Thomas. *De Republica Anglorum* (London, 1583).

Spenser, Edmund. *View of the Present State of Ireland*, edited by Andrew Hadfield and Willy Maley (Oxford, 1997).

The Statutes of the Realm, edited by A. Luders et al., 11 vols. (London, 1810–25).

Stephen, James. *The Slavery of the British West India Colonies Delineated* (London, 1824).

Stuart Royal Proclamations, edited by Paul L. Hughes and James F. Larkin, 2 vols. (Oxford, 1973–83).

T.E., *Lawes Resolutions of Women's Rights; or, The Law's Provision for Women* (London, 1632).

The Treatise on the Laws and Customs of the Realm of England Commonly Called Glanvill, edited by G.D.G. Hall (London, 1965).

Tudor Royal Proclamations, edited by Paul L. Hughes and James F. Larkin, 3 vols. (New Haven, CT, 1964–9).

Umfreville, Edward. *Lex Coronatoria: Or, the Office and Duty of Coroners* (London, 1761).

West, William. *The First Part of Simboleography, which may be termed the art, or description, of intruments and presidents* (London, 1615).

Whitford, Richard. *A Werke for Householders* (London, 1530).

Wilkinson, John. *A Treatise Collected out of the Statutes... Concerning the Office and Authorities of Coroners and Sherifes* (London, 1618 and 1657).

Wriothesley, Charles. *A Chronicle of England... by Charles Wriothesley*, edited by William Douglas Hamilton, 2 vols. Camden Society, n.s., vols. 11 and 20 (London, 1875 and 1877).

Yarington, Robert. *Two Lamentable Tragedies* (London, 1601).
York House Books, 1461–1490, edited by L.C. Atreed, 2 vols. (Stroud, 1991).

SECONDARY SOURCES

Abreu-Ferreira, Darlene. *Women, Crime and Forgiveness in Early Modern Portugal* (Farnham, 2015).
Amussen, Susan. ' "Being Stirred to Much Unquietness": Violence and Domestic Violence in Early Modern England', *Journal of Women's History* 6 (1994): pp. 70–89.
Amussen, Susan. 'Discipline and Power: The Social Meanings of Violence in Early Modern England', *Journal of British Studies* 34 (1995): pp. 1–34.
Amussen, Susan. ' "The Part of a Christian Man": The Cultural Politics of Manhood in Early Modern England'. In *Cultural Politics in Early Modern England*, edited by Susan Amussen and Mark Kishlansky (Manchester, 1995), pp. 213–33.
Andrew, Donna. 'The Code of Honour and its Critics: The Opposition to Duelling in England, 1700–1850', *Social History* 5 (1980): pp. 409–34.
Andrew, Donna. *Aristocratic Vice: The Attack on Duelling, Suicide, Adultery, and Gambling in Eighteenth-Century England* (New Haven, CT, 2013).
Baker, J.H. *The Legal Profession and the Common Law* (London, 1986).
Baker, J.H. *An Introduction to Legal History* (London, 2002).
Baker, J.H. *Oxford History of the Laws of England, vol. 6: 1483–1558* (Oxford, 2003).
Baker, J.H. *The Reinvention of Magna Carta, 1216–1616* (Cambridge, 2017).
Baker, J.H. 'R v. Saunders and Archer (1573)'. In *Landmark Cases in Criminal Law*, edited by Philip Handler et al. (London, 2017), pp. 29–57.
Baldwin, Geoff. 'The "Public" as a Rhetorical Community in Early Modern England'. In *Communities in Early Modern England*, edited by Alexandra Shepard and Phil Withington (Manchester, 2000), pp. 199–215.
Banks, Stephen. *A Polite Exchange of Bullets: The Duel and the English Gentleman, 1750–1850* (Woodbridge, 2010).
Barker-Benfield, G.J. *The Culture of Sensibility: Sex and Society in Eighteenth-Century Britain* (Chicago, 1992).
Barnes, T.G. 'The Archives and Archival Problems of the Elizabethan and Early Stuart Star Chamber'. In *Prisca Munimenta: Studies in Archival and Administrative History*, edited by F. Ranger (London, 1973), pp. 130–49.
Barnes, T.G. 'Star Chamber and the Sophistication of the Criminal Law', *Criminal Law Review* (1977): pp. 316–20.
Barnes, T.G. 'A Cheshire Seductress, Precedent, and a "Sore Blow" to Star Chamber'. In *On the Laws and Customs of England*, edited by Morris S. Arnold et al. (Chapel Hill, NC, 1981), pp. 359–82.
Barnes, T.G. 'Mr. Hudson's Star Chamber'. In *Tudor Rule and Revolution*, edited by DeLloyd J.Guth and J.W. McKenna (Cambridge, 1982), pp. 283–308.
Bartlett, Robert. *Trial by Fire and Water: The Medieval Judicial Ordeal* (Oxford, 1986).
Beattie, J.M. 'The Pattern of Crime in England, 1660–1800', *Past and Present* 62 (1974): pp. 47–95.
Beattie, J.M. *Crime and the Courts in England, 1660–1800* (Oxford, 1986).
Beattie, J.M. 'The Cabinet and the Management of Death at Tyburn after the Revolution of 1688–89'. In *The Revolution of 1688–89*, edited by Lois Schwoerer (Cambridge, 1992), pp. 218–23.
Bellamy, J.G. *Crime and Public Order in England in the Later Middle Ages* (London, 1973).

Bellamy, J.G. *Criminal Law and Society in Late Medieval and Tudor England* (New York, 1984).

Bellamy, J.G. *The Criminal Trial in Late Medieval England: Felony before the Courts from Edward I to the Sixteenth Century* (Toronto, 1998).

Bellamy, John. *Strange, Inhuman Deaths: Murder in Tudor England* (Stroud, 2005).

Bellany, Alastair. *The Politics of Court Scandal in Early Modern England* (Cambridge, 2002).

Bellany, Alastair and Thomas Cogswell. *The Murder of King James I* (New Haven, CT, 2015).

Beverley Smith, Llinos. 'A Contribution to the History of Galanas in Late-Medieval Wales', *Studia Celtica* 43 (2009): pp. 87–94.

Billacois, François. *The Duel: Its Rise and Fall in Early Modern France.* Translated by Trista Selous (New Haven, CT, 1990).

Bossy, John. 'Practices of Satisfaction, 1215–1700'. *Studies in Church History* 40 (2004): pp. 106–18.

Braddick, Michael J. *State Formation in Early Modern England, c.1550–1700* (Cambridge, 2000).

Brewer, John. *A Sentimental Murder: Love and Madness in the Eighteenth Century* (New York, 2004).

Brooks, Christopher W. *Law, Politics and Society in Early Modern England* (Cambridge, 2008).

Broude, Ronald. 'Revenge and Revenge Tragedy in Renaissance England', *Renaissance Quarterly* 28.1 (1975): pp. 38–58.

Brown, Keith M. *Bloodfeud in Scotland, 1573–1625: Violence, Justice, and Politics in an Early Modern Society* (Edinburgh, 2003).

Burney, Ian A. *Bodies of Evidence: Medicine and the Politics of the English Inquest, 1830–1926* (Baltimore, 2000).

Bush, M.L. *The English Aristocracy: A Comparative Synthesis* (Manchester, 1984).

Butler, Sara M. 'Degrees of Culpability: Suicide Verdicts, Mercy and the Jury in Medieval England', *Journal of Medieval and Early Modern Studies* 36.2 (2006): pp. 263–90.

Butler, Sara M. 'Local Concerns: Suicide and Jury Behaviour in Medieval England', *History Compass* 4.5 (2006): pp. 820–35.

Butler, Sara M. *Forensic Medicine and Death Investigation in Medieval England* (New York, 2015).

Butler, Todd. 'The Haunting of Isabell Binnington: Ghosts of Murder, Texts and Law in Restoration England', *Journal of British Studies* 50 (2011): pp. 248–76.

Campbell, Lily. 'Theories of Revenge in Renaissance England', *Modern Philology* 28.3 (1931): pp. 281–96.

Carpenter, David. *Magna Carta* (London, 2015).

Carroll, Stuart. *Blood and Violence in Early Modern France* (Oxford, 2006).

Carroll, Stuart, ed. *Cultures of Violence: Interpersonal Violence in Historical Perspective* (Houndmills, 2007).

Cavill, Paul. *The English Parliaments of Henry VII* (Oxford, 2009).

Christianson, Paul. 'Young John Selden and the Ancient Constitution, c.1610–18', *Proceedings of the American Philosophical Society* 128 (1984): pp. 271–315.

Clark, Andrew. 'An Annotated List of Lost Domestic Plays, 1578–1624', *Research Opportunities in Renaissance Drama* 18 (1975): pp. 29–44.

Cockburn, J.S. *A History of English Assizes, 1558–1714* (London, 1972).

Cockburn, J.S. 'Early Modern Assize Records as Historical Evidence', *Journal of the Society of Archivists* 5 (1975): pp. 215–31.

Cockburn, J.S. 'The Nature and Incidence of Crime in England, 1559–1625: A Preliminary Survey'. In *Crime in England, 1550–1800*, edited by J.S. Cockburn (Princeton, NJ, 1977), pp. 49–71.

Cockburn, J.S. 'Patterns of Violence in English Society: Homicide in Kent, 1560–1985', *Past and Present* 130 (1991): pp. 70–106.

Cockburn, J.S. 'Punishment and Brutalization in the English Enlightenment', *Law and History Review* 12.1 (1994): pp. 155–79.

Cockburn, J.S. and T.A. Green, eds. *Twelve Good Men and True: The English Criminal Trial Jury, 1200–1800* (Princeton, NJ, 1988).

Cogswell, Thomas. 'The Return of the "Deade Alive": The Earl of Bristol and Dr. Eglisham in the Parliament of 1626 and in Caroline Political Culture', *English Historical Review* 128 (2013): pp. 535–70.

Cohen, Esther. *The Crossroads of Justice: Law and Culture in Late Medieval France* (Leiden, 1993).

Collinson, Patrick. *Elizabethan Essays* (London, 1994).

Condren, Conal. 'Public, Private, and the Idea of the Public Sphere in Early Modern England', *Intellectual History Review* 19.1 (2009): pp. 15–28.

Cooney, Mark. 'The Decline of Elite Homicide', *Criminology* 35.3 (1997): pp. 381–407.

Crawford, Patricia. 'Charles Stuart, That Man of Blood', *Journal of British Studies* 16.2 (1977): pp. 41–61.

Cressy, David. 'Levels of Illiteracy in England, 1530–1730', *Historical Journal* 20.1 (1977): pp. 1–23.

Cust, Richard. 'Honour and Politics in Early Stuart England: The Case of Beaumont v. Hastings', *Past and Present* 149 (1995): pp. 57–94.

Cust, Richard. 'The "Public Man" in Late Tudor and Early Stuart England'. In *The Politics of the Public Sphere in Early Modern England*, edited by Peter Lake and Steven Pincus (Manchester, 2007), pp. 116–43.

Cust, Richard. *Charles I and the Aristocracy* (Cambridge, 2013).

Cust, Richard and Andrew Hopper, 'Duelling and the Court of Chivalry in Early Stuart England'. In *Cultures of Violence: Interpersonal Violence in Historical Perspective*, edited by Stuart Carroll (Basingstoke, 2007), pp. 156–74.

Daly, Martin and Margo Wilson, *Homicide* (Hawthorne, CA, 1988).

Davies, R.R. 'The Survival of the Bloodfeud in Medieval Wales', *History* 54 (1969): pp. 338–57.

Davis, Natalie Zemon. *Fiction in the Archives: Pardon Tales and their Tellers in Sixteenth-Century France* (Stanford, CA, 1987).

D'Cruze, Shani, Sandra Walklate, and Samantha Pegg. *Murder: Social and Historical Approaches to Understanding Murder and Murderers* (Cullompton, 2006).

de las Heras Santos, José Luis. *La Justicia Penal de los Austrias en la Corona de Castilla* (Salamanca, 1991).

Dickens, A.G. *The English Reformation* (University Park, PA, 1989).

Dolan, Frances, *Dangerous Familiars: Representations of Domestic Crime in England, 1550–1700* (Ithaca, NY, 1994).

Dolan, Frances. *True Relations: Reading, Literature, and Evidence in Seventeenth-Century England* (Philadelphia, PA, 2013).

Duggan, Kenneth. 'The Ritualistic Importance of Gallows in Thirteenth-Century England'. In *Crossing Borders: Boundaries and Margins in Medieval and Early Modern Britain*, edited by Sara M. Butler and K.J. Kesselring (Leiden, 2018), pp. 195–215.

Dunbabin, Jean. 'Government'. In *The Cambridge History of Medieval Political Thought, c.350–c.1450*, edited by J.H. Burns (Cambridge, 1988), pp. 477–519.

Eibach, Joachim. 'The Containment of Violence in Central European Cities, 1500–1800'. In *Crime, Law and Popular Culture in Europe, 1500–1800*, edited by Richard McMahon (Cullompton, 2008), pp. 52–73.

Eisamann Maus, Katharine, ed. *Four Revenge Tragedies* (Oxford, 1998).

Eisenstein, Elizabeth. *The Printing Press as an Agent of Change*, 2 vols. (Cambridge, 1979).

Eisner, Manuel. 'Long-Term Historical Trends in Violent Crime', *Crime and Justice: A Review of Research* 30 (2003): pp. 83–142.

Elias, Norbert. *The Civilizing Process*. Translated by Edmund Jephcott (Oxford, 1994).

Elkholst, Christine. *A Punishment for Each Criminal: Gender and Crime in Swedish Medieval Law* (Leiden, 2014).

Ellis, Karen E. 'Gaol Delivery in Yorkshire, 1399–1407', MA dissertation, Carleton University, 1983.

Ernst, D.R. 'The Moribund Appeal of Death: Compensating Survivors and Controlling Jurors in Early Modern England', *American Journal of Legal History* 28 (1984): pp. 164–88.

Fede, Andrew. *Homicide Justified: The Legality of Killing Slaves in the United States and the Atlantic World* (Athens, GA, 2017).

Finkelstein, J.J. 'The Goring Ox: Some Historical Perspectives on Deodands, Forfeiture, Wrongful Death, and the Western Notion of Sovereignty', *Temple Law Quarterly* 46 (1973): pp. 169–290.

Firth, C.H. *The House of Lords during the Civil War* (London, 1910).

Fisher, Pamela Jane. 'The Politics of Sudden Death: The Office and Role of the Coroner in England and Wales, 1726–1888', PhD dissertation, University of Leicester, 2007.

Fletcher, Richard. *Bloodfeud: Murder and Revenge in Anglo-Saxon England* (Oxford, 2003).

Forbes, T. *Surgeons at the Bailey: English Forensic Medicine to 1878* (New Haven, CT, 1985).

Fraher, Richard M. 'The Theoretical Justification for the New Criminal Law of the High Middle Ages: "Rei Publicae Interest, Ne Crimina Remaneant Impunita"', *University of Illinois Law Review* 3 (1984): pp. 577–96.

Friedland, Paul. *Seeing Justice Done: The Age of Spectacular Capital Punishment in France* (Oxford, 2012).

Gaskill, Malcolm. 'The Displacement of Providence: Policing and Prosecution in Seventeenth- and Eighteenth-Century England', *Continuity and Change* 11.3 (1996): pp. 341–79.

Gaskill, Malcolm. 'Reporting Murder: Fiction in the Archives in Early Modern England', *Social History* 23 (1998): pp. 1–30.

Gaskill, Malcolm. *Crime and Mentalities in Early Modern England* (Cambridge, 2000).

Gaspar, David Barry. '"Rigid and Inclement": Origins of the Jamaica Slave Laws of the Seventeenth Century'. In *The Many Legalities of Early America*, edited by Christopher Tomlins and Bruce H. Mann (Chapel Hill, NC, 2001), pp. 78–86.

Gauvard, Claude. *'De Grace Especial': Crime, État et Société en France au fin du Moyen Age* (Paris, 1991).

Gibson, Jeremy and Colin Rogers. *Coroners' Records in England and Wales* (Birmingham, 1988).

Given, James Buchanan. *Society and Homicide in Thirteenth-Century England* (Stanford, CA, 1977).

Gluckman, Max. 'The Peace in the Feud', *Past and Present* 8 (1955): pp. 1–14.

Godfrey, Mark. 'Rethinking the Justice of the Feud in Sixteenth-Century Scotland'. In *Kings, Lords and Men in Scotland and Britain, 1300–1625: Essays in Honour of Jenny Wormald*, edited by Stephen Boardman and Julian Goodare (Edinburgh, 2014), pp. 136–54.

Goebel, Julius. *Felony and Misdemeanor: A Study in the History of English Criminal Procedure* (New York, 1937).

Goveia, Elsa. *The West Indian Slave Laws of the Eighteenth Century* (Barbados, 1970).

Grabois, Aryeh. 'De la Trêve de Dieu à la Paix du Roi: Étude sur les Transformations du Mouvement de la Paix au XIIe Siècle'. In *Mélanges Offerts à René Crozet*, edited by Pierre Gallais and Yves-Jean Riou (Poitiers, 1966), pp. 585–96.

Grant, Alexander. 'Murder Will Out: Kingship, Kinship and Killing in Medieval Scotland'. In *Kings, Lords and Men in Scotland and Britain, 1300–1625: Essays in Honour of Jenny Wormald*, edited by Stephen Boardman and Julian Goodare (Edinburgh, 2014), pp. 193–226.

Gray, Drew D. 'The Regulation of Violence in the Metropolis: The Prosecution of Assault in the Summary Courts, *c.*1780–1820', *London Journal* 32 (2007): pp. 75–87.

Green, Ian. 'The Dissemination of the Decalogue in English and Lay Responses to its Promotion in Early Modern English Protestantism'. In *The Decalogue and its Cultural Influence*, edited by Dominik Markl (Sheffield, 2013), pp. 171–89.

Green, T.A. 'The Jury and the English Law of Homicide, 1200–1600', *Michigan Law Review* 74 (1976): pp. 414–99.

Green, T.A. *Verdict According to Conscience: Perspectives on the English Criminal Trial Jury, 1200–1800* (Chicago, 1985).

Griffiths, Paul. *Lost Londons: Change, Crime and Control in the Capital City, 1550–1660* (Cambridge, 2008).

Groundwater, Anna. *The Scottish Middle March, 1573–1623* (London, 2010).

Gunn, Steven. *Early Tudor Government, 1485–1558* (Houndmills, 1995).

Gunn, Steven. 'The Court of Henry VII'. In *The Court as a Stage: England and the Low Countries in the Later Middle Ages*, edited by Steven Gunn and Anthuen Janse (Woodbridge, 2006), pp. 132–44.

Gurr, T.R. 'Historical Trends in Violent Crime: A Critical Review of the Evidence', *Crime and Justice* 3 (1981): pp. 295–353.

Guth, DeLloyd. 'Enforcing Late-Medieval Law: Patterns in Litigation during Henry VII's Reign'. In *Legal Records and the Historian*, edited by J.H. Baker (London, 1978), pp. 80–96.

Guy, J.A. *The Cardinal's Court: The Impact of Thomas Wolsey in Star Chamber* (Hassocks, 1977).

Guy, J.A. *The Court of Star Chamber and its Records to the Reign of Elizabeth I* (London, 1985).

Hall, John, ed. *The Trial of Abraham Thornton (1817)* (Glasgow, 1926).

Halsall, Guy. 'Violence and Society in the Early Medieval West: An Introductory Survey'. In *Violence and Society in the Early Medieval West*, edited by Guy Halsall (Woodbridge, 1998), pp. 1–45.

Halttunen, Karen. *Murder Most Foul: The Killer and the American Gothic Imagination* (Cambridge, MA, 1998).

Hair, P.E.H. 'Deaths from Violence in Britain: A Tentative Secular Survey', *Population Studies* 25 (1971): pp. 5–24.

Hamil, F.C. 'The King's Approvers: A Chapter in the History of English Common Law', *Speculum* 11 (1936), pp. 238–57.

Hamil, F.C. 'Presentment of Englishry and the Murder Fine', *Speculum* 12.3 (1937): pp. 285–98.

Hammer, Carl. 'Patterns of Homicide in a Medieval University Town: Fourteenth-Century Oxford', *Past and Present* 78 (1978): pp. 3–23.

Hammer, Paul. *Elizabeth's Wars: War, Government and Society in Tudor England, 1544–1604.* (Basingstoke, 2003).

Handler, Phil. 'The Law of Felonious Assault in England, 1803–61', *Journal of Legal History* 28 (2007): pp. 183–206.

Hanham, Alison. 'Edmund de la Pole, Defector', *Renaissance Studies* 2.2 (1988), pp. 240–50.

Hanlon, Gregory. 'The Decline of Violence in the West: From Cultural to Post-Cultural History,' *English Historical Review* 128 (2013): pp. 367–400.

Hanawalt, Barbara. *Crime and Conflict in English Communities, 1300–1348* (Cambridge, MA, 1979).

Harding, Alan. *The Law Courts of Medieval England* (London, 1973).

Harley, David. 'Political Post-mortems and Morbid Anatomy in Seventeenth-Century England', *Social History of Medicine* 7 (1994): pp. 1–28.

Harvey, David J. *The Law Emprynted and Englysshed: The Printing Press as an Agent of Change in Law and Legal Culture, 1475–1642* (London, 2015).

Havard, J.D.J. *The Detection of Secret Homicide* (London, 1960).

Hay, Doug et al. *Albion's Fatal Tree: Crime and Society in Eighteenth-Century England* (London, 1975).

Helgerson, Richard. *Adulterous Alliances* (Chicago, 2003).

Herrup, Cynthia. *The Common Peace: Participation and the Criminal Law in Seventeenth-Century England* (Cambridge, 1987).

Herrup, Cynthia. *A House in Gross Disorder: Sex, Law, and the 2nd Earl of Castlehaven* (Oxford, 1999).

Hindle, Steve. *The State and Social Change in Early Modern England, c.1550–1640* (Basingstoke, 2000).

Hindle, Steve. ' "Bleedinge Afreshe"? The Affray and Murder at Nantwich, 19 December 1572'. In *The Extraordinary and the Everyday in Early Modern England*, edited by Angela McShane and Garthine Walker (Basingstoke, 2010), pp. 224–45.

Hirst, Michael. *Jurisdiction and the Ambit of the Criminal Law* (Oxford, 2003).

Hitchcock, Tim and Robert B. Shoemaker. *London Lives: Poverty, Crime and the Making of a Modern City, 1690–1800.* (Cambridge, 2015).

Holdsworth, William. *A History of English Law*, 4th edn (London, 1936).

Holstun, James. *Ehud's Dagger: Class Struggle in the English Revolution* (London, 2000).

Horder, Jeremy. 'The Duel and the English Law of Homicide', *Oxford Journal of Legal Studies* 12 (1992): pp. 419–30.

Horder, Jeremy. *Provocation and Responsibility* (Oxford, 1992).

Houston, R.A. *Punishing the Dead? Suicide, Lordship, and Community in Britain, 1500–1830* (Oxford, 2010).

Houston, R.A. *The Coroners of Northern Britain, c.1300–1700* (Basingstoke, 2014).

Howard, Sharon. *Law and Disorder in Early Modern Wales: Crime and Authority in the Denbighshire Courts, c.1660–1730* (Cardiff, 2008).

Hoyle, R.W. 'The Earl, the Archbishop and the Council: The Affray at Fulford, May 1504'. In *Rulers and Ruled in Late Medieval England*, edited by Rowena Archer and Simon Walker (London, 1995), pp. 239–56.

Hoyle, R.W. 'Faction, Feud and Reconciliation amongst the Northern English Nobility, 1525–1569', *History* 84 (1999): pp. 590–613.

Hudson, John. 'Faide, Vengeance, et Violence en Angleterre (ca 900–1200)'. In *La Vengeance, 400–1200*, edited by B. Barthélemy et al. (Rome, 2006), pp. 341–82.

Hughes, Ann. 'Men, the "Public" and the "Private" in the English Revolution'. In *The Politics of the Public Sphere in Early Modern England*, edited by Peter Lake and Steven Pincus (Manchester, 2012), pp. 191–212.

Hudson, John. *The Formation of the English Common Law* (London, 1996).

Hunnisett, R.F. 'The Origins of the Office of Coroner', *Transactions of the Royal Historical Society* 8 (1958): pp. 85–104.

Hunnisett, R.F. *The Medieval Coroner* (Cambridge, 1961).

Hunter, Joseph. *South Yorkshire: The History and Topography of the Deanery of Doncaster*, 2 vols. (York, 1828–31).

Hurnard, Naomi. *The King's Pardon for Homicide before AD 1307* (Oxford, 1969).

Hutson, Lorna. *The Invention of Suspicion: Law and Mimesis in Shakespeare and Renaissance Drama* (Oxford, 2007).

Hyams, Paul. 'Does It Matter When the English Began to Distinguish between Crime and Tort?' In *Violence in Medieval Society*, edited by Richard W. Kaeuper (Woodbridge, 2000), pp. 107–28.

Hyams, Paul. *Rancor and Reconciliation in Medieval England* (Ithaca, NY, 2003).

Hyams, Paul. 'Was There Really Such a Thing as Feud in the High Middle Ages?' In *Vengeance in the Middle Ages*, edited by Susanna Throop and Paul Hyams (Farnham, 2010), pp. 151–75.

Ingram, Martin. 'Shame and Pain: Themes and Variations in Tudor Punishments'. In *Penal Practice and Culture, 1500–1900: Punishing the English*, edited by Simon Devereaux and Paul Griffiths (Basingstoke, 2004), pp. 36–62.

Ingram, Martin. *Carnal Knowledge: Regulating Sex in England, 1470–1600* (Cambridge, 2017).

Irish, Bradley. 'Vengeance, Variously: Revenge before Kyd in Early Elizabethan Drama', *Early Theatre* 12.2 (2009): pp. 117–34.

James, Mervyn. *Society, Politics and Culture: Studies in Early Modern England* (Cambridge, 1986).

Jenkins, Philip. 'From Gallows to Prison? The Execution Rate in Early Modern England', *Criminal Justice History* 7 (1986): pp. 51–71.

Jenks, Susanne. 'Exceptions in General Pardons'. In *The Fifteenth Century XIII: Exploring the Evidence: Commemoration, Administration, and the Economy*, edited by Linda Clark (Woodbridge, 2014), pp. 153–82.

Johnstone, Nathan. *The Devil and Demonism in Early Modern England* (Cambridge, 2006).

Jones, Norman. *Governing by Virtue: Lord Burghley and the Management of Elizabethan England* (Oxford, 2015).

Kaeuper, R.W. 'Chivalry and the 'Civilizing Process'. In *Violence in Medieval Society*, edited by R.W. Kaeuper (Rochester, NY, 2000), pp. 21–35.

Kamali, Elizabeth Papp. 'The Devil's Daughter of Hell Fire: Anger's Role in Medieval English Felony Cases', *Law and History Review* 35 (2017): pp. 155–200.

Kaminsky, Howard. 'The Noble Feud in the Later Middle Ages', *Past and Present* 177 (2002): pp. 55–83.

Kane, Brendan. *The Politics and Culture of Honour in Britain and Ireland, 1541–1641* (Cambridge, 2010).

Kantorowicz, Ernst. *The King's Two Bodies: A Study in Medieval Political Theology* (Princeton, NJ, 1957).

Kaye, J.M. 'The Early History of Murder and Manslaughter', *Law Quarterly Review* 83 (1967): pp. 365–95 and 569–601.

Kelly, James. 'That Damn'd Thing Called Honour': Duelling in Ireland, 1570–1860* (Cork, 1995).

Kerr, Margaret H. 'Angevin Reform of the Appeal of Felony', *Law and History Review* 13 (1995): pp. 351–91.

Kesselring, K.J. 'A Draft of the 1531 "Acte for Poysoning" ', *English Historical Review* 116 (2001): pp. 894–9.

Kesselring, K.J. *Mercy and Authority in the Tudor State* (Cambridge, 2003).

Kesselring, K.J. 'Detecting "Death Disguised" ', *History Today* 56.4 (2006): pp. 20–7.

Kesselring, K.J. 'Felony Forfeiture in England, c.1170–1870', *Journal of Legal History* 30.3 (2009): pp. 201–26.

Kesselring, K.J. 'Making Crime Pay: Felony Forfeiture and the Profits of Crime in Early Modern England', *Historical Journal* 53.2 (2010): pp. 271–88.

Kesselring, K.J. 'License to Kill: Assassination and the Politics of Murder in Elizabethan and Early Stuart England', *Canadian Journal of History* 48 (2013): pp. 421–40.

Kesselring, K.J. 'Coverture and Criminal Forfeiture'. In *Female Transgression in Early Modern Britain*, edited by Richard Hillman and Pauline Ruberry-Blanc (Farnham, 2014), pp. 191–212.

Kesselring, K.J. 'Bodies of Evidence: Sex and Murder (or Gender and Homicide) in Early Modern England', *Gender & History* 27 (2015): pp. 245–62.

Kesselring, K.J. 'No Greater Provocation? Adultery and the Mitigation of Murder in English Law', *Law and History Review* 34 (2016): pp. 199–225.

Kesselring, K.J. 'Marks of Division: Cross-Border Remand after 1603 and the Case of Lord Sanquhar'. In *Crossing Borders: Boundaries and Margins in Medieval and Early Modern Britain*, edited by Sara M. Butler and K.J. Kesselring (Leiden, 2018), pp. 258–79.

Kiernan, V.C. *The Duel in European History* (Oxford, 1988).

King, Peter. 'Punishing Assault: The Transformation of Attitudes in the English Courts', *Journal of Interdisciplinary History* 27 (1996): pp. 43–74.

Klerman, Daniel. 'Settlement and the Decline of Private Prosecution in Thirteenth-Century England', *Law and History Review* 19.1 (2001): pp. 1–65.

Klerman, Daniel. 'Women Prosecutors in Thirteenth-Century England', *Yale Journal of Law and Humanities* 14 (2002): pp. 271–318.

Knafla, Louis A. 'New Model Lawyer: The Career of Sir Thomas Egerton, 1541–1616', PhD dissertation, University of California, Los Angeles, 1965.

Knafla, Louis A. *Law and Politics in Jacobean England* (Cambridge, 1977).

Knights, Mark. *The Devil in Disguise: Deception, Delusion, and Fanaticism in the Early English Enlightenment* (Oxford, 2011).

Krogh, Tyge. *A Lutheran Plague: Murdering to Die in the Eighteenth Century* (Leiden, 2012).

Lake, Peter. 'Puritanism, Arminianism and a Shropshire Axe-Murder', *Midland History* 15 (1990): pp. 37–64.

Lake, Peter. *Bad Queen Bess: Libellous Politics, Secret Histories, and the Politics of Publicity in the Reign of Queen Elizabeth I* (Oxford, 2016).

Lake, Peter and Michael Questier, 'Agency, Appropriation, and Rhetoric under the Gallows: Puritans, Romanists, and the State in Early Modern England', *Past and Present* 153 (1996): pp. 64–107.

Lambert, Tom. 'Introduction: Some Approaches to Peace and Protection in the Middle Ages'. In *Peace and Protection in the Middle Ages*, edited by T.B. Lambert and David Rollason (Toronto, 2009), pp. 1–18.

Lambert, Tom. 'Protection, Feud and Royal Power: Violence and its Regulation in English Law, c.850–c.1250', PhD dissertation, Durham University, 2009.

Lambert, Tom. 'Theft, Homicide and Crime in Late Anglo-Saxon Law', *Past and Present* 214 (2012): pp. 3–43.

Lambert, Tom. *Law and Order in Anglo-Saxon England* (Oxford, 2017).

Langbein, John. *Prosecuting Crime in the Renaissance* (Cambridge, MA, 1974).

Langbein, John H. *Torture and the Law of Proof* (Chicago, 1977).

Lenman, Bruce and Geoffrey Parker. 'The State, the Community, and the Criminal Law in Early Modern Europe'. In *Crime and the Law: The Social History of Crime in Western Europe Since 1500*, edited by V.A.C. Gatrell, Bruce Lenman, and Geoffrey Parker (London, 1980), pp. 11–48.

Levack, Brian. *The Civil Lawyers in England, 1603–1641* (Oxford, 1973).

Levack, Brian. *The Formation of the British State: England, Scotland, and the Union, 1603–1707* (Oxford, 1987).

Lieblein, Leanore. 'The Context of Murder in English Domestic Plays, 1590–1610', *Studies in English Literature, 1500–1900* 2 (1983): pp. 181–96.

Loar, Carol. ' "Go and Seek the Crowner": Coroners' Inquests and the Pursuit of Justice in Early Modern England', PhD dissertation, Northwestern University, 1998.

Loar, Carol. 'Medical Knowledge and the Early Modern English Coroner's Inquest', *Social History of Medicine* 23.3 (2010): pp. 475–91.

Lockwood, Matthew. *The Conquest of Death: Violence and the Birth of the Modern English State* (New Haven, CT, 2017).

Low, Jennifer. *Manhood and the Duel: Masculinity in Early Modern Drama and Culture* (London, 2003).

MacDonald, Michael. 'The Strange Death of the Earl of Essex, 1683', *History Today* 41 (1991): pp. 13–18.

MacDonald, Michael and T.R. Murphy. *Sleepless Souls: Suicide in Early Modern England* (Oxford, 1990).

Maddern, Philippa. *Violence and Social Order: East Anglia, 1422–1442* (Oxford, 1992).

Maitland, F.W. 'The Crown as Corporation', *Law Quarterly Review* 17 (1901): pp. 131–46.

Maitland, F.W. 'The Early History of Malice Aforethought'. In *The Collected Papers of Frederic William Maitland*, edited by H.A.L. Fisher, 3 vols. (Cambridge, 1911), vol. 1, pp. 304–28.

Malone, Wex S. 'The Genesis of Wrongful Death', *Stanford Law Review* 17.6 (1965): pp. 1043–76.

Manning, Roger B. *Swordsmen: The Martial Ethos in the Three Kingdoms* (Oxford, 2003).

Marshall, Alan. *The Strange Death of Edmund Godfrey: Plots and Politics in Restoration London* (Stroud, 1999).

Marshburn, J.H. ' "A Cruell Murder Donne in Kent" and its Literary Manifestations', *Studies in Philology* 46 (1949): pp. 131–40.

Martin, Randall. *Women, Murder and Equity in Early Modern England* (London, 2008).

Masschaele, James. *Jury, State and Society in Medieval England* (Basingstoke, 2008).

Mayes, C.R. 'The Sale of Peerages in Early Stuart England', *Journal of Modern History* 19 (1957): pp. 21–37.

McDiarmid, John, ed. *The Monarchical Republic of Early Modern England* (Aldershot, 2007).

McKenzie, Andrea. *Tyburn's Martyrs: Execution in England, 1675–1775* (London, 2007).

McLaren, Angus. *A Prescription for Murder: The Victorian Serial Killings of Dr Thomas Neill Cream* (Chicago, 1993).

McMahon, Vanessa. *Murder in Shakespeare's England* (London, 2004).

McSheffrey, Shannon. *Seeking Sanctuary: Crime, Mercy, and Politics in English Courts, 1400–1550* (Oxford, 2017).

Meikle, Maureen. *A British Frontier? Lairds and Gentlemen in the Eastern Borders, 1540–1603* (East Linton, 2004).

Merback, Mitchell. *The Thief, the Cross, and the Wheel: Pain and the Spectacle of Punishment in Medieval and Renaissance Europe* (London, 1999).

Minson, Stuart. 'Public Punishment and Urban Space in Early Tudor London', *London Topographical Record* 30 (2010): pp. 1–16.

Monod, Paul. *The Murder of Mr Grebell: Madness and Civility in an English Town* (New Haven, CT, 2003).

Morel, Henri. 'La Fin du Duel Judiciare en France et la Naissance du Point d'Honneur', *Revue Historique du Droit Français et Étranger* 42 (1964): pp. 575–639.

Muir, Edward. *Mad Blood Stirring: Vendetta in Renaissance Italy* (Baltimore, 1998).

Munkoff, Richelle. 'Searchers of the Dead: Authority, Marginality, and the Interpretation of Plague in England, 1574–1665', *Gender & History* 11.1 (1999): pp. 1–29.

Musson, A.J. 'Turning King's Evidence: The Prosecution of Crime in Late Medieval England', *Oxford Journal of Legal Studies* 19 (1999): pp. 467–80.

Musson, Anthony. *Public Order and Law Enforcement: The Local Administration of Criminal Justice, 1294–1350* (Woodbridge, 1996).

Musson, Anthony. 'Wergeld: Crime and the Compensation Culture in Medieval England': https://www.gresham.ac.uk/lectures-and-events/wergeld-crime-and-the-compensation-culture-in-medieval-england

Nelson, Alan H. *Monstrous Adversary: The Life of Edward de Vere, 17th earl of Oxford* (Liverpool, 2003).

Netterstrøm, Jeppe Büchert and Bjørn Poulsen, eds. *Feud in Medieval and Early Modern Europe* (Aarhus, 2009).

Neville, C.J. *Violence, Custom and Law: The Anglo-Scottish Border Lands in the Later Middle Ages.* (Edinburgh, 1998).

Neville, C.J. 'Arbitration and Anglo-Scottish Border Law in the Later Middle Ages'. In *Liberties and Identities in the Medieval British Isles*, edited by Michael Prestwich (Woodbridge, 2008), pp. 37–55.

Neville, C.J. 'Royal Mercy in Medieval Scotland', *Florilegium* 29 (2012): pp. 1–31.

Newton, Diana. *The Making of the Jacobean Regime: James VI and I and the Government of England, 1603–1605* (Woodbridge, 2005).

O'Brien, Bruce. 'From Morðor to Murdrum: The Preconquest Origin and Norman Revival of the Murder Fine', *Speculum* 71.2 (1996): pp. 321–57.

Orlin, Lena Cowen. *Private Matters and Public Culture in Post-Reformation England* (London, 1994).

Oxford Dictionary of National Biography, online edn, edited by David Cannadine (Oxford, 2004).

Parry, Glyn. *A Guide to the Records of the Great Sessions in Wales* (Aberystwyth, 1995).

Peacey, Jason. 'Reporting a Revolution: A Failed Propaganda Campaign'. In *The Regicides and the Execution of Charles I*, edited by Jason Peacey (Basingstoke, 1999), pp. 161–80.

Peltonen, Markku. *The Duel in Early Modern England: Civility, Politeness and Honour* (Cambridge, 2003).

Phillips, H.E.I. 'The Last Years of the Court of Star Chamber, 1630–41', *Transactions of the Royal Historical Society*, 4th ser., 21 (1930): pp. 103–31.

Phillpotts, Bertha Surtees. *Kindred and Clan in the Middle Ages and After* (Cambridge, 1913).

Pihlajamäki, Heikki and Mia Korpiola, 'Medieval Canon Law: The Origins of Modern Criminal Law'. In *The Oxford Handbook of Criminal Law*, edited by Markus Dirk Dubber and Tatjana Hörnle (Oxford, 2014), pp. 201–24.

Pinker, Steven. *The Better Angels of our Nature: The Decline of Violence and its Causes* (London, 2011).

Pohl-Zucker, Susanne. *Making Manslaughter: Process, Punishment and Restitution in Württemberg and Zurich, 1376–1700* (Leiden, 2017).

Pollard, A.J. 'Council, Star Chamber, and Privy Council under the Tudors: II. The Star Chamber', *English Historical Review* 37 (1922): pp. 516–39.

Pollock, Frederick. 'The King's Peace in the Middle Ages'. In Pollock, *Oxford Lectures and Other Discourses* (London, 1890), pp. 65–70.

Pollock, Frederick and F.W. Maitland, *The History of English Law before the Time of Edward I*, 2nd edn (Cambridge, 1911).

Pollock, Linda. 'Honor, Gender, and Reconciliation in Elite Culture, 1570–1700', *Journal of British Studies* 46.1 (2007): pp. 3–29.

Powell, Edward. 'Arbitration and the Law in England in the Late Middle Ages', *Transactions of the Royal Historical Society* 33 (1983): pp. 49–67.

Powell, Edward. 'Settlement of Disputes by Arbitration in Fifteenth-Century England', *Law and History Review* 2.1 (1984): pp. 21–43.

Prest, Wilfrid. 'Law and Women's Rights in Early Modern England', *The Seventeenth Century* 6 (1991): pp. 169–87.

Quint, David. 'Duelling and Civility in Sixteenth-Century Italy', *I Tatti Studies* 7 (1997): pp. 231–78.

Radelet, Michael L. and Traci L. Lacock, 'Do Executions Lower Homicide Rates?: The Views of Leading Criminologists', *Journal of Criminal Law and Criminology* 99 (2009): pp. 489–508.

Rawcliffe, Carole. 'The Great Lord as Peacekeeper: Arbitration by English Noblemen and their Councils in the Later Middle Ages'. In *Law and Social Change in British History*, edited by J.A. Guy and H.G. Beale (London, 1984), pp. 34–54.

Richardson, Catherine. *Domestic Life and Domestic Tragedy in Early Modern England* (Manchester, 2006).

Roberts, Peter. 'The English Crown, the Principality of Wales, and the Council in the Marches, 1534–1641'. In *The British Problem, c.1534–1641*, edited by Brendan Bradshaw and John Morrill (Basingstoke, 1996), pp. 118–47.

Robison, William B. 'Murder at Crowhurst: A Case Study in Early Tudor Law Enforcement', *Criminal Justice History* 9 (1988): pp. 31–62.

Rogers, Nicholas. *Mayhem: Post-War Crime and Violence in Britain, 1748–53* (New Haven, CT, 2013).

Rollison, David, 'The Spectre of the Commonalty: Class Struggle and the Commonweal in England before the Atlantic World', *William and Mary Quarterly* 63 (2006): pp. 221–52.

Rosenthal, J.T. 'Feuds and Private Peace-Making: A Fifteenth-Century Example', *Nottingham Medieval Studies* 14 (1970): pp. 84–90.

Ross, Richard J. 'The Commoning of the Common Law: The Renaissance Debate over Printing English Law, 1520–1640', *University of Pennsylvania Law Review* 146 (1998): pp. 323–461.

Roth, Randolph. 'Homicide in Early Modern England, 1549–1800: The Need for a Quantitative Synthesis', *Crime, Histoire & Sociétés* 5.3 (2001): pp. 33–67.

Roth, Randolph. *American Homicide* (Cambridge, MA, 2009).

Rowney, Ian. 'Arbitration in Gentry Disputes of the Later Middle Ages', *History* 67 (1982): pp. 367–76.

Rudolph, Julia. 'Gender and the Development of Forensic Science: A Case Study', *English Historical Review* 123 (2008): pp. 924–46.

Rugemer, Edward B. 'The Development of Mastery and Race in the Comprehensive Slave Codes of the Greater Caribbean during the Seventeenth Century', *William and Mary Quarterly* 70.3 (2013): pp. 429–58.

Samaha, Joel. *Law and Order in Historical Perspective: The Case of Elizabethan Essex* (New York, 1974).

Schwerhoff, Gerd. 'Criminalized Violence and the Process of Civilization: A Reappraisal', *Crime, Histoire & Sociétés* 6.2 (2002): pp. 103–26.

Sellar W.D.H. 'Forethocht Felony, Malice Aforethought and the Classification of Homicide'. In *Legal History in the Making*, edited by W.M. Gordon and T.D. Fergus (London, 1991), pp. 43–59.

Sellin, Thorsten. 'Two Myths in the History of Capital Punishment', *Journal of Criminal Law and Criminology* 50 (1959–60): pp. 114–17.

Shagan, Ethan. 'The Two Republics: Conflicting Views of Participatory Local Government in Early Tudor England'. In *The Monarchical Republic of Early Modern England*, edited by John McDiarmid (Aldershot, 2007), pp. 19–36.

Shagan, Ethan. *The Rule of Moderation: Violence, Religion and the Politics of Restraint in Early Modern England* (Cambridge, 2011).

Sharpe, J.A. *Defamation and Sexual Slander in Early Modern England: The Church Courts at York* (York, 1980).

Sharpe, J.A. 'Domestic Homicide in Early Modern England', *Historical Journal* 24 (1981): pp. 29–48.

Sharpe, J.A. 'The History of Violence in England: Some Observations', *Past and Present* 108 (1985): pp. 206–15.

Sharpe, J.A. '"Last Dying Speeches": Religion, Ideology and Public Execution in Seventeenth-Century England', *Past and Present* 107 (1985): pp. 144–67.

Sharpe, J.A. *Crime in Early Modern England, 1550–1750* (London, 1999).

Sharpe, J.A. *A Fiery & Furious People: A History of Violence in England* (London, 2016).

Sharpe, J.A. 'Revisiting the "Violence We Have Lost": Homicide in Seventeenth-Century Cheshire', *English Historical Review* 131 (2016): pp. 293–323.

Sharpe, J.A. and J.R. Dickinson, 'Coroners' Inquests in an English County, 1600–1800: A Preliminary Survey', *Northern History* 48.2 (2011): pp. 253–69.

Shepard, Alexandra. *Meanings of Manhood in Early Modern England* (Oxford, 2003).

Shoemaker, Robert. *The London Mob: Violence and Disorder in Eighteenth-Century England* (Hambledon, 2004).

Sim, J. and T. Ward, 'The Magistrate of the Poor? Coroners and Deaths in Custody in Nineteenth-Century England'. In *Legal Medicine in History*, edited by M. Clark and C. Crawford (Cambridge, 1994), pp. 245–67.

Skinner, Quentin. *The Foundations of Modern Political Thought*, 2 vols. (Cambridge, 1978).

Skinner, Quentin. 'Language and Political Change'. In *Political Innovation and Conceptual Change*, edited by Terence Ball et al. (Cambridge, 1989), pp. 6–23.

Skousen, Lesley. 'Have Mercy upon Me O Lord: A History of Benefit of Clergy in Early Modern England', PhD dissertation, University of Wisconsin, 2013.

Slack, Paul. *From Reformation to Improvement: Public Welfare in Early Modern England* (Oxford, 1999).

Smail, Daniel Lord. *The Consumption of Justice: Emotions, Publicity, and Legal Culture in Marseille, 1264–1423* (London, 2003).

Smith, Greg. 'Violent Crime and the Public Weal in England'. In *Crime, Law and Popular Culture in Europe, 1500–1900*, edited by Richard McMahon (Cullompton, 2008), pp. 190–218.

Smith, Molly. 'The Theatre and the Scaffold: Death as Spectacle in *The Spanish Tragedy*', *Studies in English Literature* 32 (1992): pp. 217–32.

Sobecki, Sebastian. *Unwritten Verities: The Making of England's Vernacular Legal Culture, 1463–1549* (Notre Dame, IN, 2015).

Spence, Craig. *Accidents and Violent Death in Early Modern London, 1650–1750* (Woodbridge, 2016).

Spierenburg, Pieter. *The Spectacle of Suffering* (Cambridge, 1984).

Spierenburg, Pieter. 'Violence and the Civilizing Process: Does it Work?', *Crime, Histoire & Sociétés* 5.2 (2001): pp. 87–105.

Spierenburg, Pieter. *A History of Murder: Personal Violence in Europe from the Middle Ages to the Present* (Cambridge, 2008).

Spierenburg, Pieter. 'Violence: Reflections about a Word'. In *Violence in Europe: Historical and Contemporary Perspectives*, edited by Sophie Body-Gendrot and Pieter Spierenburg (New York, 2009), pp. 13–26.

Stater, Victor. *Duke Hamilton Is Dead! A Story of Aristocratic Life and Death in Stuart Britain* (London, 2000).

Stevenson, S.J. 'The Rise of Suicide Verdicts in South-East England, 1530–1590: The Legal Process', *Continuity and Change* 2 (1987): pp. 37–75.

Stewart, Alan. 'Purging Troubled Humours: Bacon, Northampton and the Anti-Duelling Campaign of 1613–1614'. In *The Crisis of 1614 and the Addled Parliament: Literary and Historical Perspectives*, edited by Stephen Clucas and Rosalind Davies (Aldershot, 2003), pp. 81–91.

Stone, Lawrence. *The Crisis of the Aristocracy, 1558–1641* (Oxford, 1965).

Stone, Lawrence. 'Interpersonal Violence in English Society, 1300–1980,' *Past and Present* 101 (1983): pp. 22–33.

Stone, Lawrence. 'A Rejoinder', *Past and Present* 108 (1985): pp. 216–24.

Summerson, Henry. 'Attitudes to Capital Punishment in England, 1200–1350'. In *Thirteenth-Century England VIII: Proceedings of the Durham Conference, 1999*, edited by Michael Prestwich, Richard Britnell, and Robin Frame (Woodbridge, 2001), pp. 123–33.

Sutton, Teresa. 'The Deodand and Responsibility for Death', *Journal of Legal History* 18 (1997): pp. 44–55.

Sutton, Teresa. 'The Nature of the Early Law of Deodand', *Cambrian Law Review* 9 (1999): pp. 9–20.

Terpstra, Nicholas, ed. *The Art of Executing Well: Rituals of Execution in Renaissance Italy* (Kirksville, MO, 2008).

Thomas, Courtney. *If I Lose Mine Honour, I Lose Myself: Honour among the Early Modern English Elite* (Toronto, 2017).

Thompson, E.P. *Whigs and Hunters* (London, 1975).

Throop, Susanna and Paul Hyams, eds. *Vengeance in the Middle Ages* (Farnham, 2010).

Thrush, Andrew. 'Egerton, Sir John (c.1551–1614)'. In *The History of Parliament: The House of Commons, 1604–1629*, edited by Andrew Thrush and John P. Ferris (Cambridge, 2010): https://www.historyofparliamentonline.org/volume/1604-1629/member/egerton-sir-john-1551-1614

United Nations Office on Drugs and Crime, *Global Study on Homicide 2013*: https://www.unodc.org/unodc/en/data-and-analysis/statistics/publications.html

van Dülmen, R. *Theatre of Horror: Crime and Punishment in Early Modern Germany*. Translated by E. Neu (Cambridge, 1990).

Walker, Claire. '"Remember Justice Godfrey": The Popish Plot and the Construction of Panic in Seventeenth-Century Media'. In *Moral Panics, the Media and the Law in Early Modern England*, edited by D. Lemmings and C. Walker (Basingstoke, 2009), pp. 117–38.

Walker, Garthine. *Crime, Gender and Social Order in Early Modern England* (Cambridge, 2003).

Wall, Alison. 'For Love, Money, or Politics? A Clandestine Marriage and the Elizabethan Court of Arches', *Historical Journal* 38.3 (1995): pp. 511–33.

Wasser, Michael. 'Violence and the Central Criminal Courts in Scotland, 1603–1638', PhD dissertation, University of Columbia, 1995.

Watson, Katherine D. *Forensic Medicine in Western Society: A History* (New York, 2010).

Watts, John. '"Common Weal" and "Commonwealth": England's Monarchical Republic in the Making, c.1450–1630'. In *The Languages of Political Society*, edited by Andrea Gamberini et al. (Rome, 2011), pp. 147–63.

Weintraub, Jeff and Krishnan Kumar, eds., *Public and Private in Thought and Practice: Perspectives on a Grand Dichotomy* (Chicago, 1997).

Whitman, James Q. *The Origins of Reasonable Doubt: Theological Roots of the Criminal Trial* (New Haven, CT, 2008).

Whittick, Christopher. 'The Role of the Criminal Appeal in the Fifteenth Century'. In *Law and Social Change in British History*, edited by J.A. Guy and H.G. Beale (London, 1984), pp. 55–72.

Wiener, Martin. *Men of Blood: Violence, Manliness and Criminal Justice in Victorian England* (Cambridge, 2006).

Wiener, Martin. *An Empire on Trial: Race, Murder and Justice under British Rule, 1870–1935* (Cambridge, 2009).

Wilf, Steven. *Law's Imagined Republic: Popular Politics and Criminal Justice in Revolutionary America* (Cambridge, 2010).

Williams, Raymond. *Keywords: A Vocabulary of Culture and Society* (Oxford, 1976).

Willis, Jonathan. 'Repurposing the Decalogue in Reformation England'. In *The Decalogue and its Cultural Influence*, edited by Dominik Markl (Sheffield, 2013), pp. 190–204.

Wilson, Luke. *Theaters of Intention: Drama and the Law in Early Modern England* (Stanford, CA, 2000).

Wiltenburg, Joy. 'True Crime: The Origins of Modern Sensationalism', *American Historical Review* 109 (2004): pp. 1377–404.

Withington, Phil. *The Politics of Commonwealth: Citizens and Freemen in Early Modern England* (Cambridge, 2005).

Withington, Phil. 'Public Discourse, Corporate Citizenship and State Formation in Early Modern England', *American Historical Review* 112.4 (2007): pp. 1016–38.

Withington, Phil. *Society in Early Modern England: The Vernacular Origins of Some Powerful Ideas* (Cambridge, 2010).

Woodbridge, Linda. *English Revenge Drama* (Cambridge, 2010).

Woolf, Daniel R. 'Genre into Artefact: The Decline of the English Chronicle in the Sixteenth Century', *Sixteenth Century Journal* 19 (1988): pp. 321–54.

Wormald, Jenny. 'Bloodfeud, Kindred, and Government in Early Modern Scotland', *Past and Present* 87 (1980): pp. 54–97.

Wormald, Patrick. *The Making of English Law: King Alfred to the Twelfth Century* (Oxford, 1999).

Wrightson, Keith. 'Estates, Degrees, and Sorts: Changing Perceptions of Society in Tudor and Stuart England'. In *Language, History, and Class*, edited by P.J. Corfield (Oxford, 1991), pp. 30–52.

Wrightson, Keith. 'The Politics of the Parish in Early Modern England'. In *The Experience of Authority in Early Modern England*, edited by Paul Griffiths, Adam Fox, and Steve Hindle (Basingstoke, 1996), pp. 10–46.

Yetter, Leigh. *Public Execution in England, 1573–1868* (London, 2009).

Yntema, H.E. 'The *Lex Murdrorum*: An Episode in the History of English Criminal Law', *Harvard Law Review* 36 (1923): pp. 146–79.

Zook, Melinda. *Radical Whigs and Conspiratorial Politics in Late Stuart England* (University Park, PA, 1999).

Index

Abel 1–2, 144–5
abjuration of the realm 42–3
abortion 153n20
Act against Murderers (1487) 21–2, 34–5,
    43, 61–2, 68–9, 81, 83, 91, 139–40,
    142–3, 157–9
Adams, Susan 152–3
Admiralty Sessions 23–4, 152–3
adultery 29–30
almoners 42–3, 51, 64
Amussen, Susan 10–11
ancient constitution 64–5
Andrewes, Lancelot 141
anti-Catholicism 132–4, 141–4
appeal 37–8, 42–3, 68–70, 78–93,
    141–3, 148
approvers 79–80, 99
Apsley, Peter 112
arbitration 73–6, 78, 85–7
Arden, Alice 135–6
Arden, Thomas 135–6
Arden of Faversham 135–6
Armstrong, Edward 74–5
Armstrong, John 74–5
Armstrong, Richard 91
Armstrong *v* Lisle (1696) 91
assassination 4–5, 57, 145–6
assault 29–30, 33–4, 105
Assize of Clarendon (1166) 20–1
assythment 75–8, 92–3
attempted murder 34
autopsies 56–7, 56n85

Babington, Zachary 142–3
Bacon, Francis 30–1, 97, 100–2, 107, 109,
    116–17
bail and committal statutes 43
Baker, J.H. 29, 80–1
Baldwin, Geoff 7–8, 146
Barnes, Roger 57
Barnes, Thomas G. 111
battery 33, 105
Beattie, John 11, 156
Beaumont, Agnes 50–1
Bellamy, J.G. 24–5, 123–4, 130–1
Bellany, Alastair 143–4
Bellingham, Thomas 109–10
benefit of clergy 21–5, 28–9, 81–3, 91,
    148–50, 152–3
Bible 1–2, 31, 92–3, 140, 145–6
bills, parliamentary 106–7, 114–15
bills of mortality 127–8
Blackstone, William 18–19

blood
    cold 14, 23–4, 141–2
    guilt 143–5
    hot 23–5, 29, 32, 83–4
border
    Anglo-Scottish 74–5, 83–4
    Anglo-Welsh 44–5, 61–2, 77–8, 83–4
Borough, Henry 81–2
Braddick, Michael 17–18
Braddon, Laurence 65–6
Brewen, John 131–2
Broude, Ronald 138
Buckingham, George Villiers, first duke of 4–5,
    109–10
Buckingham, George Villiers, second duke of
    114, 150
Burney, Ian 40–1
Butler, Sara 38
Butler, Todd 131
Byer, John 53

Cain 1–2, 109, 132–3
Calverley, Walter 136
Campbell, Lily 138
canon law 6–7, 20–1
Carroll, Stuart 95–6
Cavill, Paul 81
Caxton, William 130–1
chance medley 21–2, 22n71, 30–1, 63
Chapman, George 117–18
Charles I, king of England, Scotland, and
    Ireland 4–5, 68, 112–14, 143–5
Charles II, king of England, Scotland, and
    Ireland 143–6, 150
Cheshire 11, 128–9, 158
Chester 46–7
Chivalry, Court of 107, 112–15
Christmas, Brice 109–10
chronicles 123–6, 130–1
Cicero 6–7
civilizing process 12–13, 17–18, 95–6,
    121n2
Cockburn, J.S. 11, 47–8, 80–1, 157–8
Cogswell, Thomas 143–4
Cohen, Esther 124–5
Coke, Edward 3, 22n71, 24n80, 28–9, 31,
    64–5, 81–2, 105–9, 153–4
Combermere, abbey of 52–3
commorth, see *cymhortha*
compensation 69–70, 74–8, 81–9, 92–3
Constable, John 57
Cook, John 144–5
Cooney, Mark 118

Cooper, Thomas 133–4, 141–2
Cornwallis, Charles, lord 150–1
coroners 13, 37, 83–4, 139–40
　coroners' juries 38–9
　elections of 44–5, 64–5, 139–40
　guidebooks for 43–4
Cotton, Daniel 68
Council of Trent 98–9
courtesy 97–8, 100, 103
Coventry, John 34
coverture 87–8
Cowper, Spencer 92
Cressy, David 46–7
Crompton, Richard 29, 139–40
Cromwell, Oliver 114, 145–6
Cromwell, Thomas 6–7, 126
Crown, the (concept of) 18–19, 18n59, 23–4,
　54, 156
cruentation 38, 56n85
Cumberland, Henry Clifford, earl of 73
Cust, Richard 7–8, 107, 117–18
cymhortha 83–4

D'Ambois, Bussy 117–18
Dacre, Thomas Fiennes, lord 26, 73, 149
Danvers, Henry 65–6
Danvers, John 71–2
Darcy, Conyers, lord 109, 116–17
Darcy, George 85–7
Darcy, John 85–7
Davies, John 8, 84
Dean, John 68
Decalogue 140–1
Denmark 124–5
deodands 41–3, 48, 51, 64, 51n66, 90n98
Devil, *see* Satan
Devon 128–9
Dolan, Frances 5–6, 131–2
domestic homicide 14–15, 131–2
domestic tragedy (genre) 137
Done, John 73
Dorset, Edward Sackville, earl of 94–5
duel 75–6, 94–119, 142–3, 147–8
Durham 46–7, 74, 126
Dyer, James (judge) 83

Eden, Garden of 1–2
Eden, William 92
Egerton, John 147
Ehud 145–6
éiric 77–8, 84
Eisenstein, Elizabeth 130–1
Eisner, Manuel 11–12
Elias, Norbert 12–13, 17–18
Elizabeth I, queen of England and Ireland 7–8,
　76–7, 82–3, 103–4, 126–7
Ellesmere, Thomas Egerton, lord 109, 148
Ernst, Daniel 69
Essex 128–9
Essex, Arthur Capel, earl of 65–6, 143–4

Eve 1–2
evolutionary psychology 12–13, 17–18

Fairfax, William 85–6
felony merger 90
Ferguson, Robert 65–6
feud 20–1, 69–77, 88, 95–7
Filmer, Robert 4
Finch, Heneage 150–2
Fisher, Pamela 40–1
Fitzherbert, Anthony 139–40
Fleetwood, William 139–40
Foljambe, Henry 73–4
Foljambe, Hercules 73–4
forensic medicine 38, 51, 56–7
forfeitures 18–19, 22–3, 32, 41–3, 42n23,
　48, 51, 51n66, 54, 58, 64, 68, 70,
　115–16, 156
Foucault, Michel 123n9
Fowle, Magnus 55
Foxe, John 60
France 80n42, 95–6, 124–5
Friedland, Paul 124–5

galanas 77–8, 83–4
gaols, deaths in 42–3, 45–6, 58–9
Gascoigne, William (chief justice) 87–8
Gaskill, Malcolm 10–11, 38, 120–1, 131
Glamorgan 44–5
Glanvill 20–1, 87–8
Godfrey, Edmund Berry 143–4
Golding, Arthur 132–3, 136–7
Goring, Henry 89–90
Green, T.A. 24–5, 31, 38–9, 116
Gurr, T.R. 9–10

Habermas, Jürgen 18–19, 146
Hamilton, James Hamilton, fourth duke of
　(d. 1712) 114
Harrison, William 2n4, 45–6, 125n19
Hartgill, John 72–3
Hartgill, William 72–3
Havard, J.D.J. 41–3
Hawarde, John 62–3
Heath, Robert (attorney general) 112
Heath, Robert (coroner,) 48–9
Henrickson, Jacob 152–3
Henry II, king of England 3, 20–1, 70, 77–8
Henry VII, king of England 3–5, 34–6, 43,
　68n2, 81, 149
Henry VIII, king of England and Ireland 3, 26,
　60, 82–3, 85, 126
Herbert case 27, 147
heresy 122, 126–7
Herrup, Cynthia 38–9, 116
Heywood, Thomas 135–8
Hobart, Henry (attorney general) 107–8
Hockenhell, Henry 54–5
Holcroft, Thomas 73, 81–2
Holdsworth, William 79

Holinshed, Raphael 135–7
Holt, John (chief justice) 91–2
homicide
    distinction between murder and manslaughter
        19–23, 26–32, 105, 108–9, 116, 141–3
    excusable 19–20
    impulsive 16–18
    incidence 9–18
    judicial 121–2, 129
    justifiable 19–20
    misadventure 21–2, 41–4, 48, 153–4, 158–9
    self-defence 14–15, 19–20, 24–6, 11
    see also domestic homicide; infants, killings
        of; manslaughter verdict; murder;
        self-murder
honour 12–13, 95–9, 102–4, 107, 117–18,
    150–1
Hopper, Andrew 107
Horder, Jeremy 29–30
Hoyle, R.W. 73
Hudson, William 63, 110–11
Hughes, Ann 7–8
Hull 126
humanism 3, 6–7
humours 1–2, 23–4, 100–1, 132–3
Hunne, Richard 59–60, 130–1
Hunnisett, R.F. 41–3, 64–5, 157–9
Hunter, Joseph 85–6
Hutchest, George 107–8
Hyams, Paul 71

infanticide, *see* infants, killings of
infants, killings of 14–15
Ingram, Martin 123–4
inquests 13, 37–7, 147, 149
Ireland 68n1, 77–8, 84, 99n28
Irish, Bradley 138
Ivy, George 103

Jamaica 154–5
James VI/I, king of Scotland/king of England and
    Ireland 3–5, 35–6, 75–7, 95–7, 106–7,
    109–10, 113–14, 119, 143–4, 147–9
James, Mervyn 117–18
Jarnac, Guy Chabot de 98–9
Jeaffreson, James Cordy 128–9, 157
Jenkins, Philip 125–6, 128–9
Jenks, Susanne 20–1
Jennings, Abraham 56–7
jurisdiction, territorial 105–7, 153
jurors
    literacy, social status 46–7
    on coroners' inquests, juries 38–9, 45–7,
        49–51, 54–60, 63
jury nullification 38–9, 58, 64

Kane, Brendan 117–18
Kelke, Isabel 85
Kelyng, John (chief justice) 31
Kent 11, 47–9

keywords 5–6, 156
Kiernan, Victor 103
King's Bench, Court of 13, 48, 61, 72–3, 80–1,
    86–7, 99, 106–7, 157–8
king's peace (concept of) 18–21, 19n60, 153–6
Kinloss, Edward Bruce, lord of 94
Kroge, Tyge 124–5
Kyd, Thomas 137–8

Lake, Peter 132
Lambarde, William 23–4, 139–40
Lambert, Thomas 19n60, 20–1
Lamech 109
Langbein, John 43
Laud, William, archbishop of Canterbury 112
law officers
    killings by 28
    killings of 28
law reformers 141–2
law reports 5–6
Leeke, Francis 73–4
Leeke, Henry 73–4
legal fictions 19–20, 26, 32
Leslie, John 74
letters of slain 75–6
Levack, Brian 75
Lewis, David 83–4
libel 109, 111–12
Lincolnshire 47
Lisle, Thomas 91
Lloyd, Philip 89–90
Loar, Carol 38–40, 51
Locke, John 4
Lockwood, Matthew 13n38, 18n56, 38–9,
    51n66, 158–60
London Gazette, The 138–9
Long, Henry 71–2
Long, Walter 62–3, 71–2
Longueville, Edward 89
Lord High Steward, Court of the 150–2
Lucas, Thomas 115–16

MacDonald, Michael 32–3
Machyn, Henry 34, 86–7, 126–7
Mackalley's Case 28–9
maiming 34
Maitland, F.W. 18–19
malice (forethought, constructive, implied)
    19–22, 21n67, 25–32, 108–9, 144–5, 147
Manning, Roger 95–7
manslaughter verdict
    early development of 19–25
    effects of 24–5, 31–2, 64, 81–3, 148, 150–2
    opposition to 31, 93, 141–3
    provocation, role in 29–30
March, John 141–2
Marches, Council in the 4n10, 61–2
Markham, Gervase 109
Martin, Randall 131
Mary I, queen of England and Ireland 43, 126–7

Mary, queen of Scots 4–5, 76–7
Massachusetts 141–2
Masschaele, James 39–40
Mawgridge's Case 29–30
mayhem 34
McKenzie, Andrea 138–9
McSheffrey, Shannon 22–3
Middlesex 128–9
Middleton, Thomas 136–7
Milton, John 1–2
Minson, Stuart 123–4
misadventure, *see* homicide
Mohun, Charles, lord 114, 150–1
monarchical republic(anism) 7–8
Monmouth, James [Crofts] Scott, first
    duke of 150
Moody, Henry 103
More, Thomas 60
Morgan, Edward 147–8
Morley, Thomas, lord 150
Mosaic law 93n104
Munday, Anthony 136–7
murder fine, *see murdrum*
murder
    Coke's definition of 31, 153–15
    see also homicide, distinction between
        murder and manslaughter
murdrum 20–1, 41–2
Musson, Anthony 78–80

Nashe, John 55–6
Newcastle upon Tyne 46, 75
newsbooks, newspapers 138–9
Nicholls, John 152–3
Noah 1–2, 4
Norris, Edward 103
Northampton, Henry Howard, first earl of 107
Northumberland 74, 83–4
Northumberland, Henry Algernon Percy, fifth
    earl of 71–2
Northumberland, Henry Percy, eighth
    earl of 60–1
Nurse, Mark 89–90

Oates, Titus 143–4
oaths 65
Old Bailey *Proceedings* 138–9
Ordinary of Newgate's *Accounts* 138–9
outlaws, outlawry 41–3, 153–4
Overbury, Thomas 143–4, 149
Oxford 53–4, 126–7
Oxford, Edward de Vere, seventeenth earl of
    103, 149

Packington Robert 15–16
pamphlets 60, 120–1, 130–5
pardons 19–22, 58–9, 68–9, 75–6, 82–3,
    144–5, 147–50, 152–3, 156
parricide 14–15
passions 1–2, 89, 132–3

peace of God 18–19
Peltonen, Markku 95, 97, 107
Pembroke and Montgomery, Philip Herbert,
    earl of 88–9, 150–1
Penryn *v* Corbet (1595) 82–3
petty treason 14–15, 23–4, 34, 122, 135–6
physicians 38, 56–7
pirates 23–4, 126–7, 145–6
plays 130, 135–8
Plowden, Edmund 139–40
Pollock, Frederick 18–19
Pollock, Linda 95–6, 117–18
Ponet, John 4
Popish Plot (1678) 143–4
population 3, 13, 128–9
Powell, Edward 78
Prest, William 107–8, 116–17
printing 121, 130–6, 138–46
    legal 3, 130–1, 139–40
Privy Council 4, 34–5, 44, 61–4, 72–4, 160
proclamations 28, 43, 106–9, 111–12, 114–16
property qualifications 39–40, 45–6
providence 120–1, 131, 133–4, 136–40
provocation 28–32, 108–9
Pulton, Ferdinando 139–40
punishment (public, capital) 121–30

Queen's Bench, Court of, *see* King's Bench
Quint, David 98–9

Raleigh, Walter 100–1
Reade, Richard 83
regicide 144–5
retaining 71–2
revenge tragedies (genre) 137
Revolution of 1688/9 3–5, 65–6, 143,
    149–50, 156
Reynolds, John 133
Richard III, king of England 4–5
Richmond, Henry 103
Robson, Simon 103
Rochfort, James 115–16
Romei, Annibale 98–9, 103
Roth, Randolph 12–13
Royer, Katherine 123
Rye House Plot (1683) 65–6, 143–4

Salisbury's Case 27
sanctuary 21–3, 85–7
Sanquhar, Robert Crichton, lord 30–1,
    88–9, 149
Satan 1–2, 132–3
satisfaction 134–5, 142–3
    see also compensation; duel; feud
Saunders, George 136–7
Saunders case 27–8, 132–3
Savage, Thomas, archbishop of York 71–2
Saviolo, Vincentio 100, 102–3
Scotland 74–8, 80n42, 92–3, 99n25, 105
searchers of the dead 52

Segar, William 100, 102–3
Selden, John 64–5, 104
self-murder 32–3, 38–9, 42–3, 51, 64, 90, 157
serfs 153–4
servants 14–15, 58
Sexby, Edward 145–6
Sharpe, James A. 11, 17–18, 39–40, 117–18, 123–4, 128–9, 157–9
Shepard, Alexandra 101–2, 117–18
Sheppard, William 141–2
Shoemaker, Robert 118
Sidney, Philip 103
sin 1–2, 6–7, 19–20, 132–4
Slack, Paul 6–7
slaves 154–5
Smith, Thomas 43–4, 50, 64
Society of Antiquaries 100–1
Somerset, Edward Seymour, first duke of ('Lord Protector of England') 6–7
Somerset, Frances Carr, countess of 149
Somerset, Robert Carr, earl of 149
Spanish Tragedy, The 137–8
Spenser, Edmund 84
Spierenburg, Pieter 12–13, 16–17
stabbing, statute of 29
stage, commercial 3, 135–6
Stanger, Elizabeth 87
Star Chamber, Court of 3, 34, 60–3, 65, 72–4, 85, 97, 100–2, 104, 106–14, 116–17, 160
state (concept of the) 9, 12, 17–18, 156
Staunford, William 139–40
Stone, Lawrence 10–11, 95
Stourton, Lord Charles 72–3, 149
Stout, Sarah 92
Stow, John 135–6
Suffolk 46–7, 133–4
Suffolk, Edmund de la Pole, sixth earl of 149
suicide, *see* self-murder
Summerson, Henry 123
surgeons 52, 55–6, 56n84
Sweden 77n33, 92–3
Symondes, Elizabeth 87

T.E. (author of *Lawes Resolution of Women's Rights*) 88
Taverner, Richard 108–9
Ten Commandments 140–1
Thomas, Courtney 117–18
torture 4
Tower (of London) 122–4, 143–4
treason 122, 126–7, 144–5
trial by battle 86–7, 98–101
Turner, John 30–1

Tyburn 122–4, 126–7
Tyndale, William 60
tyrannicide 144–6

union of the crowns (1603) 75

Vavasour, Thomas 103
villeinage 153–4
violence, definitions of 33–4, 129–30

Wales 13n39, 44–5, 77–8, 83–4, 153
Walker, Garthine 23–4, 116
Wapping Dock 122–4, 126–7
Warburton, Emmet 54
Warwick and Holland, Edward Rich, earl of 150–1
Wasser, Michael 75–6
Watts, John 6–7
Watts v Brains 29
weapons 15–16
Webbe, Margaret 85
Webbe, William 48
Weber, Max 17–18
Welles, William 81
wergeld 20–1, 79, 84
West, Lewis 85–6
West, Margaret 85–7
West, William 85–6
Westminster (sanctuary) 85–7
Wharton, Thomas, lord 73
Whitelocke, James 104–5
Whittick, Christopher 80–1
widows 69–70, 84–90
Wigges, Thomas 81–2
Wilkins, George 136
Wilkinson, John 65
Wiltenburg, Joy 134
Windebank, Francis 112
witchcraft 14, 57–8
Withington, Phil 6–7, 18–19
Wolfe, Alice 122
Wolsey, Thomas, cardinal 85
Woodbridge, Linda 138
Wormald, Jenny 92–3
Wright, Richard 107–8, 116–17
Wriothesley, Charles 126
wrongful death 90
Wrote, Catherine 81–2
Wrote, Robert 81–2

Yetter, Leigh 131
York 81, 126
Yorkshire 85–6, 136